Family Law Arbitration

SECOND EDITION

Other titles available from Law Society Publishing:

Children and Families Act 2014
Noel Arnold

Family Law Protocol (4th edn)
The Law Society

Good Practice in Child Care Cases (3rd edn)
The Law Society

Unbundling Family Legal Services Toolkit
Ursula Rice and Mena Ruparel

Titles from Law Society Publishing can be ordered from all good bookshops or direct (telephone 0370 850 1422, email **lawsociety@prolog.uk.com** or visit our online shop at **bookshop.lawsociety.org.uk**).

Family Law Arbitration

Practice and Precedents

SECOND EDITION

Dennis Sheridan and Suzanne Kingston

The Law Society

© The Law Society 2017

Crown copyright material is reproduced with the permission of the Controller of Her Majesty's Stationery Office

ISBN-13: 978-1-78446-074-7

First edition published in 2014

This second edition published in 2017 by the Law Society
113 Chancery Lane, London WC2A 1PL

Typeset by Columns Design XML Ltd, Reading
Printed by Hobbs the Printers Ltd, Totton, Hants

The paper used for the text pages of this book is FSC® certified. FSC (the Forest Stewardship Council®) is an international network to promote responsible management of the world's forests.

Contents

PART II – APPENDICES

Foreword

This is a very timely and useful guide to arbitration in family matters. Over the last five years the use of arbitration in family disputes has become increasingly accepted, and increasingly resourced. The senior courts have indicated their approval of arbitration in family matters, both in court decisions and in extrajudicial statements. The Institute of Family Law Arbitrators (IFLA) has ensured that there is a cadre of suitably trained and qualified arbitrators able to do the arbitrations and a body of rules that are flexible and readily applicable by practitioners in family matters. Arbitration is now available both in financial disputes and in relation to issues concerning children in private law cases.

The use of arbitration as a means of resolving disputes in family matters is now something that the family practitioner will wish to consider in very many cases. Arbitration allows the parties confidentiality, and is a process where they are much more in control than they would be if the case was being heard by the conventional court system.

The development of arbitration in the family justice system is a new and exciting development in family law. This guide provides much needed and authoritative guidance as to the applicable law and the meaning of the procedural rules, and sensible practical advice as to when to use arbitration and how to go about it. It also contains many valuable documentary precedents that are so vital in the course of a family arbitration.

Family arbitration will inevitably expand in the years to come. It needs an authoritative textbook. This work provides it and will be of invaluable use to family practitioners. I commend the work of Dennis Sheridan and Suzanne Kingston.

Lord Falconer of Thoroton
House of Lords
London
January 2017

Preface

When the Institute of Family Law Arbitrators (IFLA) was formed five years ago, the steering group took the firm decision that in its initial stages IFLA should only promote a scheme that would deal with financial matters. The stakeholders in IFLA – the Chartered Institute of Arbitrators, the Family Law Bar Association, Resolution (the solicitors' family law group) and the Centre for Child and Family Law Reform – were content with that approach.

Rules were drawn up, together with a training scheme, and IFLA was formed as a not-for-profit company. The Financial Scheme was launched in the confident expectation that its jurisprudential basis would be accepted as sound and that the senior courts would back both the thinking behind and operation of the Scheme. It was a novel concept in family law and there were those who initially expressed doubts about its validity. Now, after five years have passed, there have been leading judgments supporting the Scheme and various extrajudicial statements of approval at the highest levels. Over 140 arbitrators have been trained in financial arbitrations, and the post-separation distributions of many millions of pounds of family assets have been successfully arbitrated upon. The speed, confidentiality and cost-effectiveness of the Scheme have been recognised.

When it became clear that the concept of arbitration in financial matters was acceptable to the courts and the profession, strong arguments were advanced that there was really no reason why arbitration should not also be applied in a range of children matters. Both Sir Hugh Bennett and Sir Peter Singer presented compelling arguments in its favour, and so the Advisory Committee asked His Honour Michael Horowitz QC to chair a committee to take the matter forward.

A very able team of lawyers with experience in children work was asked to report. They did so positively and prepared a set of draft rules that were presented to the Advisory Committee and then the Rules Subcommittee. It was agreed that the Scheme should be launched in July 2016, following a model similar to the launch of the Financial Scheme and with very comparable Rules. Existing arbitrators have been further trained in children work, and a new group of arbitrators doing only children work have also been trained.

Obviously, the first edition of this very helpful book was going to need updating to include the new Scheme – and this was also a good opportunity to incorporate the amendments to the Rules for the Financial Scheme. The up-to-date Rules for both the Financial and Children Schemes are set out in this new edition, which has been co-written with Suzanne Kingston. Suzanne has played a leading part in IFLA and in its training since the start; with her experience in training and as a leading family solicitor, I can think of no one better to have on board.

The Rules can be found on the IFLA website, but this book provides much more material besides and will prove a very useful guide to both new and seasoned practitioners who will increasingly be asked to advise their clients about the advantages of arbitration in both financial and children work. IFLA and their fellow arbitrators should be very grateful to Dennis Sheridan and Suzanne Kingston for this timely and useful guide to family arbitration under the IFLA Schemes.

Donald Cryan (Hon) LLD
One of Her Majesty's Circuit Judges
Chairman of the Advisory Committee of IFLA
Treasurer of the Honourable Society of the Inner Temple
January 2017

Acknowledgements

Thanks are given to the following people for their assistance and contribution:

- Hugh Bennett, of Queen Elizabeth Buildings
- Andrzej Bojarski MCIArb, barrister, head of the Family Team, 36 Bedford Row
- Rachael Kelsey, of Sheehan Kelsey Oswald
- Sir Peter Singer MCIArb, of 1 Hare Court

We also gratefully acknowledge the contributions of the following resources and organisations:

- FamilyArbitrator (**www.familyarbitrator.com**)
- *Family Law Journal*
- IFLA (**www.ifla.org.uk**)
- Resolution (**www.resolution.org.uk**)

Finally, a huge thanks to our respective secretaries – Anita Kerley and Lisa Harman – and to all our friends, family and colleagues who have supported us with this venture.

Dennis Sheridan and Suzanne Kingston
January 2017

Part I

Family law arbitration in practice

Chapter 1

Introduction

1.1 Background

The essence of family law arbitration is that it is a contractually binding agreement between parties to a dispute to accept the decision of an arbitrator to whom they have agreed to submit an issue or issues which they cannot resolve between themselves. An arbitrator is in effect a 'private judge' who is able, once appointed to undertake an arbitration, to make decisions in respect of family financial or property disputes or children disputes to which, as between themselves, the parties agree in advance to be bound. The 'award' (which is the document in which arbitrators set out their decisions in financial cases) and the 'determination' (which is the document in which arbitrators set out their decisions in relation to children disputes) may still be subject to final approval by a court. Accredited family law arbitrators operate in accordance with and subject to either the Family Law Arbitration Financial Scheme Arbitration Rules 2016 ('the Financial Scheme' and 'the Financial Rules') (see **Appendix 1.1**)[1] or the Family Law Arbitration Children Scheme Arbitration Rules 2016 ('the Children Scheme' and 'the Children Rules') (see **Appendix 1.2**)[2] and the Arbitration Act 1996 (**Appendix 1.3**).

Both Schemes are administered by the Institute of Family Law Arbitrators (IFLA), a not-for-profit company. The Rules for both Schemes are very similar. They are produced in the same format and there are only some minor differences between them. The Children Rules concentrate on issues specific to children disputes (namely safeguarding and the voice of the child) but generally speaking the rule numberings are exactly the same and should be easily recognised. When the Financial Scheme first started it was the only Scheme and so the one application form was simply called Form ARB1. However, now there are two Schemes there are also two different forms. Form ARB1 is now known as Form ARB1FS (**Appendix 2.1**) and the application form for arbitration in a children case is known as Form ARB1CS (**Appendix 2.2**).

1.2 The Financial Scheme

1.2.1 Scope

The arbitrator deals with financial and property disputes arising from marriage, civil partnership or cohabitation and their respective breakdown, or arising from parenting or between those sharing parenting responsibilities, and also in respect of provision from the estate of a deceased person for his or her dependants.[3] Article 2.2 of the Rules lists the statutes under which claims within the Scheme are most usually brought:

---

[1] Article references in the text are to the Family Law Arbitration Financial Scheme Arbitration Rules 2016 (5th edn, effective 18 July 2016).
[2] Article references in the text are to the Family Law Arbitration Children Scheme Arbitration Rules 2016 (1st edn, effective 1 November 2016).
[3] Article 2.1.

2.2 . . .

    (a)   the Married Women's Property Act 1882, s.17;
    (b)   the Matrimonial Causes Act 1973, Part II;
    (c)   the Inheritance (Provision for Family and Dependants) Act 1975;
    (d)   the Matrimonial and Family Proceedings Act 1984, s.12 (financial relief after overseas divorce);
    (e)   the Children Act 1989, Sched.1;
    (f)   the Trusts of Land and Appointment of Trustees Act 1996;
    (g)   the Civil Partnership Act 2004 Sched.5, or Sched.7, Part 1, para.2 (financial relief after overseas dissolution).

The Scheme does not apply to disputes directly concerning:

- the liberty of individuals;

- the status of individuals or of their relationship;

- bankruptcy or insolvency;

- welfare benefits;

- jurisdictional stay cases;

- issues over recognition of a foreign marriage or divorce;

- any person or organisation which is not a party to the arbitration (unless they agree).

Although the arbitrator may have regard to and admit evidence in respect of laws of another country in so far and in the same way as a judge who exercises the jurisdiction of the High Court would do, the arbitrator in reaching his[4] decision must apply the law of England and Wales.[5]

1.2.2 Case study

> In this case study, Dennis Sheridan explains a case that he was involved in and the conversation that he had with his client in relation to a financial arbitration.

Does this ring a bell? You sit opposite a client whose face gradually lengthens, whose mouth drops and whose eyes widen in dismay and disbelief as you describe how long it takes to bring matrimonial financial issues to a conclusion through the court litigation process.

You have advised of the other ways there are to resolve his or her case, but no matter how enthusiastically you describe mediation the response is negative and you hear the comment: my ex-husband/wife will only listen to a judge. You encouragingly mention the collaborative procedure and sadly that too is dismissed.

The case itself does not represent a great value in terms of the assets and capital, far more high street than high net worth – but the parties are at loggerheads on all aspects of their marriage and its financial aftermath.

The one thing that your client does not want is for the matter to go on for what appears an interminable period with the prospect of expensive, lengthy and stressful court appearances, most likely before different judges on each occasion. What do you offer?

In a recent case I was acting for a client in such a situation and I suggested arbitration. After explaining what arbitration meant and how the financial issues between the parties could be dealt

---

[4]   The masculine form when referring to the arbitrator is used for simplicity throughout the book and encompasses both genders.
[5]   Article 3.

with more speedily and with less formality than through the courts, and with a final and binding arbitrator's award as the outcome, the client agreed that I should propose arbitration to the other side's solicitors.

Fortunately the parties agreed and the arbitration process kicked into action.

We agreed between us on two arbitrators we would both be happy to engage, the Institute of Family Law Arbitrators (IFLA) Form ARB1FS was completed setting out the basic issues and then submitted to IFLA and within days one of our nominated arbitrators confirmed his agreement to be appointed and an initial meeting was arranged. Everybody agreed the date and time of the initial pre-commitment meeting and location.

The first benefit had already occurred. Up to this point the parties had not been able to agree on anything, and yet here they were agreeing to come outside the obvious 'box' and resolve their financial matters through arbitration.

The proposal to arbitrate led immediately to arbitration's second benefit, the immediate rapport between myself and my opposite number when it came to completing the IFLA Form ARB1FS and setting out the issues that we both considered the arbitrator should deal with. This led to the third benefit which was that at the initial meeting with the arbitrator there had already been good communication between solicitors and the atmosphere was therefore friendly.

At that initial pre-commitment hearing the arbitrator explained to both parties and to the solicitors present what arbitration was all about and how he suggested they should proceed, and explained the Family Law Arbitration Scheme Arbitration Rules by which the process would be governed. Most importantly he reiterated what we solicitors had already told our clients: that once they agreed to arbitration, and the process was underway, a central part of their agreement was to be bound by the arbitrator's decision which would be final and binding upon them.

This initial hearing was extremely important as during its course the parties, who had hardly spoken to each other for quite some time, were now at least engaging in making points jointly to the arbitrator, and it was clear that a rapport and a clear connection were building up between them and the arbitrator as well as between the solicitors and the arbitrator. For the first time the parties were able to look straight at the decision-maker and hear him talk to them as they in turn were able to talk to him. Towards the conclusion of the initial hearing the arbitrator left the room to let us talk to our clients and for them to decide whether they were happy to agree to confirm their wish to appoint him as arbitrator, or whether either of them wanted time to reflect before deciding. In fact the atmosphere was such that they agreed to confirm the appointment there and then.

These formalities concluded, the preliminary hearing at which fundamentals would be discussed (similar perhaps to a First Directions Appointment (FDA)) was the next step. The practicalities as to where and when the preliminary hearing should take place were swiftly agreed, and what should be done in the meantime. In fact a date convenient to all was selected, just two weeks later. Also within that timeframe checklists were to be completed and documents exchanged.

The preliminary hearing enabled a full discussion on the issues that had been listed in Form ARB1FS, enabling all parties including the arbitrator to play a full part in prioritising what each of the parties was seeking and what was really important to each of them. Very soon it became clear which matters were likely to take up a great deal of time at the arbitration 'final' hearing which was then envisaged, and those which perhaps might be settled even prior to that hearing. This was a very powerful meeting with the confidence of the clients becoming more obvious, enhanced by the very fact of the continuity of the same arbitrator. Judicial continuity is something we rarely get in court: here was a chance to see how very important it is and what immense assistance and confidence it gives the clients.

At the preliminary hearing's conclusion directions were given to prepare for the final hearing (including, again, agreeing a date, time and location to suit everyone). The solicitors were asked to provide written submissions by a specific date, which proved a very beneficial exercise. With submissions exchanged I raised with the arbitrator whether he would be agreeable to a variation of his directions allowing the parties by a specific date to file counter-arguments. The arbitrator readily agreed, enabling everything to be ready for the final hearing. This was yet another benefit of the continuity of the arbitrator as the decision-maker throughout.

The approach adopted and the atmosphere of confidence generated by the arbitrator encouraged a recognition by us all that rather than the clients incurring the additional expense of a full oral hearing, with cross-examination, the arbitrator should be asked to arrive at his award as a paper exercise. By this stage he had the relevant documents, arguments and counter-arguments before him. The relief to the clients was palpable, the pressure and tensions lifted from them, and now all that they wanted was to have the decision as soon as possible. Their wish was granted when the detailed award was received which enabled the clients to get on with their lives – and their respective solicitors to archive their files.

This arbitration from start to finish (final award) took four months. If, on the same day as we filed Form ARB1FS with IFLA to start the arbitration process, I or my opponent had filed with the court a Form A to kick-start proceedings for financial remedies, we would in that same period of four months not even have reached first base, the First Directions Appointment (FDA) hearing date. Had this particular matter been referred to the courts, it is likely that it would have proceeded through the FDA to the Financial Dispute Resolution (FDR) hearing, and who knows when a hearing date would be given for that.

I can honestly state that arbitration certainly reduced the anxiety and the misery for the clients, and disposing of their case so satisfactorily and swiftly leaves me better able to deal with the next matrimonial client who comes through my door. 'Have you heard about the Arbitration Scheme?' I shall ask them …

1.3 The Children Scheme

1.3.1 Scope

The arbitrator deals with children disputes concerning the exercise of parental responsibility and other private law issues about the welfare of children. Article 2.1 sets out the scope of the Children Scheme and makes it clear that it covers issues between parents.

The areas that *are* covered by the Children Scheme are:

- any issue between parents or other persons holding parental responsibility or sufficient interest in a child's present or future welfare;

- where a child should be living, including shared living arrangements;

- visiting arrangements and time spent with a non-residential parent;

- education issues;

- disputes concerning routine and non-life-threatening medical treatment.

The following disputes and issues are *not* within the scope of the Children Scheme:

- applications to have a child returned to this jurisdiction from another country – whether or not that country is a signatory to the Hague Convention on the Civil Aspects of International Child Abduction ('the 1980 Hague Convention');

- applications to remove a child from this jurisdiction to another country, whether permanently or for a temporary period;

- disputes relating to the authorisation of life-changing or life-threatening medical treatment or the progress of such treatment;

- where a party lacks capacity under the Mental Capacity Act 2005;

- where any person with parental responsibility for the child or who seeks to be a party to the arbitration is a minor;

- where the child concerned has party status in existing proceedings relating to the same or similar issues, or should – in the opinion of the arbitrator – be separately represented in the arbitration.

As with the Financial Scheme, the arbitrator has the same power to make orders or determinations as would a High Court judge.

1.3.2 Children Scheme

The Children Scheme is so new that at the time of publication there has only been one case which has been through the arbitration process. However, in principle, the advantages are the same as set out in the case study at **1.2.2**. Indeed, some may say that in children disputes the need to have a speedy resolution is even more pressing. It is for this reason that many commentators expect that the Children Scheme will prove extremely popular, particularly when considering discrete urgent issues (for example, arrangements for the summer or Christmas holidays).

Like financial arbitrations, children arbitrations offer a bespoke flexible process. It should be noted, however, that the Children Scheme has been very carefully drafted to deal with the important issues of safeguarding and listening to the voice of the child – see further at **2.6.2**.

1.4 Arbitration forms

It is imperative to ensure that the correct form is used for the commencement of an arbitration. The most reliable source for up-to-date rules and forms is the IFLA website (**ifla.org.uk**). Both forms contain a new feature: a box marked 'Important' which sets out the binding nature of arbitration. This box is reproduced below.

Important

Parties should be aware that:

- by signing this form they are entering into a binding agreement to arbitrate (within the meaning of s.6 of the Arbitration Act 1996).

- after signing, neither party may avoid arbitration (unless they both agree to do so). Either party may rely on the arbitration agreement to seek a stay of court proceedings commenced by the other.

- arbitration is a process whose outcome is generally final. There are very limited bases for raising a challenge or appeal, and it is only in exceptional circumstances that a court will exercise its own discretion in substitution for the [award/determination].

In addition to understanding the binding nature of arbitration, under the Children Scheme the parties must comply with the safeguarding procedures as set out in paragraph 8.3 of Form ARBICS and Article 17 of the Children Rules. These requirements will be dealt with fully in **Chapter 2**.

Chapter 2
Procedure

2.1 Pre-commitment meeting

It is envisaged that most arbitrations will start with a pre-commitment meeting or telephone call so that the parties can meet the arbitrator and ensure that it is the right process for them. This process effectively enables the arbitrator to showcase the arbitration process and enables the parties to raise questions with the arbitrator before they are contractually bound.

Although a pre-commitment meeting is not an absolute requirement, many arbitrators will consider a pre-commitment discussion helpful to them and to the parties and legal representatives. The purpose of the pre-commitment discussion is to enable all parties to meet with the arbitrator, to confirm the issues that the parties wish the arbitrator to consider and, if possible, list the issues in order of importance. The discussion enables the parties and their legal representatives to learn how the arbitration is to proceed and to understand their obligations within the arbitration process. It is imperative that the parties understand that any decision by the arbitrator is final and binding and the meeting gives an opportunity to both parties to check the extent of their commitment to the arbitration.

The parties must be informed that, should one or other become dissatisfied with the way in which the arbitration is working and disengage from or demand the termination of the arbitration, the arbitrator remains in control, the arbitration remains operative, and, if and when an award is made, it will remain binding on both parties.

The list of issues before the arbitrator may change or be reformulated during or following the pre-commitment meetings as a result of the discussions and input of the arbitrator. It also enables the parties to agree the arbitrator's fees, the location of the arbitration proceedings and if possible the timescale over which the matters will be dealt with.

If the arbitrator offers a pre-commitment meeting he may do so without a fee and without commitment. The arbitrator must be satisfied that all parties involved fully understand that an award at the conclusion of the process will, as between the parties, be binding.

2.2 Specific issues for pre-commitment meetings for financial matters

The benefit of a pre-commitment discussion is that the parties will have a full understanding of the procedure that they are now entering into and will be fully aware of the binding nature of arbitration.

During this meeting the parties may wish to discuss the terms of the arbitrator's engagement and the conditions of his appointment, and to consider some very specific issues – for example, whether the arbitrator should incorporate the *Calderbank* principles and whether rights to appeal should be dismissed.

2.3   Specific issues for pre-commitment meetings in children cases

It is important for the arbitrator, the parties and their representatives to think about safeguarding – both before and during the arbitration – and how to ascertain the wishes and feelings of the child. In a children arbitration, the arbitrator will want to know that all of the safeguarding procedures have been undertaken and that the dispute in question is within scope. In addition, the arbitrator will need to give early consideration as to whether an independent social worker (ISW) will be appointed to ascertain the wishes and feelings of the children. If an ISW is to be appointed, the arbitrator may suggest suitable potential ISWs, and it may be agreed at the pre-commitment meeting that a specific ISW will be approached to find out their availability and costs estimate. See also **2.6.2**.

2.4   Signing up to arbitration

Once the parties to a dispute have decided that they both want their dispute to be referred to arbitration, either they or their legal representatives suggest arbitrators' names to their opposite number as being suitable. The names of qualified family arbitrators can be found on the Institute of Family Law Arbitrators (IFLA) website – **www.ifla.org.uk**. The arbitrators' areas of expertise are denoted on the website by (F) for financial arbitration or (C) for children matters; arbitrators denoted with (F)(C) are trained in both. The website has been designed specifically to enable each arbitrator to set out a short profile so that an arbitrator may be selected from a particular locality or branch of the legal profession – perhaps a solicitor, barrister or a retired judge from one of a number of different levels of court. The list can also be searched to identify an arbitrator who has particular expertise or skills, including a foreign language or knowledge of religious or cultural customs. If they would prefer, the parties may request that IFLA nominate an arbitrator.

Sample letters for confirming the appointment of the chosen arbitrator (**Appendix 2.3**) and corresponding with the parties regarding choosing an arbitrator (**Appendix 2.4**) are included in this book.

It is important to emphasise that a matter being referred to arbitration must first be notified to IFLA (regardless of whether the name of the arbitrator is already agreed or the nomination is left to IFLA). The notification to IFLA is by way of either Form ARB1FS for financial matters (see **Appendix 2.1**) or Form ARB1CS for children matters (see **Appendix 2.2**).

2.5   Financial – Form ARB1FS

Form ARB1FS requests details of the parties, and of their legal representatives (if any). Most importantly the main issues requiring arbitration must be set out. The Form itself is not complex but it is important, as this document constitutes a binding agreement between the parties (as stated at **2.2**). Form ARB1FS records basic details concerning each party, each solicitor and barrister (if any); the issues that are in contention; and (if agreed) the name of the proposed arbitrator.

Each of the parties (or, in the first instance at least, their respective lawyers) must sign Form ARB1FS.

As in litigation there must be a lead party and generally the party who signs Form ARB1FS first will be referred to as the applicant. It must, however, be understood that there is no significance within an arbitration as to which party is designated applicant and which is the respondent, and that the arbitrator has the power to treat either as the applicant.

The completed and signed Form ARB1FS, after having been reviewed by the other party, must then be forwarded to IFLA; IFLA will then refer the case either to the chosen arbitrator or, if requested, to an arbitrator that it has nominated. The nominated arbitrator will then contact all parties to confirm that theirs is a suitable case on which the arbitrator can adjudicate.

2.6   Children – Form ARB1CS

Form ARB1CS is almost the same as Form ARB1FS and is treated in the same way.

The main difference centres around the issue of safeguarding.

2.6.1   Safeguarding

The safeguarding requirements are set out in Article 17 of the Children Rules and paragraphs 7 and 8 of Form ARB1CS.

Article 17.1.1 of the Children Rules makes it clear that both parties have a duty prior to the commencement of the arbitration to provide accurate information regarding safeguarding in Form ARB1CS and in the Safeguarding Questionnaire they are obliged to complete. In addition, the parties are obliged to obtain a Basic Disclosure from Disclosure Scotland and to send it to the arbitrator and every other party. Also, if either party has a relevant letter or report prepared by the Children and Family Court Advisory and Support Service (Cafcass) or any local authority children's services department or similar agency in relation to the welfare or safeguarding of any child who is the subject of the proposed arbitration, then that must be sent to the arbitrator and to every other party.

The precise information that the parties are to disclose is set out in art.17.1.2. Such disclosure would generally include, but is not limited to, criminal convictions, cautions or involvement (concerning any child) with children's services.

If the arbitrator believes that there are safeguarding issues either prior to or during the arbitration then the arbitrator must consider whether the arbitration may safely continue (art.17.2.1). If the arbitrator concludes that the dispute is no longer suitable for arbitration then he must inform the parties in writing of that decision and of the grounds, and will then terminate the proceedings (arts.7.3 and 15.2(b)). Under art.17.3.1, if the arbitrator becomes aware of any matters which lead him reasonably to apprehend that a child or any party has suffered or is likely to suffer significant harm by reason of the likely future behaviour of any party, then these concerns must be communicated to the relevant local authority or appropriate government agency as soon as possible. In those circumstances, there is no need for the arbitrator to inform the parties that he is going to contact the relevant local authority or appropriate government agency. The arbitrator may also inform IFLA of a decision to decline an appointment or to terminate an arbitration on safeguarding or welfare grounds.

2.6.2   Voice of the child

It is clear from Article 8.3 of the Children Rules that the arbitrator may not meet with the child who is the subject of the arbitration at any time, not even to communicate the decision made in arbitration. However, it is important that the arbitrator has a way of determining the wishes and feelings of the child – this will generally be facilitated by the instruction of an ISW, who will ascertain the wishes and feelings of the child and report to the arbitrator and the parties. Instruction of an ISW can either be proposed by the parties, subject to the confirmation and approval of the arbitrator (Article 8.2.3), or the arbitrator may of his own motion appoint an ISW (Article 8.2.4).

2.6.3 The 'no order' principle

Section 1(5) of the Children Act (CA) 1989 makes it clear that a court should not make an order unless it is considered better for the child than making no order at all. In children arbitration, the arbitrator must apply s.1 of CA 1989 and therefore must consider whether or not it is better to make an order at the end of the case or not. If the arbitrator believes it is not necessary, he should make that clear in his determination. Please note that although the final adjudication in financial cases is called an award, in children arbitration it is called a determination.

2.6.4 Other principles the arbitrator must consider

When dealing with a children arbitration, the arbitrator should have s.1 of CA 1989 firmly in mind – in other words, the child's welfare should be the paramount consideration. In order to do that, the arbitrator should pay particular attention to the welfare checklist as follows:

1. the ascertainable wishes and feelings of the child concerned (considered in the light of his or her age and understanding);

2. his or her physical, emotional and educational needs;

3. the likely effect on him or her of any change in his or her circumstances;

4. the child's age, sex, background and any other characteristics which the court considers relevant;

5. any harm which he or she has suffered or is at risk of suffering;

6. how capable each parent (and any other person in relation to whom the court considers the question to be relevant) is of meeting the child's needs;

7. the range of powers available to the court under this Act in the proceedings in question.

Another important point is for the tribunal to ensure that there are no unnecessary delays when considering the child's welfare. This is probably less of a problem in an arbitration than it would be in a court setting, since one of the main benefits of arbitration is that the pacing and speed can be adjusted to suit the case and the needs of the parties.

2.7 Contact with the arbitrator – Financial and Children

2.7.1 Communication with the arbitrator

Once the arbitrator confirms his agreement to arbitrate, generally he will contact the legal representatives by telephone or email to confirm whether there is to be a pre-commitment meeting or a telephone conference, or to suggest whether either is deemed necessary in the circumstances of the case. The arbitrator may also at this point, to assist him as well as the parties, forward or arrange for the checklist of matters for discussion at the first meeting in an IFLA family arbitration to be completed by both parties. Although the checklist is a lengthy document it can be completed quickly, and the contents assist the arbitration as many of the questions that the parties wish to raise with the arbitrator may already have been dealt with or the points narrowed down (see the checklist at **Appendix 2.7**). The arbitrator may decide such a checklist need not be completed in a particular arbitration if the issues in the matter are clear and it is apparent from the outset how the arbitration should be conducted.

2.7.2 Consideration as to process

Once the parties have agreed and the arbitrator has agreed to undertake the matter and has before him the issues he has been asked to consider, he will discuss with the parties by either telephone conference or email his initial thoughts. He will consider with the parties whether it would be beneficial to have:

(a)   a pre-commitment meeting by way of a hearing or telephone conference; or

(b)   an alternative that the parties themselves may suggest.

A great advantage of arbitration is its flexibility.

2.8   The contract

Each arbitrator has his own form of letter of engagement. A typical example of a letter of engagement in a financial case is to be found at **Appendix 2.8**. The children letter of engagement will be very similar but will specifically mention issues such as safeguarding and the voice of the child. If there has been a pre-commitment discussion, the contents of the letter will have been discussed. If there has been no previous discussion the letter of engagement will be submitted by the arbitrator to the legal representatives of the parties for them to discuss its contents with their clients, ensuring they fully understand the terms of the arbitration before signing up to it. It is appropriate to confirm the appointment of an arbitrator with your client – draft letters to this effect can be found at **Appendices 2.3** (Financial) and **2.4** (Children).

2.9   The arbitration process – Financial and Children

Depending on the matter(s) to be resolved by arbitration it may be appropriate for a hearing to take place to consider directions, documentation and evidence required, expert evidence and dates by which steps should be completed. The parties 'own' the process and the arbitrator will ordinarily be keen to follow the course suggested by the parties if they are in agreement. If the parties are not in agreement as to the specific process the arbitrator will intervene by giving directions which are binding upon them. Generally, the arbitrator will guide all parties through the process. Hearings may take place at a specific venue, time and date with all parties and lawyers present or they may be conducted by telephone, Skype or other form of video-conferencing. Alternatively, the process may proceed by email – with each party submitting to the other and to the arbitrator what they seek and the arbitrator then preparing appropriate directions. The arbitrator's directions are in many ways similar to those given in court and the following topics and provisions are set out by way of example:

(a)   written statements of case;

(b)   disclosure and production of documents as between the parties;

(c)   the exchange of witness statements;

(d)   the number and type of expert witnesses, exchange of their reports and any meetings they may have had (it is envisaged that in children arbitration cases, ISWs will be appointed to ascertain the wishes and feelings of the children);

(e)   arrangements for any meeting or hearing and the procedures to be adopted;

(f)   time limits to be imposed on oral submissions, the examination of witnesses, and any other procedure for controlling the length of hearings.

If the issue of directions is to proceed by way of a face-to-face hearing or by another form of audio process, e.g. Skype or telephone, this hearing is not intended to be a mediation or collaborative procedure. However, at this hearing, what may have been thought intractable might, through discussion, become less so and could, through the arbitration process, be resolved.

The directions hearing involves all five parties at the table (or on the telephone), all of whom have the opportunity to express their views. At the end of the hearing, directions will be discussed and the arbitrator will usually advise of the likely directions he is going to make. The directions will then be drafted by the arbitrator and will be forwarded to the parties within 7–14 days.

It must be emphasised that directions will be given in writing/emails, although it is possible the arbitrator may be able to provide printed directions at the hearing itself and hand them out at that hearing.

2.10 Directions

Sometimes directions given following either a hearing or paper exchanges themselves suggest an avenue for substantive discussion because there is direct contact between legal representatives. In such circumstances the arbitrator can, where requested, assist by giving guidance or further direction in order to facilitate settlement of the case. Once the parties in such circumstances consider that they have reached agreement the content can be forwarded to the arbitrator for his comments and approval and, if appropriate, for an award/determination to be prepared.

The arbitrator may, with the agreement of all involved, recommend that a particular aspect of the case be referred to mediation or to a specific expert, e.g. an independent financial adviser or pensions expert. This generally would occur if the parties are close to a potential settlement and the arbitrator believes that a full agreement can be reached if more advice is made available to them.

If there is no possibility of settlement the parties must comply with the directions and all disclosure/ evidence must be submitted by the due date to the arbitrator for his consideration. The arbitrator may consider that the documents before him are sufficient to enable the matter to be decided by way of documents only or by way of a full hearing with oral evidence from the parties or perhaps from experts. The parties may themselves express preference as to how the hearing should be dealt with. In either case, the arbitrator has to consider whether he has sufficient documentation, information and detail to enable him to proceed to grant an award/determination without further written documentation and evidence. He must also consider whether it is appropriate, even though a paper exercise has been requested, that the parties should be asked to give oral evidence and he must also consider whether it is appropriate for expert evidence to be provided either orally or in writing. The arbitrator may, particularly if the matter proceeds by way of a paper exercise, request that the parties file and serve on him and each other their submissions, and following such service may direct that each provides a counter-submission. This gives the legal representatives the opportunity to put further argument following the review of the other party's initial submission. Once the arbitrator has all the documents and information he will prepare the award/determination.

It should be remembered that the arbitrator has authority to adapt the process of arbitration according to the case and the concerns of the parties involved, and may consider with the parties that they recommend that the matter which is giving rise to the impasse (as mentioned above) be referred to a particular expert in the field or may recommend an expert be called to give evidence.

2.11 The final hearing

If the case is to proceed by way of a full hearing it is the responsibility of the parties to find a venue which has at least one sufficiently sized room for the hearing to take place and two separate rooms where meetings can be held by the parties individually. The arbitration generally follows a similar pattern to what would happen in court; however, since the process is more flexible, the parties and their lawyers can provide their thoughts about how the hearing should be undertaken. The arbitrator will generally discuss how the room is going to be set up with the legal representatives and the usual approach is one of informality. A bundle of papers and any other documents that the arbitrator considers appropriate must be prepared and be made available to him. The preparation of documents is normally dealt with by the applicant's solicitors in conjunction with the respondent's legal representatives. However, a benefit of arbitration is that as there will have been communication between each of the legal representatives from the start of the arbitration they will be able to discuss what steps each party needs to take to complete the preparation for the forthcoming hearing. The arbitrator will, together with the legal representatives, timetable the delivery and duration of their respective arguments, the length of time allowed for any witnesses to give evidence and decide whether the parties themselves will need to give evidence and if so the timescale for that evidence. The arbitrator will advise and finalise the timetable in preparation for the final hearing.

The arbitrator will want to make sure that refreshments are made available to the parties and legal representatives throughout the final hearing and will need to have the necessary equipment to administer oaths if live evidence is to be heard. Further, it is necessary to consider whether and how a transcript of the hearing is going to be undertaken – e.g. through a formal transcript service, a recording of all or part of the evidence, or a note taker. The arbitrator will want to discuss these issues prior to the final hearing and ensure that provision is properly made and costs for undertaking this factored in.

2.12 Award/determination

The final adjudication in a financial case is known as the award, whereas in a children case it is called a determination. At the conclusion of the hearing, the arbitrator will reserve his award/determination and advise the parties when it will be ready. It is common practice for the award/determination to be finalised well within 28 days and generally it will be forwarded to the parties to check that factual matters such as dates and times are correct. However, the arbitrator will require payment of his fees before releasing even a draft award.

It is important for the arbitrator to ensure that all relevant issues have been determined in the award/determination and that this document could serve as a standalone adjudication. At **Appendices 2.9** (Finance) and **2.10** (Children) there are examples of drafting checklists which set out all of the main points to be contained in the document. Once the award/determination is finalised (signed and dated), it is sent out to the parties via email and post; the date on the arbitral award is the date from which any time for appeal will run.

2.13 Enforcement of the financial award

The arbitral award is intended to be final, subject to any right to challenge (see **3.3**).

Most parties will also obtain a court order from the Family Court to mirror and confirm the terms of the award. A draft letter to the HM Courts and Tribunals Service can be found at **Appendix 2.11**. This will assist with enforcement, although in some instances an award can be enforced directly in the same way as a judgment or order of the court and to the same effect (Arbitration Act 1996, s.66). This may be the appropriate route for a Trusts of Land and Appointment of Trustees Act (TOLATA) 1996 award but it is not appropriate in the case of a financial remedies award.

The draft consent order reflecting the decisions and directions contained in the arbitrator's award should be lodged at court for approval. It should follow the relevant paragraphs of the standard form for financial remedy orders. There will be a recital making it clear that settlement has been reached through the arbitration process and that the consent order reflects the terms of the arbitral award – see **Appendices 2.12–2.15**. The president of the Family Division (Sir James Munby) issued 'Arbitration in the Family Court – practice guidance' on 23 November 2015 and this contains all of the relevant information regarding the lodging of the consent order (see **Appendix 1.4**). Further, Sir James Munby endorsed the use of a streamlined procedure in the High Court to fast track the review of draft consent orders which are the products of arbitral awards under the IFLA Scheme or something similar. The process was first used in *S* v. *P* [2008] 2 FLR 2040.

In order to use the streamlined procedure, the following documents must be lodged:

- a signed copy of the proposed order and the terms agreed;
- Forms A and D81;
- the arbitral award;
- the agreement to arbitrate (Form ARB1FS).

The confidentiality of the award can be preserved by lodging it at court in a sealed envelope clearly marked with the name and number of the case and the words 'arbitration award – confidential'. The award will then remain on the court file, which should be placed in an envelope clearly marked as above and with the words 'not to be opened without the permission of the Judge of the Family Court'.

Although it is not possible for parties to give undertakings within arbitration, it is envisaged that these will be set out in a Schedule of Agreement attached to the award/determination. These could then be made into full undertakings when the award/determination is made into a court order.

Where one party seeks to resile from an arbitral award, the other party should apply to the court under the 'notice to show cause' procedure.

If the attempt to resile from the arbitral award lacks merit, the court may summarily make an order reflecting the terms of the arbitral award and provide for its enforcement (see para.26 of *S* v. *S* [2014] EWHC 7 (Fam) at **Appendix 4.1**).

If a further hearing is necessary the court will be 'appropriately robust' in defining the issues in dispute and will fix a short and focused hearing. The focus will usually be on whether the party who is seeking to resile from the award can formulate one of the grounds of challenge or appeal under the Arbitration Act 1996 (see **3.3**). In the case of *S* v. *S*, Sir James Munby expressly approved the formulation that awards should be upheld by the courts save in 'the most exceptional circumstances' and unless there are 'overwhelmingly strong considerations' why they should not be. For further information refer to Sir James Munby's 'Arbitration in the Family Court – practice guidance' (**Appendix 1.4**) and see Suzanne Kingston and Rachael Kelsey's article at **Appendix 3.2**.

Consideration is currently being given to the extent to which the Convention on the Recognition and Enforcement of Foreign Arbitral Awards (the 'New York Convention') may apply in the recognition and enforcement of arbitral awards.

2.14 Orders within arbitration

The provisions relating to an arbitration claim most likely to be sought in the course of a financial remedies arbitration are:

- stay pursuant to section 9 of the Arbitration Act 1996;

- enforcement of peremptory orders of the arbitrator (Arbitration Act 1996, s.42);

- securing the attendance of witnesses (Arbitration Act 1996, s.43).

The following standard orders have been issued to meet each of these contingencies:

- 'Stay pursuant to Arbitration Act 1996 section 9' (see **Appendix 2.13**);

- 'Enforcement of an arbitrator's peremptory order under Arbitration Act 1996 s.42' (see **Appendix 2.14**); and

- 'Order securing the attendance of witnesses under Arbitration Act 1996 s.43' (see **Appendix 2.15**).

2.15 Enforcement of the children determination

The arbitrator must consider whether an order is necessary at the end of the proceedings or whether, following s.1(5) of the Children Act 1989, no order is necessary. It is envisaged that, in most cases, an order will be made and the way in which an order is sought from the court and issues of enforcement will be the same in children matters as they are in financial cases. The Children Scheme is so new that so far we have not received any further guidance from the president of the Family Division in relation to this area of work but it is anticipated that it will be forthcoming shortly.

Chapter 3

Guidance

3.1 The arbitrator

3.1.1 Responsibility of the arbitrator

Section 33 of the Arbitration Act 1996 sets out in specific terms the general duty of a tribunal (in IFLA arbitrations this will be a single arbitrator).

General duty of the tribunal

1. The tribunal shall:

   (a) act fairly and impartially as between the parties, giving each party a reasonable opportunity of putting his case and dealing with that of his opponent, and

   (b) adopt procedures suitable to the circumstances of the particular case, avoiding unnecessary delay or expense, so as to provide a fair means for the resolution of the matters falling to be determined.

2. The tribunal shall comply with that general duty in conducting the arbitral proceedings in its decisions on matters of procedure and evidence and in the exercise of all other powers conferred on it.

3.1.2 How to address the arbitrator

Most arbitrators will refer to the parties and their legal representatives by their title and surname and would expect to be addressed in the same way.

3.1.3 Does it matter where you sit?

No, but generally the client should be closer to the arbitrator than the legal representative.

3.1.4 Does it matter where the arbitration takes place?

No, although there should be three rooms available, one for the arbitration itself, and two more for the parties to separately hold individual discussions with their legal representatives.

3.1.5 Time

The time should be convenient to all parties and the arbitrator.

3.1.6 Contact with the arbitrator

Contact with the arbitrator should usually be by way of email or, in an emergency, by telephone, but all communication must be copied in to the other party. The parties (who are not the legal representatives) unless acting as litigant in person should not contact the arbitrator direct, unless authorised by both the arbitrator and all other parties involved.

3.2 Benefits of arbitration

1. Immediate engagement with the other party, as early agreement has to be reached regarding the fact that the case will be dealt with by way of arbitration and regarding the appointment of the arbitrator.

2. Direct and easy communication with the arbitrator once the nomination has been accepted. This saves time and is a positive experience for the parties.

3. The parties together with legal representatives take an active part in the discussions as to location, date and time of the initial pre-commitment hearing. The parties are therefore involved from the outset in their matter rather than considering themselves 'outsiders'. The process is far more 'their own' than conventional litigation in which the court's procedures and requirements often leave litigants feeling disempowered. In particular, it should be noted that the whole concept of party autonomy is key in the arbitral process and parties are encouraged to participate and feel engaged throughout.

4. A further benefit is that if it is necessary for hearings to take place in the evening and/or at a weekend, the arbitrator will if possible accommodate this.

5. Takes place at a location suitable to all parties and representatives. This is a significant benefit; many courts are closing, meaning parties and representatives may live a long distance from the nominated court – sometimes this results in travel times that exceed an hour by car. Public transport to the court's location is often unobtainable or, if available, very expensive and time consuming.

6. Continuity of the arbitrator (as decision-maker) throughout the matter. This leads to reassurance for all involved that the arbitrator will be fully aware of all the issues that need to be decided upon and is not a decision-maker who merely picks the papers up immediately prior to the attendance of the parties before him at a hearing, as frequently happens in court.

7. Arbitration, although a formal process, is less formal than the court process and takes place in a more informal setting. All attending at the various hearings before the arbitrator, including the arbitrator, will sit at the same table on the same level. It means all parties will feel able to communicate when necessary in the knowledge that all present will listen and be able to contribute within the hearing. The parties gain confidence that, when appropriate, they may directly contribute and that their comments will be heard and listened to by all others present, including the arbitrator. A further benefit of the somewhat less formal setting is that most arbitrators will have refreshments such as coffee, tea and water available.

8. If during a hearing any individual present wants a short adjournment (a party may wish to have a few minutes away from the arbitration setting) the arbitrator will normally grant it, either immediately or when it is appropriate to take a break during the hearing. The arbitration process can be very sensitive to the needs of all attending.

9. Early discussions will take place between the arbitrator, the parties and their legal representatives about how the arbitration will be recorded. There are various different methods which can be deployed, including recording the proceedings (video recording or just voice recording) or employing a minute taker. Sometimes it will be agreed that the parties' representatives will take notes and then prepare minutes of the directions hearing which will be circulated for all to consider and review.

10. The speed at which the arbitration deals with the issues is determined by the arbitrator with the legal representatives and the parties. The potential costs savings through arbitration result from the comparatively speedy resolution achievable when contrasted with the delay inherent in

court procedures. Concluding the matter expeditiously with a final and binding award means the parties can move on with their lives. Arbitration, by its ability to conclude matters speedily, removes the burden of outstanding and unsettled financial and children issues from the parties and enables them to continue their lives and their work (if employed) without the constant concern of court proceedings and endless involvement with lawyers (see the case study at **1.2.2**).

11. The parties can discuss with the arbitrator how the arbitration procedures are to move forward and the timetable to be complied with.

12. The general principle is that the arbitration and its outcome are confidential and remain so, and only the parties themselves can disclose what has happened at the arbitration if they are minded to do so. Any note or transcript of the proceedings is confidential and will be used solely for the purpose of the arbitration, its implementation and (if need be) in connection with any necessary application to the court, or the enforcement of the award.

13. The arbitrator may at any point in the process agree that it would be appropriate for another dispute resolution procedure to be used, e.g. mediation or negotiation, in which case the arbitration will be adjourned until that has been attempted. Thus the arbitrator will do what he can to promote an amicable settlement of the issues separating the parties.

14. The award of the arbitrator is final and binding upon the parties, and although there is provision for appeal the grounds for appeal are extremely limited. The parties can agree to waive their rights to appeal which provides even greater certainty and finality to the process.

3.3 How can an arbitral decision be challenged?

In a commercial award, when the parties agree to arbitration they 'buy the right to get the wrong answer'[1] – in other words, the grounds to correct or to challenge an award are very circumscribed. Similarly, when the parties sign the application form (ARB1FS or ARB1CS) they are agreeing to be bound by the adjudication of the arbitrator, and the grounds for challenging that arbitral decision are limited. Nevertheless, there are two possible options, which apply to both Financial and Children arbitration.

3.3.1 Corrective jurisdiction

Under s.57(1) of the Arbitration Act 1996, the parties are free to agree on the powers of the tribunal to correct an award or make an additional award. If they do not agree, then either party may, under s.57(3)–(4) of the Act, apply to the arbitrator within 28 days of the award to either:

> (3) . . .
>
> > (a) correct an award so as to remove any clerical mistake or error arising from an accidental slip or omission or clarify or remove any ambiguity in the award, or
> > (b) make an additional award in respect of any claim (including a claim for interest or costs) which was presented to the tribunal but was not dealt with in the award.

3.3.2 Appeal

The grounds of appeal against the arbitrator's decision are deliberately very limited. The overall experience in commercial arbitration cases has been that, in general, courts tend to support the arbitration process and to discourage appeals. The Arbitration Act 1996 provides for the following potential routes:

---

[1] Sir Bernard Eder in his speech 'Challenges to the arbitral awards at the seat' at the 2014 Mauritius International Arbitration Conference.

- challenging an award of the arbitral tribunal as to its 'substantive jurisdiction' (s.67);

- challenging an award on the grounds of 'serious irregularity'(s.68); or

- appealing to the court on a 'question of law' arising out of an award made in the proceedings (s.69).

As stated in s.70, to bring an application or appeal the applicant must have exhausted arbitral processes of appeal and review. Any application or appeal must be brought within 28 days of the award.

Challenges to the substantive jurisdiction are dealt with under s.30(1)(a)–(c) of the Act – namely:

   (1) . . .

   (a)   whether there is a valid arbitration agreement;
   (b)   whether the tribunal is properly constituted; and
   (c)   what matters have been submitted to arbitration in accordance with the arbitration agreement.

Instances of 'serious irregularity' include:

- failure by the tribunal to act fairly;

- the tribunal exceeding its powers;

- procedural failure;

- failure by the tribunal to deal with all the issues that were put to it;

- uncertainty or ambiguity as to the effect of the award; and

- the award being obtained by fraud or the way in which it was procured being contrary to public policy.

The court will not generally give leave to appeal or substitute its own decision for that of the tribunal on points that might be said to involve a question of law (e.g. whether on the particular facts a party has wrongfully repudiated or renounced a contract), unless the court decides that the arbitral tribunal had or might have misdirected itself in a point of law.

The first 'notice to show cause' case in the Family Court following the making of a family arbitral award was *DB* v. *DLJ* [2016] EWHC 324 (**Appendix 4.2**). The case underlines the fact that clients and their legal advisers can be confident that the circumstances in which an arbitral award may be challenged remain very limited indeed.

In this case, Mostyn J considered the traditional grounds for challenging a financial remedy order in family court proceedings – mistake, fraud, non-disclosure and the existence of a supervening event.

He contrasted the situation in arbitration, where fraud is a ground of challenge under s.68(2)(g) of the Arbitration Act 1996 and mistake can only be raised if it falls within s.57 of the Act and will not extend to error in the production of evidence. Mostyn J concluded, however, that if – following an arbitral award – evidence emerges that would (had the award been an order of the court) entitle the court to set aside its order on the grounds of mistake or supervening event, then the court is entitled to refuse to incorporate the arbitral award.

It may be possible for the court to make a different order reflecting the new evidence.

Furthermore, in his judgment Mostyn J commented positively about arbitration and said that the award was a 'thorough, conscientious and clear piece of work. Its quality is a testament to the merit of opting for arbitration'.

3.4 Points to note

3.4.1 Consent by both parties

Arbitration, like all other dispute resolution procedures, needs the consent of all parties before it can proceed. This is unlike court proceedings where one of the parties can (subject to the requirement for mediation first to be considered) make the decision to pursue litigation through the courts whether that is the wish of the other party or not.

3.4.2 Costs

The arbitrator will be paid a fee (often a fixed fee negotiated during the pre-commitment meeting) and expenses may be incurred for the use of a venue, recording equipment and the arbitrator's travel.

3.5 International arbitration

It has been very interesting to speak with different practitioners and review details of how arbitration is conducted both in England and overseas. It is also interesting to note how different arbitration would be in England and Wales if it had been established by statute. The following articles (appended at **Part II**) review arbitration in Canada and internationally:

1. 'Family law arbitration in Ontario, Canada' – Ann Wilton and Gary Joseph (see **Appendix 3.1**).
2. 'ADR: wide focus and global view' – Suzanne Kingston and Rachael Kelsey (see **Appendix 3.2**).
3. 'Family arbitration' – Sir Hugh Bennett (see **Appendix 3.3**).

3.6 Conclusion

One of the current concerns about family matters in the courts are the delays. As s.33 of the Arbitration Act 1996 ensures that the arbitrator must adopt procedures to avoid unnecessary delays and expense, the arbitration process should be widely encouraged as a form of private dispute resolution in financial and child related family cases. Hopefully, as the merits and advantages of the arbitration process become more widely known, the pressure will be taken off the courts and access to justice for all will increase.

Part II

Appendices

Appendix 1

Legislation and rules

1.1

Family Law Arbitration Financial Scheme: Arbitration Rules 2016[1]

[Fifth edition, effective 18 July 2016]

Article 1 – Introductory

1.1 The Family Law Arbitration Financial Scheme ('the Financial Scheme') is a scheme under which financial or property disputes with a family background may be resolved by arbitration.

1.2 The Financial Scheme is administered and run by the Institute of Family Law Arbitrators Limited ('IFLA'), a company limited by guarantee whose members are the Chartered Institute of Arbitrators ('CIArb'), Resolution and the Family Law Bar Association ('FLBA').

1.3 Disputes referred to the Financial Scheme will be arbitrated in accordance with:

(a) the provisions of the Arbitration Act 1996 ('the Act'), both mandatory and non-mandatory;

(b) these Rules, to the extent that they exclude, replace or modify the non-mandatory provisions of the Act; and

(c) the agreement of the parties, to the extent that that excludes, replaces or modifies the non-mandatory provisions of the Act or these Rules; except that the parties may not agree to exclude, replace or modify Art.3 (Applicable Law).

1.4 The parties may not amend or modify these Rules or any procedure under them after the appointment of an arbitrator unless the arbitrator agrees to such amendment or modification; and may not amend or modify Art.3 (Applicable Law) in any event.

1.5 Expressions used in these Rules which are also used in the Act have the same meaning as they do in the Act and any reference to a section number means the section of the Act so numbered, unless otherwise indicated.

Article 2 – Scope of the Financial Scheme

2.1 The Financial Scheme covers financial and property disputes arising from:

(a) marriage and its breakdown (including financial provision on divorce, judicial separation or nullity);

(b) civil partnership and its breakdown;

(c) co-habitation and the ending of co-habitation;

(d) parenting or those sharing parental responsibility;

(e) provision for dependants from the estate of the deceased.

2.2 The Financial Scheme covers (but is not limited to) claims which would come within the following statutes:

(a) the Married Women's Property Act 1882, s.17;

(b) the Matrimonial Causes Act 1973, Part II;

(c) the Inheritance (Provision for Family and Dependants) Act 1975;

---

[1] © IFLA 2016.

(d) the Matrimonial and Family Proceedings Act 1984, s.12 (financial relief after overseas divorce);

(e) the Children Act 1989, Sched.1;

(f) the Trusts of Land and Appointment of Trustees Act 1996;

(g) the Civil Partnership Act 2004 Sched.5, or Sched.7, Part 1, para.2 (financial relief after overseas dissolution).

2.3 The Financial Scheme does not apply to disputes directly concerning:

(a) the liberty of individuals;

(b) the status either of individuals or of their relationship;

(c) the care or parenting of children;

(d) bankruptcy or insolvency;

(e) any person or organisation which is not a party to the arbitration.

Article 3 – Applicable law

3.1 The arbitrator will decide the substance of the dispute only in accordance with the law of England and Wales. The arbitrator may have regard to, and admit evidence of, the law of another country insofar as, and in the same way as, a Judge exercising the jurisdiction of the High Court would do so.

Article 4 – Starting the arbitration

4.1 The parties may refer a dispute to arbitration under the Financial Scheme by making an agreement to arbitrate in Form ARB1FS, signed by both parties or their legal representatives, and submitting it to IFLA.

4.2 IFLA has set up the IFLA Financial Panel of arbitrators ('the Financial Panel') comprising Members of the Chartered Institute of Arbitrators who are experienced family law professionals with particular expertise in financial matters and who have received specific training in the determination of family disputes relating to financial matters by means of arbitration.

4.3.1 The parties may agree to nominate a particular arbitrator from the Financial Panel; and may, if they are agreed, approach a particular arbitrator directly. Any arbitrator directly approached must refer the approach to IFLA before accepting appointment in order to facilitate the completion of Form ARB1FS before the arbitration commences. IFLA will offer the appointment to the agreed arbitrator. If the appointment is not accepted by their first choice of arbitrator the parties may, if they agree, make a second or subsequent choice. Otherwise, it will be offered to another member of the Financial Panel chosen by IFLA in accordance with paragraph 4.3.3 below.

4.3.2 Alternatively, the parties may agree on a shortlist of arbitrators from the Financial Panel any one of whom would be acceptable to them, and may ask IFLA to select one of the arbitrators on the shortlist without reference to any criteria. In this case, IFLA will offer the appointment to one of the shortlisted arbitrators chosen at random. If the appointment is not accepted by the first choice of arbitrator, IFLA will offer the appointment to a second or subsequent shortlisted arbitrator, similarly chosen at random. If none of the shortlisted arbitrators accepts the appointment, IFLA will inform the parties and invite them to submit further agreed names.

4.3.3 In all other cases (including if so requested by the parties) IFLA will offer the appointment to a sole arbitrator from the Financial Panel whom it considers appropriate having regard to the nature of the dispute; any preferences expressed by the parties as to the qualifications, areas of experience, expertise or other attributes of the arbitrator; any preference expressed by the parties as to the geographical location of the arbitration; and any other relevant circumstances.

4.4 If, after considering Form ARB1FS and any representations from the parties, either IFLA or the arbitrator considers that the dispute is not suitable for arbitration under the Financial Scheme, then the parties will be so advised and their reference of the matter to the Financial Scheme will be treated as withdrawn.

4.5 The arbitration will be regarded as commenced when the arbitrator communicates to the parties his or her acceptance of the appointment.

4.6 Except as provided in Art.4.7, a party to an arbitration under the Financial Scheme may be represented in the proceedings by a lawyer or other person chosen by him; or, if he is acting in person, may receive the advice and assistance of a McKenzie Friend.

4.7 If at any time the arbitrator forms the view that the participation of a non-lawyer representative or the assistance given by a McKenzie Friend unreasonably impedes or is likely to impede the conduct of the arbitral proceedings or the administration of justice, he may direct that the relevant party should not continue to be so represented or assisted, as the case may be, and will state his reasons in writing.

Article 5 – Arbitrator's appointment

5.1 Before accepting the appointment or as soon as the relevant facts are known, the arbitrator will disclose to the parties any actual or potential conflict of interest or any matter that might give rise to justifiable doubts as to his or her impartiality.

5.2 In the event of such disclosure, the parties, or either of them (as appropriate), may waive any objection to the arbitrator continuing to act, in which case the arbitrator may commence or continue with the arbitration. If an objection is maintained, the arbitrator will decide whether to continue to act, subject to any agreement by the parties to revoke his or her authority or intervention by the court.

5.3 After accepting appointment, the arbitrator may not subsequently act in relation to the same dispute in a different capacity.

5.4 If the arbitrator ceases to hold office through revocation of his or her authority, removal by the court, resignation or death, or is otherwise unable, or refuses, to act, and either party or the existing arbitrator so requests, IFLA may appoint a replacement arbitrator from the Financial Panel.

5.5 The replacement arbitrator may determine whether and if so to what extent the previous proceedings should stand.

Article 6 – Communications between parties, the arbitrator and IFLA

6.1 Any communication between the arbitrator and either party will be copied to the other party.

6.2 Unless agreed by the parties, the arbitrator will designate one party as the lead party. For the purposes of the Act, the lead party will equate to a claimant, but will be formally referred to in the arbitration as the 'Applicant'. The other party will equate to a respondent, and will be formally referred to in the arbitration as the 'Respondent'.

6.3 The arbitrator will not discuss any aspect of the dispute or of the arbitration with either party or their legal representatives in the absence of the other party or their legal representatives, unless such communication is solely for the purpose of making administrative arrangements.

6.4 Neither IFLA, the CIArb, Resolution nor the FLBA will be required to enter into any correspondence concerning the arbitration or its outcome.

Article 7 – Powers of the arbitrator

7.1 The arbitrator will have all the powers given to an arbitrator by the Act including those contained in section 35 (consolidation of proceedings and concurrent hearings); and section 39 (provisional orders), but limited as provided by Art.7.2.

7.2 In relation to substantive relief of an interim or final character, the arbitrator will have the power to make orders or awards to the same extent and in the same or similar form as would a Judge exercising the jurisdiction of the High Court. (For the avoidance of doubt, the arbitrator's power does not extend to interim injunctions; committal; or jurisdiction over non-parties without their agreement.)

7.3 The arbitrator will have the power to award interest in accordance with section 49 (interest) whether or not it is specifically claimed.

7.4 If the arbitrator considers that the dispute is not suitable for arbitration under the Financial Scheme the arbitrator will have the power to terminate the proceedings.

Article 8 – Powers of the arbitrator concerning procedure

8.1 The arbitrator will decide all procedural and evidential matters (including, but not limited to, those referred to in section 34(2)), subject to the right of the parties to agree any matter (if necessary, with the concurrence of the arbitrator (see Art.1.4)).

8.2 In accordance with section 37 (power to appoint experts), the arbitrator may appoint experts to report on specific issues or prepare valuations.

8.3 The arbitrator may limit the number of expert witnesses to be called by any party or may direct that no expert be called on any issue or issues or that expert evidence may be called only with the permission of the arbitrator.

8.4 Further, and/or in particular, the arbitrator will have the power to:

(a) direct a party to produce information, documents or other materials in a specified manner and/or within a specified time;

(b) give directions in relation to any property which is the subject of the proceedings or as to which any question arises in the proceedings, and which is owned by or is in the possession or control of a party to the proceedings for the inspection, photographing, valuation, preservation, custody or detention of the property by the tribunal, an expert or a party.

8.5 If, without showing sufficient cause, a party fails to comply with its obligations under section 40 (general duty of parties) or with these Rules, or is in default as set out in section 41(4) (failure to attend a hearing or make submissions), then, after giving that party due notice, the arbitrator may continue the proceedings in the absence of that party or without any written evidence or submissions on their behalf and may make an award on the basis of the evidence before him or her.

8.6 The parties agree that if one of them fails to comply with a peremptory order made by the arbitrator and another party wishes to apply to the court for an order requiring compliance under s.42 (enforcement of peremptory orders of tribunal), the powers of the court under that section are available.

Article 9 – Form of procedure

9.1 The parties are free to agree as to the form of procedure (if necessary, with the concurrence of the arbitrator (see Art.1.4)) and, in particular, to adopt a documents-only procedure or some other simplified or expedited procedure.

9.2 If there is no such agreement, the arbitrator will have the widest possible discretion to adopt procedures suitable to the circumstances of the particular case in accordance with section 33 (general duty of the tribunal).

Article 10 – General procedure

10.1 Generally, on commencement of the arbitration, the arbitrator will invite the parties to make submissions setting out briefly their respective views as to the nature of the dispute, the issues, what form of procedure should be adopted, the timetable and any other relevant matters.

10.2 If appropriate, the arbitrator may convene a preliminary meeting, telephone conference or other suitable forum for exchange of views.

10.3 Within a reasonable time of ascertaining the parties' views, the arbitrator will give directions and set a timetable for the procedural steps in the arbitration, including (but not limited to) the following:

(a)   written statements of case;

(b)   disclosure and production of documents as between the parties;

(c)   the exchange of witness statements;

(d)   the number and type of expert witnesses, exchange of their reports and meetings between them;

(e)   arrangements for any meeting or hearing and the procedures to be adopted at these events;

(f)   time limits to be imposed on oral submissions or the examination of witnesses, or any other procedure for controlling the length of hearings.

10.4   The arbitrator may at any time direct any of the following to be delivered in writing:

(a)   submissions on behalf of any party;

(b)   questions to be put to any witness;

(c)   answers by any witness to specific questions.

Article 11 – Applications for directions as to procedural or evidential matters

11.1   The arbitrator may direct a time limit for making or responding to applications for directions as to procedural or evidential matters.

11.2   Any application by a party for directions as to procedural or evidential matters will be accompanied by such evidence and/or submissions as the applicant may consider appropriate or as the arbitrator may direct.

11.3   A party responding to such an application will, if feasible, have a reasonable opportunity to consider and agree the order or directions proposed.

11.4   Any agreement will be communicated to the arbitrator promptly and will be subject to the arbitrator's concurrence, if necessary (see Art.1.4).

11.5   Unless the arbitrator convenes a meeting, telephone conference or other forum for exchange of views, any response to the application will be followed by an opportunity for the party applying to comment on that response; and the arbitrator will give directions within a reasonable time after receiving the applicant's comments.

Article 12 – Alternative procedure

12.1   In any case where it is appropriate, the parties may agree or the arbitrator may decide to adopt the procedure set out in this Article.

12.2   The parties may at any stage agree (with the concurrence of the arbitrator) or the arbitrator may direct any variation or addition to the following steps and/or timetable. In particular, the arbitrator may at any stage allow time for the parties to consider their positions and pursue negotiations with a view to arriving at an amicable settlement (see, also, Arts.17.1 and 17.2).

12.3   Within 56 days of the arbitrator communicating to the parties his or her acceptance of the appointment, each party will complete and send to the arbitrator and to the other party a sworn statement as to their financial situation (in the form of the 'Form E' or 'Form E1' Financial Statement in accordance with the Family Procedure Rules 2010, as appropriate) together with such further evidence or information as the arbitrator may direct.

12.4   Within 28 days of receipt of the other party's financial statement, each party may send to the arbitrator and to the other party a questionnaire raising questions and/or requesting information and/or documents.

12.5   Within 14 days of receipt of a questionnaire, a party may send to the arbitrator and to the other party reasoned objections to answering any of the questions or meeting any of the requests, together with a submission as to whether a preliminary meeting is required.

12.6   Within 14 days of receipt of objections or, if there is a preliminary meeting, within a reasonable time after that meeting, the arbitrator will direct in respect of each party:

(a)   which questions are to be answered and which requests are to be met, together with the time within which these things are to be done;

(b)   which property is to be valued, who is to undertake the valuation, how they are to be appointed and the time within which the valuation is to be carried out; and

(c)   any other steps for providing information, dealing with enquiries or clarifying issues as may be appropriate.

12.7   Within a reasonable time of receipt from both parties of replies to questionnaires, valuations and any other information as may have been required, the arbitrator may convene a further meeting to review progress, address outstanding issues and consider what further directions are necessary.

12.8   The arbitrator will give detailed directions for all further procedural steps in the arbitration including (but not limited to) the following:

(a)   the drawing up of lists of issues and schedules of assets;

(b)   written submissions;

(c)   arrangements for any meeting or hearing and the procedures to be adopted at these events;

(d)   time limits to be imposed on oral submissions or the examination of witnesses, or any other procedure for controlling the length of hearings.

Article 13 – Awards

13.1   The arbitrator will deliver an award within a reasonable time after the conclusion of the proceedings or the relevant part of the proceedings.

13.2   Any award will be in writing, will state the seat of the arbitration, will be dated and signed by the arbitrator, and (unless the parties agree otherwise or the award is by consent) will contain sufficient reasons to show why the arbitrator has reached the decisions it contains.

13.3   Once an award has been made, it will be final and binding on the parties, subject to the following:

(a)   any challenge to the award by any available arbitral process of appeal or review or in accordance with the provisions of Part 1 of the Act;

(b)   insofar as the subject matter of the award requires it to be embodied in a court order (see Art.13.4), any changes which the court making that order may require;

(c)   insofar as the award provides for continuing payments to be made by one party to another, or to a child or children, a subsequent award or court order reviewing and varying or revoking the provision for continuing payments, and which supersedes an existing award.

13.4   If and so far as the subject matter of the award makes it necessary, the parties will apply to an appropriate court for an order in the same or similar terms as the award or the relevant part of the award and will take all reasonably necessary steps to see that such an order is made. In this context, 'an appropriate court' means a court which has jurisdiction to make a substantive order in the same or similar terms as the award, whether on primary application or on transfer from another division of the court.

13.5   The arbitrator may refuse to deliver an award to the parties except upon full payment of his or her fees or expenses. Subject to this entitlement, the arbitrator will send a copy of the award to each party or its legal representatives.

Article 14 – Costs

14.1   In this Article any reference to costs is a reference to the costs of the arbitration as defined in section 59 (costs of the arbitration) including the fees and expenses of IFLA, unless otherwise indicated.

14.2   The arbitrator may require the parties to pay his or her fees and expenses accrued during the course of the arbitration at such interim stages as may be agreed with the parties, and in the absence of agreement, at reasonable intervals.

14.3   The arbitrator may order either party to provide security for the arbitrator's fees and expenses and the fees and expenses of IFLA.

14.4   Unless otherwise agreed by the parties, the arbitrator will make an award allocating costs as between the parties in accordance with the following general principle:

(a)   the parties will bear the arbitrator's fees and expenses and the fees and expenses of IFLA in equal shares;

(b)   there will be no order or award requiring one party to pay the legal or other costs of another party.

This principle is subject to the arbitrator's overriding discretion set out in Art.14.5.

14.5   Where it is appropriate to do so because of the conduct of a party in relation to the arbitration (whether before or during it), the arbitrator may at any stage order that party:

(a)   to bear a larger than equal share, and up to the full amount, of the arbitrator's fees and expenses and the fees and expenses of IFLA;

(b)   to pay the legal or other costs of another party;

and may make an award accordingly.

14.6   In deciding whether, and if so, how to exercise the discretion set out in Art.14.5, the arbitrator will have regard to the following:

(a)   any failure by a party to comply with these Rules or any order or directions which the arbitrator considers relevant;

(b)   any open offer to settle made by a party;

(c)   whether it was reasonable for a party to raise, pursue or contest a particular allegation or issue;

(d)   the manner in which a party has pursued or responded to a claim or a particular allegation or issue;

(e)   any other aspect of a party's conduct in relation to the arbitration which the arbitrator considers relevant; and

(f)   the financial effect on the parties of any costs order or award.

14.7   Unless the parties agree otherwise, no offer to settle which is not an open offer to settle shall be admissible at any stage of the arbitration.

14.8   These rules as to costs will not apply to applications made to the court where costs fall to be determined by the court.

Article 15 – Conclusion of the arbitration

15.1   The agreement to arbitrate will be discharged (and any current arbitration will terminate) if:

(a)   a party to the arbitration agreement dies; or

(b)   a party to the arbitration agreement lacks, or loses, capacity (within the meaning of the Mental Capacity Act 2005); except that:

(i)   if the party is represented by an attorney who has the power so to act, the attorney may, in his or her discretion, continue with the arbitration or terminate it;

(ii)   if a Deputy is appointed by the Court of Protection in relation to that party and has the power so to act, the Deputy may, in his or her discretion, continue with the arbitration or terminate it.

15.2   The arbitration will be terminated:

(a)   If the arbitrator considers that the dispute is not suitable for arbitration under the Financial Scheme and terminates the proceedings;

(b)   If and insofar as a court entertains concurrent legal proceedings and declines to stay them in favour of arbitration;

(c)   If the parties settle the dispute and, in accordance with section 51 (settlement), the arbitrator terminates the proceedings;

(d)   If the parties agree in writing to discontinue the arbitration and notify the arbitrator accordingly;

(e)   On the arbitrator making a final award dealing with all the issues, subject to any entitlement of the parties to challenge the award by any available arbitral process of appeal or review or in accordance with the provisions of Part 1 of the Act.

Article 16 – Confidentiality

16.1 The general principle is that the arbitration and its outcome are confidential, except insofar as disclosure may be necessary to challenge, implement, enforce or vary an award (see Art.13.3(c)), in relation to applications to the court or as may be compelled by law.

16.2 All documents, statements, information and other materials disclosed by a party will be held by any other party and their legal representatives in confidence and used solely for the purpose of the arbitration, unless otherwise agreed by the disclosing party or compelled by law.

16.3 Any transcript of the proceedings will be provided to all parties and to the arbitrator. It will similarly be confidential and used solely for the purpose of the arbitration, implementation or enforcement of any award or applications to the court, unless otherwise agreed by the parties or compelled by law.

16.4 The arbitrator will not be called as a witness by any party either to testify or to produce any documents or materials received or generated during the course of the proceedings in relation to any aspect of the arbitration, unless with the agreement of the arbitrator or compelled by law.

Article 17 – General

17.1 At relevant stages of the arbitration, the arbitrator may encourage the parties to consider using an alternative dispute resolution procedure other than arbitration, such as mediation, negotiation or early neutral evaluation, in relation to the dispute or a particular aspect of the dispute.

17.2 If the parties agree to use an alternative dispute resolution procedure such as mediation, negotiation or early neutral evaluation, then the arbitrator will facilitate its use and may, if appropriate, stay the arbitration or a particular aspect of the arbitration for an appropriate period of time for that purpose.

17.3 In the event that the dispute is settled (following a mediation or otherwise), the parties will inform the arbitrator promptly and section 51 (settlement) will apply. Fees and expenses accrued due to arbitrator by that stage will remain payable.

17.4 The parties will inform the arbitrator promptly of any proposed application to the court and will provide him or her with copies of all documentation intended to be used in any such application.

17.5 IFLA, the CIArb, Resolution, the FLBA, their employees and agents will not be liable:

    (a)   for anything done or omitted in the actual or purported appointment or nomination of an arbitrator, unless the act or omission is shown to have been in bad faith;

    (b)   by reason of having appointed or nominated an arbitrator, for anything done or omitted by the arbitrator (or his employees or agents) in the discharge or purported discharge of his functions as an arbitrator;

    (c)   for any consequences if, for whatever reason, the arbitral process does not result in an award or, where necessary, a court order embodying an award by which the matters to be determined are resolved.

Family Law Arbitration Children Scheme: Arbitration Rules 2016[1]

[First edition, effective 1 November 2016]

Safety and welfare of children

The safety and welfare of children is of the utmost importance to the Family Law Arbitration Children Scheme. Measures providing for safeguarding appear at Article 17 (below) and in the Form ARB1CS and Safeguarding Questionnaire which has to be completed by the parties. These steps are intended to ensure that matters accepted for arbitration are suitable for that process, and that the child(ren) concerned will be safe from harm.

Article 1 – Introductory

1.1   The Family Law Arbitration Children Scheme ('the Children Scheme') is a scheme under which disputes concerning the exercise of parental responsibility and other private law issues about the welfare of children may be resolved by the determination of an arbitrator.

1.2   The Children Scheme is administered and run by the Institute of Family Law Arbitrators Limited ('IFLA'), a company limited by guarantee whose members are the Chartered Institute of Arbitrators ('CIArb'), Resolution and the Family Law Bar Association ('FLBA').

1.3   Disputes referred to the Children Scheme will be determined by arbitration in accordance with:

(a)   the provisions of the Arbitration Act 1996 ('the Act') both mandatory and non-mandatory;

(b)   these Rules, to the extent that they exclude, replace or modify the non-mandatory provisions of the Act; and

(c)   the agreement of the parties, to the extent that that excludes, replaces or modifies the non-mandatory provisions of the Act or these Rules; except that the parties may not agree to exclude, replace or modify Art.3 (Applicable Law).

1.4   The parties may not amend or modify these Rules or any procedure under them after the appointment of an arbitrator unless the arbitrator agrees to such amendment or modification; and may in any event neither amend nor modify Art.3 (Applicable Law) nor agree to exclude the right of any party to appeal to the court on a question of law (section 69).

1.5   Expressions used in these Rules which are also used in the Act have the same meaning as they do in the Act, except that in these Rules 'determine' and 'determination' have an equivalent meaning to 'award' in the Act; and any reference to a section number means the section of the Act so numbered, unless otherwise indicated.

Article 2 – Scope of the Children Scheme

2.1   Save as provided by Art.2.2 below, the Children Scheme covers issues between parents (or other persons holding parental responsibility or with a sufficient interest in the child's welfare)

---

[1]   © IFLA 2016.

which relate to the exercise of parental responsibility or the present or future welfare of the child concerned (including the child's upbringing, present or future living arrangements, contact and education) and extends but is not limited to matters which could be the subject of an application to the Family Court under section 8 of the Children Act 1989.

2.2 The following disputes and issues are not within the scope of the Children Scheme:

(a) any application under the inherent jurisdiction for the return of a child to England and Wales ('this jurisdiction') from a country which is not a signatory to the 1980 Hague Convention on the Civil Aspects of International Child Abduction ('the 1980 Hague Convention');

(b) any application for a child's summary return to this or another jurisdiction under the 1980 Hague Convention;

(c) any application for permanent or temporary removal of a child from this jurisdiction;

(d) any application for the court 'to examine the question of custody of the child' under Art.11(7) of Council Regulation (EC) No 2201/2003 after an order of a foreign court on non-return to this jurisdiction made pursuant to Art.13 of the 1980 Hague Convention;

(e) any application for cross-border access within the scope of Art.41 of the said Council Regulation which, if a judgment, would require a court to issue an Annex III Certificate;

(f) any dispute relating to the authorisation of life-changing or life-threatening medical treatment or the progress of such treatment;

(g) any case where a party lacks capacity under the Mental Capacity Act 2005;

(h) any case where any person with parental responsibility for the child or who seeks to be a party to an arbitration under the Children Scheme is a minor; and any case where any person with parental responsibility for the child is not a party to the arbitration;

(i) any case where the child concerned has party status in existing proceedings relating to the same or similar issues, or should in the opinion of the arbitrator be separately represented in the arbitration.

Article 3 – Applicable law

3.1 The arbitrator will determine the substance of the dispute only in accordance with the law of England and Wales. The arbitrator may have regard to, and admit evidence of, the law of another country insofar as, and in the same way as, a Judge exercising the jurisdiction of the High Court would do so.

3.2 When determining any question relating to the upbringing of a child, the welfare of the child shall be the arbitrator's paramount consideration and in considering welfare the arbitrator shall have regard in particular to the welfare checklist set out in section 1(3) of the Children Act 1989.

Article 4 – Starting the arbitration

4.1.1 The parties may refer a dispute to arbitration under the Children Scheme by making an agreement to arbitrate in Form ARB1CS, signed by both parties or their legal representatives, and submitting it to IFLA.

4.1.2 Form ARB1CS and the Safeguarding Questionnaire shall be in the form of Annex 1 to these Rules.

4.2 IFLA has established the IFLA Children Panel of arbitrators ('the Children Panel') comprising Members of the Chartered Institute of Arbitrators who are experienced family law professionals with particular expertise in children matters and who have received specific training in the determination of family disputes relating to children by means of arbitration.

4.3.1 The parties may agree to nominate a particular arbitrator from the Children Panel; and may, if they are agreed, approach a particular arbitrator directly. Any arbitrator directly approached must refer the approach to IFLA before accepting appointment in order to facilitate the completion of Form ARB1CS and the Safeguarding Questionnaires before the arbitration commences. IFLA will offer the appointment to the agreed arbitrator. If the appointment is not accepted by their first choice of arbitrator the parties may, if they agree, make a second or subsequent choice. Otherwise, it will be offered to another member of the Children Panel chosen by IFLA in accordance with paragraph 4.3.3 below.

4.3.2   Alternatively, the parties may agree on a shortlist of arbitrators from the Children Panel any one of whom would be acceptable to them, and may ask IFLA to select one of the arbitrators on the shortlist without reference to any criteria. In this case, IFLA will offer the appointment to one of the shortlisted arbitrators chosen at random. If the appointment is not accepted by the first choice of arbitrator, IFLA will offer the appointment to a second or subsequent shortlisted arbitrator, similarly chosen at random. If none of the shortlisted arbitrators accepts the appointment, IFLA will inform the parties and invite them to submit further agreed names.

4.3.3   In all other cases (including if so requested by the parties) IFLA will offer the appointment to a sole arbitrator from the Children Panel whom it considers appropriate having regard to the nature of the dispute; any preferences expressed by the parties as to the qualifications, areas of experience, expertise or other attributes of the arbitrator; any preference expressed by the parties as to the geographical location of the arbitration; and any other relevant circumstances.

4.4   If, after considering Form ARB1CS, the Safeguarding Questionnaires and any representations from the parties, either IFLA or the arbitrator considers that the dispute is not suitable for arbitration under the Children Scheme, the parties will be so advised and their reference of the matter to the Children Scheme will be treated as withdrawn.

4.5   The arbitration will be regarded as commenced when the arbitrator communicates to the parties his or her acceptance of the appointment.

4.6   Except as provided in Art.4.7, a party to an arbitration under the Children Scheme may be represented in the proceedings by a lawyer or other person chosen by him; or, if a party is acting in person, may receive the advice and assistance of a McKenzie Friend.

4.7   If at any time the arbitrator forms the view that the participation of a non-lawyer representative or the assistance given by a McKenzie Friend unreasonably impedes or is likely to impede the conduct of the arbitral proceedings or the administration of justice, the arbitrator may direct that the relevant party should not continue to be so represented or assisted, as the case may be, and will state the reasons in writing.

Article 5 – Arbitrator's appointment

5.1   Before accepting the appointment or as soon as the relevant facts are known, the arbitrator will disclose to the parties any actual or potential conflict of interest or any matter that might give rise to justifiable doubts as to his or her impartiality.

5.2   In the event of such disclosure, the parties, or either of them (as appropriate) may waive any objection to the arbitrator continuing to act, in which case the arbitrator may commence or continue with the arbitration. If an objection is maintained, the arbitrator will decide whether to continue to act, subject to any agreement by the parties to revoke his or her authority or intervention by the court.

5.3   After accepting appointment, the arbitrator may not subsequently act in relation to the same dispute in a different capacity.

5.4   If the arbitrator ceases to hold office through revocation of his or her authority, removal by the court, resignation or death, or is otherwise unable, or refuses, to act, and either party or the existing arbitrator so requests, IFLA may appoint a replacement arbitrator from the Children Panel.

5.5   The replacement arbitrator may determine whether and if so to what extent previous proceedings shall stand.

Article 6 – Communications between the parties, the arbitrator and IFLA

6.1   Any communication between the arbitrator and either party will be copied to the other party.

6.2 Unless agreed by the parties, the arbitrator will designate one party as the lead party. For the purposes of the Act, the lead party will equate to a claimant, but will be formally referred to in the arbitration as the 'Applicant'. The other party will equate to a respondent, and will be formally referred to in the arbitration as the 'Respondent'.

6.3 The arbitrator will not discuss any aspect of the dispute or of the arbitration with either party or their legal representatives in the absence of the other party or their legal representatives, unless such communication is solely for the purpose of making administrative arrangements.

6.4 Neither IFLA, the CIArb, Resolution nor the FLBA will be required to enter into any correspondence concerning the arbitration or its outcome.

Article 7 – Powers of the arbitrator

7.1 The arbitrator will have all the powers given to an arbitrator by the Act including those contained in section 35 (consolidation of proceedings and concurrent hearings); and section 39 (provisional orders), but limited as provided by Art.7.2.

7.2 In relation to substantive relief of an interim or final character, the arbitrator will have the power to make orders or determinations to the same extent and in the same or similar form as would a Judge exercising the jurisdiction of the High Court. (For the avoidance of doubt, the arbitrator's power does not extend to interim injunctions; committal; or jurisdiction over non-parties without their agreement.)

7.3 If the arbitrator at any stage prior to determination of the issues considers that the dispute is no longer suitable for arbitration under the Children Scheme on welfare or other grounds the arbitrator will have the power to terminate the proceedings (see Arts.15.2(b) and 17.2).

Article 8 – Powers of the arbitrator concerning procedure

8.1 The arbitrator will decide all procedural and evidential matters (including, but not limited to, those referred to in section 34(2)), subject to the right of the parties to agree any matter (if necessary, with the concurrence of the arbitrator (see Art.1.4)).

8.2.1 In accordance with section 37 (power to appoint experts), the arbitrator may appoint experts to report on specific issues.

8.2.2 The arbitrator may limit the number of expert witnesses to be called by any party or may direct that no expert is to be called on any issue or issues or that expert evidence may be called only with the permission of the arbitrator.

8.2.3 Where the parties propose the instruction as an expert of an independent social worker to ascertain the wishes and feelings of a child or otherwise to advise on welfare issues and to report, such instruction will be subject to the confirmation and approval of the arbitrator who will decide the identity of the independent social worker if the parties cannot agree.

8.2.4 The arbitrator may of his or her own motion appoint as an expert an independent social worker of appropriate expertise and standing to ascertain the wishes and feelings of a child or otherwise to advise on welfare issues and to report if the arbitrator considers that such evidence will assist in determining the issues. Such an appointment may be made irrespective of whether or not the parties agree.

8.3 The arbitrator may not meet with the child concerned at any stage of the proceedings including any meeting with the child to discuss or explain the determination or its implementation.

8.4 Further, and/or in particular, the arbitrator will have the power to:

(a) direct a party to produce information, documents or other materials in a specified manner and/or within a specified time;

(b) give directions in relation to any documents or other materials as to which any question arises in the proceedings, and which are owned by or are in the possession or control of a party to the proceedings for the inspection, photographing, valuation, preservation, custody or detention of the property by the tribunal, an expert or a party.

8.5   If, without showing sufficient cause, a party fails to comply with his or her obligations under section 40 (general duty of parties) or with these Rules, or is in default as set out in section 41(4) (failure to attend a hearing or make submissions), then, after giving that party due notice, the arbitrator may continue the proceedings in the absence of that party or without any written evidence or submissions on their behalf and may make a determination on the basis of the evidence before the arbitrator.

8.6   The parties agree that if one of them fails to comply with a peremptory order made by the arbitrator and another party wishes to apply to the court for an order requiring compliance under section 42 (enforcement of peremptory orders of tribunal), the powers of the court under that section are available.

Article 9 – Form of procedure

9.1   The parties are free to agree as to the form of procedure (if necessary, with the concurrence of the arbitrator (see Art.1.4)) and, in particular, to adopt a documents-only procedure or some other simplified or expedited procedure.

9.2   If there is no such agreement, the arbitrator will have the widest possible discretion to adopt procedures suitable to the circumstances of the particular case in accordance with section 33 (general duty of the tribunal).

Article 10 – General procedure

10.1   Generally, on commencement of the arbitration, the arbitrator will invite the parties to make submissions setting out briefly their respective views as to the nature of the dispute, the issues, the outcome they seek, what form of procedure should be adopted, the timetable and any other relevant matters.

10.2   If appropriate, the arbitrator may convene a preliminary meeting, telephone conference or other suitable forum for the exchange of a summary of each party's position on the matters set out in Art.10.1.

10.3   Within a reasonable time of ascertaining the parties' views but in any event not more than 14 days, the arbitrator will give such directions as appear appropriate and set a timetable for the procedural steps in the arbitration, including (but not limited to) the following:

(a)   written statements of case;
(b)   disclosure and production of documents as between the parties;
(c)   the exchange of witness statements;
(d)   the number and type of expert witnesses, exchange of their reports and meetings between them;
(e)   arrangements for any meeting or hearing and the procedures to be adopted at these events;
(f)   time limits to be imposed on oral submissions or the examination of witnesses, or any other procedure for controlling the length of hearings.

10.4   The arbitrator may at any time direct any of the following to be delivered in writing:

(a)   submissions on behalf of any party;
(b)   questions to be put to any witness;
(c)   answers by any witness to specific questions.

Article 11 – Applications for directions as to procedural or evidential matters

11.1   The arbitrator may direct a time limit for making or responding to applications for directions as to procedural or evidential matters.

11.2   Any application by a party for directions as to procedural or evidential matters will be accompanied by such evidence and/or submissions as the applicant may consider appropriate or as the arbitrator may direct.

11.3   A party responding to such an application will have a reasonable opportunity to consider and agree the order or directions proposed.

11.4   Any agreement shall be communicated to the arbitrator promptly and will be subject to the arbitrator's concurrence, if necessary (see Art.1.4).

11.5   Unless the arbitrator convenes a meeting, telephone conference or other forum for exchange of views, any response to the application will be followed by an opportunity for the party applying to comment on that response; and the arbitrator shall give directions within a reasonable time after receiving the applicant's comments.

Article 12 – Alternative procedure

12.1   In any case where it is appropriate, the parties may agree or the arbitrator may decide to adopt the procedure set out in this Article.

12.2   The parties may at any stage agree (with the concurrence of the arbitrator) or the arbitrator may direct any variation or addition to the following steps and/or timetable. In particular, the arbitrator may at any stage allow time for the parties to consider their positions and pursue negotiations with a view to arriving at an amicable settlement (see, also, Arts.18.1 and 18.2).

12.3   Within 14 days of the arbitrator communicating to the parties his or her acceptance of the appointment, each party will complete and send to the other party a sworn statement setting out their case, a brief outline of the facts upon which they rely and the outcome that they seek, together with such further evidence or information as the arbitrator may direct.

12.4   Within 14 days of receipt of the other party's statement, each party may send to the arbitrator and to the other party a questionnaire raising questions and/or requesting information and/or documents.

12.5   Within 7 days of receipt of a questionnaire, a party may send to the arbitrator and to the other party reasoned objections to answering any of the questions together with a submission as to whether a preliminary meeting is required.

12.6   In the absence of any such objection, the party in receipt of the questionnaire shall within 14 days provide succinct answers and/or documents.

12.7   In the event of such objection, the arbitrator will consider and decide in writing whether and to what extent the request should be answered together with a time limit or, alternatively, convene a meeting between the parties face-to-face or in such other form as he or she may decide to be the most appropriate having regard to convenience and costs and may require short written submissions in support of each party's position.

12.8   14 days after exchange of statements or, in the event that questionnaires have been served and allowed, within a reasonable time of receipt from both parties of the responses thereto, the arbitrator may convene a further meeting to review progress, address outstanding issues and consider what further directions are necessary, if he or she deems it appropriate having regard to costs and the avoidance of delay.

12.9   If he or she considers it appropriate having regard to the scope of the dispute between the parties, the arbitrator will give detailed directions for all further procedural steps in the arbitration including (but not limited to) the following:

    (a)   the drawing up of a list of issues and/or a schedule of points of agreement or disagreement;
    (b)   written submissions;
    (c)   arrangements for any meeting or hearing and the procedures to be adopted at these events;
    (d)   time limits to be imposed on oral submissions or the examination of witnesses, or any other procedure for controlling the length of hearings.

Article 13 – The arbitrator's determination

13.1   The arbitrator will deliver a determination within a reasonable time after the conclusion of the proceedings or the relevant part of the proceedings.

13.2   Any determination will be in writing, will state the seat of the arbitration, will be dated and signed by the arbitrator, and, unless it merely records a full agreement the parties have reached during the course of the proceedings, will contain sufficient reasons to show why the arbitrator has reached the decisions it contains.

13.3   Once a determination has been made, it will be final and binding on the parties, subject only to the following:

   (a)   any challenge to the determination by any available arbitral process of appeal or review or in accordance with the provisions of Part 1 of the Act;

   (b)   insofar as the subject matter of the determination requires it to be embodied in a court order (see Art.13.4), any changes which the court making that order may require;

   (c)   any subsequent determination superseding the determination; or any changes to the determination or subsequent order superseding the determination which the Family Court considers ought to be made in the exercise of its statutory and/or inherent jurisdiction whether under the Children Act 1989 or otherwise.

13.4   If and so far as the subject matter of the determination makes it necessary, the parties will apply to an appropriate court for an order in the same or similar terms as the determination or the relevant part of the determination or to assist or enable its implementation and will take all reasonably necessary steps to see that such an order is made. In this context, 'an appropriate court' means the Family Court or such other court in England and Wales which has jurisdiction to make a substantive order in the same or similar terms as the determination.

13.5   Where the terms of the determination require any party to give an undertaking, the determination shall not take effect unless and until a suitable form of undertaking has been lodged with and accepted by an appropriate court.

13.6   The arbitrator may refuse to deliver the determination to the parties except upon full payment of his or her fees or expenses. Subject to this entitlement, the arbitrator will send a copy of the determination to each party or their legal representatives.

Article 14 – Costs

14.1   In this Article any reference to costs is a reference to the costs of the arbitration as defined in section 59 (costs of the arbitration) including the fees and expenses of IFLA and the fees of any expert, unless otherwise stated.

14.2   The arbitrator may require the parties to pay his or her fees and expenses accrued during the course of the arbitration at such interim stages as may be agreed with the parties or, in the absence of agreement, at reasonable intervals.

14.3   The arbitrator may order either party to provide security for the arbitrator's fees and expenses and the fees and expenses of IFLA.

14.4   Unless otherwise agreed by the parties, the arbitrator will make a determination allocating costs as between the parties in accordance with the following general principles:

   (a)   the parties will bear the arbitrator's fees and expenses, the costs of any expert and the fees and expenses of IFLA in equal shares;

   (b)   there will be no order or determination requiring one party to pay the legal or other costs of another party.

These principles are subject to the arbitrator's overriding discretion set out in Arts.14.5 and 14.6.

14.5   Where it is appropriate to do so because of the conduct of a party in relation to the arbitration (whether before or during it), the arbitrator may at any stage order that party:

   (a)   to bear a larger than equal share, and up to the full amount, of the arbitrator's fees and expenses and the fees and expenses of IFLA;

(b)   to pay the legal or other costs of another party;

and may make a determination accordingly.

14.6   In deciding whether, and if so, how to exercise the discretion set out in Art.14.5, the arbitrator will have regard to the following:

(a)   the principles applied by the courts in relation to cases concerning child welfare;
(b)   any failure by a party to comply with these Rules or any order or directions which the arbitrator considers relevant;
(c)   any open offer to settle made by a party;
(d)   whether it was reasonable for a party to raise, pursue or contest a particular allegation or issue;
(e)   the manner in which a party has pursued or responded to a claim or a particular allegation or issue;
(f)   any other aspect of a party's conduct in relation to the arbitration which the arbitrator considers relevant;
(g)   the financial effect on the parties of any costs order or determination.

14.7   Unless the parties agree otherwise, no offer to settle which is not an open offer to settle shall be admissible at any stage of the arbitration.

14.8   These rules as to costs will not apply to applications made to the court where costs fall to be determined by the court.

Article 15 – Conclusion of the arbitration

15.1   The agreement to arbitrate will be discharged (and any current arbitration will terminate) if:

(a)   a party to the arbitration agreement dies; or
(b)   a party to the arbitration agreement lacks, or loses, capacity (within the meaning of the Mental Capacity Act 2005).

15.2   The arbitration will be terminated:

(a)   if the arbitrator considers that the dispute is not suitable for arbitration under the Children Scheme and terminates the proceedings;
(b)   if the arbitrator at any time after the commencement of the arbitration considers that the dispute is no longer suitable for arbitration under the Children Scheme on welfare or other grounds (see Arts.7.3 and 17.2);
(c)   if and insofar as a court entertains concurrent legal proceedings and declines to stay them in favour of arbitration;
(d)   if the parties settle the dispute and, in accordance with section 51 (settlement), the arbitrator terminates the proceedings;
(e)   if the parties agree in writing to discontinue the arbitration and notify the arbitrator accordingly;
(f)   on the arbitrator making a final determination dealing with all the issues, subject to any entitlement of the parties to challenge the determination by any available arbitral process of appeal or review or in accordance with the provisions of Part 1 of the Act.

Article 16 – Confidentiality

16.1   The general principle is that the arbitration and its outcome are confidential, except insofar as disclosure may be necessary:

(a)   to challenge, implement, enforce or vary a determination, or in relation to applications to the court;
(b)   in the performance under Art.17 of an arbitrator's duty to convey information relating to the welfare of the child to any appropriate local authority or government agency, or in the exercise of an arbitrator's choice to inform IFLA of a decision to decline an appointment or to terminate an arbitration; or
(c)   as may otherwise be compelled by law.

16.2.1 All documents, statements, information and other materials disclosed by a party to the arbitration will be held by any other party and their legal representatives in confidence and used solely for the purpose of the arbitration unless otherwise agreed by the disclosing party; or if required to be disclosed to any appropriate protection/safeguarding authority; or as may otherwise be compelled by law; or as may be provided for by a direction given by the arbitrator under Art.16.2.2 below.

16.2.2 Upon application by a party to the arbitration, the arbitrator may direct that any document, statement, information or other material disclosed in the arbitration by any party may be disclosed to any person mentioned in Art.16.2.3 below (the person and purpose of disclosure being identified in the direction), upon that person agreeing in writing to confine their use of the disclosure to the terms of the direction.

16.2.3 The arbitrator may permit disclosure under Art.16.2.2 above to a professional acting in furtherance of the protection of children; or to any other person to whom disclosure is necessary, for one or more of the following purposes:

(a)   to enable that person to provide expert or other evidence for the purposes of the arbitration or related legal proceedings;

(b)   to enable a party to the arbitration, by confidential discussion, to obtain support, advice (whether legal or other professional) or assistance in the conduct of the arbitration or related legal proceedings;

(c)   to enable a party to the arbitration to make and pursue a complaint against a person or body concerned in the arbitration;

(d)   to make and pursue a complaint regarding the law, policy or procedure relating to arbitration as it concerns children.

16.3   Any transcript of the proceedings will be provided to all parties and to the arbitrator. It will similarly be confidential and used solely for the purpose of the arbitration, implementation or enforcement of any determination or applications to the court unless otherwise agreed by the parties, or if it forms part of any necessary disclosure to any appropriate protection/safeguarding authority, or as may otherwise be compelled by law, or as directed by the arbitrator under Art.16.2.2 above.

16.4   The arbitrator will not be called as a witness by any party either to testify or to produce any documents or materials received or generated during the course of the proceedings in relation to any aspect of the arbitration unless with the agreement of the arbitrator, or in connection with any necessary disclosure to any appropriate protection/safeguarding authority, or as may otherwise be compelled by law.

Article 17 – Disclosure of issues relating to safeguarding and welfare

17.1.1 Prior to the formal commencement of the arbitration each party shall have a duty:

(a)   to provide accurate information regarding safeguarding and protection from harm in their Form ARB1CS and Safeguarding Questionnaire;

(b)   to obtain a Basic Disclosure from Disclosure Scotland and promptly send it to the arbitrator and to every other party;

(c)   to send to the arbitrator and to every other party any relevant letter or report prepared by CAFCASS or any local authority children's services department or similar agency in relation to the welfare or safeguarding of any child who is the subject of the proposed arbitration.

17.1.2 Prior to the formal commencement of the arbitration and at every stage of the process each party shall have a continuing duty to disclose fully and completely to the arbitrator and to every other party any fact, matter or document in their knowledge, possession or control which is or appears to be relevant to the physical or emotional safety of any other party or to the safeguarding or welfare of any child the subject of the proceedings, or to a decision by the arbitrator under Art.17.2.1. Such disclosure shall include (but not be limited to) any criminal conviction, caution or involvement (concerning any child) with children's services in respect of any party or any person with whom the child is likely to have contact.

17.2.1 If at any time prior to or during the arbitration but prior to communication of the determination to the parties the arbitrator (whether as a result of information received or by reason of behaviour on the part of either party) forms the view that there are reasonable grounds to believe that there may be a risk to the physical or emotional safety of any party or to the safeguarding or welfare of any child, it is the arbitrator's duty to consider whether the arbitration may safely continue.

17.2.2 If in such a case the arbitrator concludes that the dispute is no longer suitable for arbitration under the Children Scheme then he or she must inform the parties in writing of that decision and of its grounds, and will terminate the proceedings (see Arts.7.3 and 15.2(b)). The arbitrator may also inform IFLA of a decision to decline an appointment or to terminate an arbitration on safeguarding or welfare grounds.

17.3.1 If at any time during the arbitration but prior to communication of the determination to the parties the arbitrator becomes aware of any matters which lead him or her reasonably to apprehend that a child or any party has suffered or is likely to suffer significant harm by reason of the actual or likely future behaviour of any party, it is the arbitrator's duty to communicate his or her concerns as soon as possible to the relevant local authority or appropriate government agency.

17.3.2 In such a case the arbitrator shall be entitled, if he or she considers it appropriate, to communicate such concerns to the relevant local authority or appropriate government agency without prior intimation to any party of an intention so to do.

Article 18 – General

18.1 At relevant stages of the arbitration, the arbitrator may encourage the parties to consider using an alternative dispute resolution procedure other than arbitration, such as mediation, negotiation or early neutral evaluation, in relation to the dispute or a particular aspect of the dispute.

18.2 If the parties agree to use an alternative dispute resolution procedure such as mediation, negotiation or early neutral evaluation, then the arbitrator will facilitate its use and may, if appropriate, stay the arbitration or a particular aspect of the arbitration for an appropriate period of time for that purpose.

18.3 In the event that the dispute is settled (following a mediation or otherwise), the parties will inform the arbitrator promptly and section 51 (settlement) will apply. Fees and expenses accrued due to the arbitrator by that stage will remain payable.

18.4 In the event that an arbitrator under the Children Scheme is at the same time conducting a parallel financial arbitration under the IFLA Financial Scheme which involves one or more of the same parties, then in the event of any conflict between the two Scheme Rules, the arbitrator shall have sole discretion to decide which will prevail. For the avoidance of doubt, subject to the discretion of the arbitrator, all evidence adduced and all reports and documents disclosed in each arbitration shall stand as evidence in the other.

18.5 The parties will inform the arbitrator promptly of any proposed application to the court and will provide him or her with copies of all documentation intended to be used in any such application.

18.6 IFLA, the CIArb, Resolution, and the FLBA, their employees and agents will not be liable:

    (a)   for anything done or omitted in the actual or purported appointment or nomination of an arbitrator, unless the act or omission is shown to have been in bad faith;

    (b)   by reason of having appointed or nominated an arbitrator, for anything done or omitted by the arbitrator (or his employees or agents) in the discharge or purported discharge of his functions as an arbitrator;

    (c)   for any consequences if, for whatever reason, the arbitral process does not result in a determination or, where necessary, a court order embodying a determination by which the matters to be determined are resolved.

1.3

Arbitration Act 1996[1]

[1996 Chapter 23]

An Act to restate and improve the law relating to arbitration pursuant to an arbitration agreement; to make other provision relating to arbitration and arbitration awards; and for connected purposes

PART I: Arbitration pursuant to an arbitration agreement

Introductory

The arbitration agreement

Stay of legal proceedings

Commencement of arbitral proceedings

The arbitral tribunal

---

[1] Crown copyright material is reproduced here with the permission of the Controller of HMSO.

Part I: Arbitration pursuant to an arbitration agreement

Introductory

1   General principles

The provisions of this Part are founded on the following principles, and shall be construed accordingly –

(a)   the object of arbitration is to obtain the fair resolution of disputes by an impartial tribunal without unnecessary delay or expense;

(b)   the parties should be free to agree how their disputes are resolved, subject only to such safeguards as are necessary in the public interest;

(c)   in matters governed by this Part the court should not intervene except as provided by this Part.

2   Scope of application of provisions

(1)   The provisions of this Part apply where the seat of the arbitration is in England and Wales or Northern Ireland.

(2)   The following sections apply even if the seat of the arbitration is outside England and Wales or Northern Ireland or no seat has been designated or determined –

(a)   sections 9 to 11 (stay of legal proceedings, &c), and

(b)   section 66 (enforcement of arbitral awards).

(3)   The powers conferred by the following sections apply even if the seat of the arbitration is outside England and Wales or Northern Ireland or no seat has been designated or determined –

(a)   section 43 (securing the attendance of witnesses), and

(b)   section 44 (court powers exercisable in support of arbitral proceedings);

but the court may refuse to exercise any such power if, in the opinion of the court, the fact that the seat of the arbitration is outside England and Wales or Northern Ireland, or that when designated or determined the seat is likely to be outside England and Wales or Northern Ireland, makes it inappropriate to do so.

(4)   The court may exercise a power conferred by any provision of this Part not mentioned in subsection (2) or (3) for the purpose of supporting the arbitral process where –

(a)   no seat of the arbitration has been designated or determined, and

(b)   by reason of a connection with England and Wales or Northern Ireland the court is satisfied that it is appropriate to do so.

(5)   Section 7 (separability of arbitration agreement) and section 8 (death of a party) apply where the law applicable to the arbitration agreement is the law of England and Wales or Northern Ireland even if the seat of the arbitration is outside England and Wales or Northern Ireland or has not been designated or determined.

3   The seat of the arbitration

In this Part 'the seat of the arbitration' means the juridical seat of the arbitration designated –

(a)   by the parties to the arbitration agreement, or

(b)   by any arbitral or other institution or person vested by the parties with powers in that regard, or

(c)   by the arbitral tribunal if so authorised by the parties,

or determined, in the absence of any such designation, having regard to the parties' agreement and all the relevant circumstances.

4   Mandatory and non-mandatory provisions

(1)   The mandatory provisions of this Part are listed in Schedule 1 and have effect notwithstanding any agreement to the contrary.

(2)   The other provisions of this Part (the 'non-mandatory provisions') allow the parties to make their own arrangements by agreement but provide rules which apply in the absence of such agreement.

(3)   The parties may make such arrangements by agreeing to the application of institutional rules or providing any other means by which a matter may be decided.

(4)   It is immaterial whether or not the law applicable to the parties' agreement is the law of England and Wales or, as the case may be, Northern Ireland.

(5)   The choice of a law other than the law of England and Wales or Northern Ireland as the applicable law in respect of a matter provided for by a non-mandatory provision of this Part is equivalent to an agreement making provision about that matter.

For this purpose an applicable law determined in accordance with the parties' agreement, or which is objectively determined in the absence of any express or implied choice, shall be treated as chosen by the parties.

5   Agreements to be in writing

(1)   The provisions of this Part apply only where the arbitration agreement is in writing, and any other agreement between the parties as to any matter is effective for the purposes of this Part only if in writing.

The expressions 'agreement', 'agree' and 'agreed' shall be construed accordingly.

(2)   There is an agreement in writing –

(a)   if the agreement is made in writing (whether or not it is signed by the parties),
(b)   if the agreement is made by exchange of communications in writing, or
(c)   if the agreement is evidenced in writing.

(3)   Where parties agree otherwise than in writing by reference to terms which are in writing, they make an agreement in writing.

(4)   An agreement is evidenced in writing if an agreement made otherwise than in writing is recorded by one of the parties, or by a third party, with the authority of the parties to the agreement.

(5)   An exchange of written submissions in arbitral or legal proceedings in which the existence of an agreement otherwise than in writing is alleged by one party against another party and not denied by the other party in his response constitutes as between those parties an agreement in writing to the effect alleged.

(6)   References in this Part to anything being written or in writing include its being recorded by any means.

The arbitration agreement

6   Definition of arbitration agreement

(1)   In this Part an 'arbitration agreement' means an agreement to submit to arbitration present or future disputes (whether they are contractual or not).

(2)   The reference in an agreement to a written form of arbitration clause or to a document containing an arbitration clause constitutes an arbitration agreement if the reference is such as to make that clause part of the agreement.

7 Separability of arbitration agreement

Unless otherwise agreed by the parties, an arbitration agreement which forms or was intended to form part of another agreement (whether or not in writing) shall not be regarded as invalid, non-existent or ineffective because that other agreement is invalid, or did not come into existence or has become ineffective, and it shall for that purpose be treated as a distinct agreement.

8 Whether agreement discharged by death of a party

(1) Unless otherwise agreed by the parties, an arbitration agreement is not discharged by the death of a party and may be enforced by or against the personal representatives of that party.

(2) Subsection (1) does not affect the operation of any enactment or rule of law by virtue of which a substantive right or obligation is extinguished by death.

Stay of legal proceedings

9 Stay of legal proceedings

(1) A party to an arbitration agreement against whom legal proceedings are brought (whether by way of claim or counterclaim) in respect of a matter which under the agreement is to be referred to arbitration may (upon notice to the other parties to the proceedings) apply to the court in which the proceedings have been brought to stay the proceedings so far as they concern that matter.

(2) An application may be made notwithstanding that the matter is to be referred to arbitration only after the exhaustion of other dispute resolution procedures.

(3) An application may not be made by a person before taking the appropriate procedural step (if any) to acknowledge the legal proceedings against him or after he has taken any step in those proceedings to answer the substantive claim.

(4) On an application under this section the court shall grant a stay unless satisfied that the arbitration agreement is null and void, inoperative, or incapable of being performed.

(5) If the court refuses to stay the legal proceedings, any provision that an award is a condition precedent to the bringing of legal proceedings in respect of any matter is of no effect in relation to those proceedings.

10 Reference of interpleader issue to arbitration

(1) Where in legal proceedings relief by way of interpleader is granted and any issue between the claimants is one in respect of which there is an arbitration agreement between them, the court granting the relief shall direct that the issue be determined in accordance with the agreement unless the circumstances are such that proceedings brought by a claimant in respect of the matter would not be stayed.

(2) Where subsection (1) applies but the court does not direct that the issue be determined in accordance with the arbitration agreement, any provision that an award is a condition precedent to the bringing of legal proceedings in respect of any matter shall not affect the determination of that issue by the court.

11 Retention of security where Admiralty proceedings stayed

(1) Where Admiralty proceedings are stayed on the ground that the dispute in question should be submitted to arbitration, the court granting the stay may, if in those proceedings property has been arrested or bail or other security has been given to prevent or obtain release from arrest –

(a) order that the property arrested be retained as security for the satisfaction of any award given in the arbitration in respect of that dispute, or

(b)   order that the stay of those proceedings be conditional on the provision of equivalent security for the satisfaction of any such award.

(2)   Subject to any provision made by rules of court and to any necessary modifications, the same law and practice shall apply in relation to property retained in pursuance of an order as would apply if it were held for the purposes of proceedings in the court making the order.

Commencement of arbitral proceedings

12   Power of court to extend time for beginning arbitral proceedings, &c

(1)   Where an arbitration agreement to refer future disputes to arbitration provides that a claim shall be barred, or the claimant's right extinguished, unless the claimant takes within a time fixed by the agreement some step –

(a)   to begin arbitral proceedings, or
(b)   to begin other dispute resolution procedures which must be exhausted before arbitral proceedings can be begun,

the court may by order extend the time for taking that step.

(2)   Any party to the arbitration agreement may apply for such an order (upon notice to the other parties), but only after a claim has arisen and after exhausting any available arbitral process for obtaining an extension of time.

(3)   The court shall make an order only if satisfied –

(a)   that the circumstances are such as were outside the reasonable contemplation of the parties when they agreed the provision in question, and that it would be just to extend the time, or
(b)   that the conduct of one party makes it unjust to hold the other party to the strict terms of the provision in question.

(4)   The court may extend the time for such period and on such terms as it thinks fit, and may do so whether or not the time previously fixed (by agreement or by a previous order) has expired.

(5)   An order under this section does not affect the operation of the Limitation Acts (see section 13).

(6)   The leave of the court is required for any appeal from a decision of the court under this section.

13   Application of Limitation Acts

(1)   The Limitation Acts apply to arbitral proceedings as they apply to legal proceedings.

(2)   The court may order that in computing the time prescribed by the Limitation Acts for the commencement of proceedings (including arbitral proceedings) in respect of a dispute which was the subject matter –

(a)   of an award which the court orders to be set aside or declares to be of no effect, or
(b)   of the affected part of an award which the court orders to be set aside in part, or declares to be in part of no effect,

the period between the commencement of the arbitration and the date of the order referred to in paragraph (a) or (b) shall be excluded.

(3)   In determining for the purposes of the Limitation Acts when a cause of action accrued, any provision that an award is a condition precedent to the bringing of legal proceedings in respect of a matter to which an arbitration agreement applies shall be disregarded.

(4)   In this Part 'the Limitation Acts' means –

(a)   in England and Wales, the Limitation Act 1980, the Foreign Limitation Periods Act 1984 and any other enactment (whenever passed) relating to the limitation of actions;
(b)   in Northern Ireland, the Limitation (Northern Ireland) Order 1989, the Foreign Limitation Periods (Northern Ireland) Order 1985 and any other enactment (whenever passed) relating to the limitation of actions.

14 Commencement of arbitral proceedings

(1) The parties are free to agree when arbitral proceedings are to be regarded as commenced for the purposes of this Part and for the purposes of the Limitation Acts.

(2) If there is no such agreement the following provisions apply.

(3) Where the arbitrator is named or designated in the arbitration agreement, arbitral proceedings are commenced in respect of a matter when one party serves on the other party or parties a notice in writing requiring him or them to submit that matter to the person so named or designated.

(4) Where the arbitrator or arbitrators are to be appointed by the parties, arbitral proceedings are commenced in respect of a matter when one party serves on the other party or parties notice in writing requiring him or them to appoint an arbitrator or to agree to the appointment of an arbitrator in respect of that matter.

(5) Where the arbitrator or arbitrators are to be appointed by a person other than a party to the proceedings, arbitral proceedings are commenced in respect of a matter when one party gives notice in writing to that person requesting him to make the appointment in respect of that matter.

The arbitral tribunal

15 The arbitral tribunal

(1) The parties are free to agree on the number of arbitrators to form the tribunal and whether there is to be a chairman or umpire.

(2) Unless otherwise agreed by the parties, an agreement that the number of arbitrators shall be two or any other even number shall be understood as requiring the appointment of an additional arbitrator as chairman of the tribunal.

(3) If there is no agreement as to the number of arbitrators, the tribunal shall consist of a sole arbitrator.

16 Procedure for appointment of arbitrators

(1) The parties are free to agree on the procedure for appointing the arbitrator or arbitrators, including the procedure for appointing any chairman or umpire.

(2) If or to the extent that there is no such agreement, the following provisions apply.

(3) If the tribunal is to consist of a sole arbitrator, the parties shall jointly appoint the arbitrator not later than 28 days after service of a request in writing by either party to do so.

(4) If the tribunal is to consist of two arbitrators, each party shall appoint one arbitrator not later than 14 days after service of a request in writing by either party to do so.

(5) If the tribunal is to consist of three arbitrators –

(a) each party shall appoint one arbitrator not later than 14 days after service of a request in writing by either party to do so, and

(b) the two so appointed shall forthwith appoint a third arbitrator as the chairman of the tribunal.

(6) If the tribunal is to consist of two arbitrators and an umpire –

(a) each party shall appoint one arbitrator not later than 14 days after service of a request in writing by either party to do so, and

(b) the two so appointed may appoint an umpire at any time after they themselves are appointed and shall do so before any substantive hearing or forthwith if they cannot agree on a matter relating to the arbitration.

(7) In any other case (in particular, if there are more than two parties) section 18 applies as in the case of a failure of the agreed appointment procedure.

17 Power in case of default to appoint sole arbitrator

(1) Unless the parties otherwise agree, where each of two parties to an arbitration agreement is to appoint an arbitrator and one party ('the party in default') refuses to do so, or fails to do so within the time specified, the other party, having duly appointed his arbitrator, may give notice in writing to the party in default that he proposes to appoint his arbitrator to act as sole arbitrator.

(2) If the party in default does not within 7 clear days of that notice being given –

    (a) make the required appointment, and
    (b) notify the other party that he has done so,

the other party may appoint his arbitrator as sole arbitrator whose award shall be binding on both parties as if he had been so appointed by agreement.

(3) Where a sole arbitrator has been appointed under subsection (2), the party in default may (upon notice to the appointing party) apply to the court which may set aside the appointment.

(4) The leave of the court is required for any appeal from a decision of the court under this section.

18 Failure of appointment procedure

(1) The parties are free to agree what is to happen in the event of a failure of the procedure for the appointment of the arbitral tribunal.

There is no failure if an appointment is duly made under section 17 (power in case of default to appoint sole arbitrator), unless that appointment is set aside.

(2) If or to the extent that there is no such agreement any party to the arbitration agreement may (upon notice to the other parties) apply to the court to exercise its powers under this section.

(3) Those powers are –

    (a) to give directions as to the making of any necessary appointments;
    (b) to direct that the tribunal shall be constituted by such appointments (or any one or more of them) as have been made;
    (c) to revoke any appointments already made;
    (d) to make any necessary appointments itself.

(4) An appointment made by the court under this section has effect as if made with the agreement of the parties.

(5) The leave of the court is required for any appeal from a decision of the court under this section.

19 Court to have regard to agreed qualifications

In deciding whether to exercise, and in considering how to exercise, any of its powers under section 16 (procedure for appointment of arbitrators) or section 18 (failure of appointment procedure), the court shall have due regard to any agreement of the parties as to the qualifications required of the arbitrators.

20 Chairman

(1) Where the parties have agreed that there is to be a chairman, they are free to agree what the functions of the chairman are to be in relation to the making of decisions, orders and awards.

(2) If or to the extent that there is no such agreement, the following provisions apply.

(3) Decisions, orders and awards shall be made by all or a majority of the arbitrators (including the chairman).

(4) The view of the chairman shall prevail in relation to a decision, order or award in respect of which there is neither unanimity nor a majority under subsection (3).

21 Umpire

(1)   Where the parties have agreed that there is to be an umpire, they are free to agree what the functions of the umpire are to be, and in particular –

(a)   whether he is to attend the proceedings, and

(b)   when he is to replace the other arbitrators as the tribunal with power to make decisions, orders and awards.

(2)   If or to the extent that there is no such agreement, the following provisions apply.

(3)   The umpire shall attend the proceedings and be supplied with the same documents and other materials as are supplied to the other arbitrators.

(4)   Decisions, orders and awards shall be made by the other arbitrators unless and until they cannot agree on a matter relating to the arbitration.

In that event they shall forthwith give notice in writing to the parties and the umpire, whereupon the umpire shall replace them as the tribunal with power to make decisions, orders and awards as if he were sole arbitrator.

(5)   If the arbitrators cannot agree but fail to give notice of that fact, or if any of them fails to join in the giving of notice, any party to the arbitral proceedings may (upon notice to the other parties and to the tribunal) apply to the court which may order that the umpire shall replace the other arbitrators as the tribunal with power to make decisions, orders and awards as if he were sole arbitrator.

(6)   The leave of the court is required for any appeal from a decision of the court under this section.

22 Decision-making where no chairman or umpire

(1)   Where the parties agree that there shall be two or more arbitrators with no chairman or umpire, the parties are free to agree how the tribunal is to make decisions, orders and awards.

(2)   If there is no such agreement, decisions, orders and awards shall be made by all or a majority of the arbitrators.

23 Revocation of arbitrator's authority

(1)   The parties are free to agree in what circumstances the authority of an arbitrator may be revoked.

(2)   If or to the extent that there is no such agreement the following provisions apply.

(3)   The authority of an arbitrator may not be revoked except –

(a)   by the parties acting jointly, or

(b)   by an arbitral or other institution or person vested by the parties with powers in that regard.

(4)   Revocation of the authority of an arbitrator by the parties acting jointly must be agreed in writing unless the parties also agree (whether or not in writing) to terminate the arbitration agreement.

(5)   Nothing in this section affects the power of the court –

(a)   to revoke an appointment under section 18 (powers exercisable in case of failure of appointment procedure), or

(b)   to remove an arbitrator on the grounds specified in section 24.

24 Power of court to remove arbitrator

(1)   A party to arbitral proceedings may (upon notice to the other parties, to the arbitrator concerned and to any other arbitrator) apply to the court to remove an arbitrator on any of the following grounds –

(a)   that circumstances exist that give rise to justifiable doubts as to his impartiality;

(b)   that he does not possess the qualifications required by the arbitration agreement;

(c)   that he is physically or mentally incapable of conducting the proceedings or there are justifiable doubts as to his capacity to do so;

(d)   that he has refused or failed –

    (i)   properly to conduct the proceedings, or

    (ii)   to use all reasonable despatch in conducting the proceedings or making an award,

and that substantial injustice has been or will be caused to the applicant.

(2)   If there is an arbitral or other institution or person vested by the parties with power to remove an arbitrator, the court shall not exercise its power of removal unless satisfied that the applicant has first exhausted any available recourse to that institution or person.

(3)   The arbitral tribunal may continue the arbitral proceedings and make an award while an application to the court under this section is pending.

(4)   Where the court removes an arbitrator, it may make such order as it thinks fit with respect to his entitlement (if any) to fees or expenses, or the repayment of any fees or expenses already paid.

(5)   The arbitrator concerned is entitled to appear and be heard by the court before it makes any order under this section.

(6)   The leave of the court is required for any appeal from a decision of the court under this section.

25   Resignation of arbitrator

(1)   The parties are free to agree with an arbitrator as to the consequences of his resignation as regards –

(a)   his entitlement (if any) to fees or expenses, and

(b)   any liability thereby incurred by him.

(2)   If or to the extent that there is no such agreement the following provisions apply.

(3)   An arbitrator who resigns his appointment may (upon notice to the parties) apply to the court –

(a)   to grant him relief from any liability thereby incurred by him, and

(b)   to make such order as it thinks fit with respect to his entitlement (if any) to fees or expenses or the repayment of any fees or expenses already paid.

(4)   If the court is satisfied that in all the circumstances it was reasonable for the arbitrator to resign, it may grant such relief as is mentioned in subsection (3)(a) on such terms as it thinks fit.

(5)   The leave of the court is required for any appeal from a decision of the court under this section.

26   Death of arbitrator or person appointing him

(1)   The authority of an arbitrator is personal and ceases on his death.

(2)   Unless otherwise agreed by the parties, the death of the person by whom an arbitrator was appointed does not revoke the arbitrator's authority.

27   Filling of vacancy, &c

(1)   Where an arbitrator ceases to hold office, the parties are free to agree –

(a)   whether and if so how the vacancy is to be filled,

(b)   whether and if so to what extent the previous proceedings should stand, and

(c)   what effect (if any) his ceasing to hold office has on any appointment made by him (alone or jointly).

(2)   If or to the extent that there is no such agreement, the following provisions apply.

(3)   The provisions of sections 16 (procedure for appointment of arbitrators) and 18 (failure of appointment procedure) apply in relation to the filling of the vacancy as in relation to an original appointment.

(4)   The tribunal (when reconstituted) shall determine whether and if so to what extent the previous proceedings should stand.

This does not affect any right of a party to challenge those proceedings on any ground which had arisen before the arbitrator ceased to hold office.

(5)   His ceasing to hold office does not affect any appointment by him (alone or jointly) of another arbitrator, in particular any appointment of a chairman or umpire.

28   Joint and several liability of parties to arbitrators for fees and expenses

(1)   The parties are jointly and severally liable to pay to the arbitrators such reasonable fees and expenses (if any) as are appropriate in the circumstances.

(2)   Any party may apply to the court (upon notice to the other parties and to the arbitrators) which may order that the amount of the arbitrators' fees and expenses shall be considered and adjusted by such means and upon such terms as it may direct.

(3)   If the application is made after any amount has been paid to the arbitrators by way of fees or expenses, the court may order the repayment of such amount (if any) as is shown to be excessive, but shall not do so unless it is shown that it is reasonable in the circumstances to order repayment.

(4)   The above provisions have effect subject to any order of the court under section 24(4) or 25(3)(b) (order as to entitlement to fees or expenses in case of removal or resignation of arbitrator).

(5)   Nothing in this section affects any liability of a party to any other party to pay all or any of the costs of the arbitration (see sections 59 to 65) or any contractual right of an arbitrator to payment of his fees and expenses.

(6)   In this section references to arbitrators include an arbitrator who has ceased to act and an umpire who has not replaced the other arbitrators.

29   Immunity of arbitrator

(1)   An arbitrator is not liable for anything done or omitted in the discharge or purported discharge of his functions as arbitrator unless the act or omission is shown to have been in bad faith.

(2)   Subsection (1) applies to an employee or agent of an arbitrator as it applies to the arbitrator himself.

(3)   This section does not affect any liability incurred by an arbitrator by reason of his resigning (but see section 25).

Jurisdiction of the arbitral tribunal

30   Competence of tribunal to rule on its own jurisdiction

(1)   Unless otherwise agreed by the parties, the arbitral tribunal may rule on its own substantive jurisdiction, that is, as to –

(a)   whether there is a valid arbitration agreement,
(b)   whether the tribunal is properly constituted, and
(c)   what matters have been submitted to arbitration in accordance with the arbitration agreement.

(2)   Any such ruling may be challenged by any available arbitral process of appeal or review or in accordance with the provisions of this Part.

31 Objection to substantive jurisdiction of tribunal

(1) An objection that the arbitral tribunal lacks substantive jurisdiction at the outset of the proceedings must be raised by a party not later than the time he takes the first step in the proceedings to contest the merits of any matter in relation to which he challenges the tribunal's jurisdiction.

A party is not precluded from raising such an objection by the fact that he has appointed or participated in the appointment of an arbitrator.

(2) Any objection during the course of the arbitral proceedings that the arbitral tribunal is exceeding its substantive jurisdiction must be made as soon as possible after the matter alleged to be beyond its jurisdiction is raised.

(3) The arbitral tribunal may admit an objection later than the time specified in subsection (1) or (2) if it considers the delay justified.

(4) Where an objection is duly taken to the tribunal's substantive jurisdiction and the tribunal has power to rule on its own jurisdiction, it may –

(a) rule on the matter in an award as to jurisdiction, or
(b) deal with the objection in its award on the merits.

If the parties agree which of these courses the tribunal should take, the tribunal shall proceed accordingly.

(5) The tribunal may in any case, and shall if the parties so agree, stay proceedings whilst an application is made to the court under section 32 (determination of preliminary point of jurisdiction).

32 Determination of preliminary point of jurisdiction

(1) The court may, on the application of a party to arbitral proceedings (upon notice to the other parties), determine any question as to the substantive jurisdiction of the tribunal.

A party may lose the right to object (see section 73).

(2) An application under this section shall not be considered unless –

(a) it is made with the agreement in writing of all the other parties to the proceedings, or
(b) it is made with the permission of the tribunal and the court is satisfied –

(i) that the determination of the question is likely to produce substantial savings in costs,
(ii) that the application was made without delay, and
(iii) that there is good reason why the matter should be decided by the court.

(3) An application under this section, unless made with the agreement of all the other parties to the proceedings, shall state the grounds on which it is said that the matter should be decided by the court.

(4) Unless otherwise agreed by the parties, the arbitral tribunal may continue the arbitral proceedings and make an award while an application to the court under this section is pending.

(5) Unless the court gives leave, no appeal lies from a decision of the court whether the conditions specified in subsection (2) are met.

(6) The decision of the court on the question of jurisdiction shall be treated as a judgment of the court for the purposes of an appeal.

But no appeal lies without the leave of the court which shall not be given unless the court considers that the question involves a point of law which is one of general importance or is one which for some other special reason should be considered by the Court of Appeal.

The arbitral proceedings

33   General duty of the tribunal

(1)   The tribunal shall –

    (a)   act fairly and impartially as between the parties, giving each party a reasonable opportunity of putting his case and dealing with that of his opponent, and

    (b)   adopt procedures suitable to the circumstances of the particular case, avoiding unnecessary delay or expense, so as to provide a fair means for the resolution of the matters falling to be determined.

(2)   The tribunal shall comply with that general duty in conducting the arbitral proceedings, in its decisions on matters of procedure and evidence and in the exercise of all other powers conferred on it.

34   Procedural and evidential matters

(1)   It shall be for the tribunal to decide all procedural and evidential matters, subject to the right of the parties to agree any matter.

(2)   Procedural and evidential matters include –

    (a)   when and where any part of the proceedings is to be held;

    (b)   the language or languages to be used in the proceedings and whether translations of any relevant documents are to be supplied;

    (c)   whether any and if so what form of written statements of claim and defence are to be used, when these should be supplied and the extent to which such statements can be later amended;

    (d)   whether any and if so which documents or classes of documents should be disclosed between and produced by the parties and at what stage;

    (e)   whether any and if so what questions should be put to and answered by the respective parties and when and in what form this should be done;

    (f)   whether to apply strict rules of evidence (or any other rules) as to the admissibility, relevance or weight of any material (oral, written or other) sought to be tendered on any matters of fact or opinion, and the time, manner and form in which such material should be exchanged and presented;

    (g)   whether and to what extent the tribunal should itself take the initiative in ascertaining the facts and the law;

    (h)   whether and to what extent there should be oral or written evidence or submissions.

(3)   The tribunal may fix the time within which any directions given by it are to be complied with, and may if it thinks fit extend the time so fixed (whether or not it has expired).

35   Consolidation of proceedings and concurrent hearings

(1)   The parties are free to agree –

    (a)   that the arbitral proceedings shall be consolidated with other arbitral proceedings, or

    (b)   that concurrent hearings shall be held,

on such terms as may be agreed.

(2)   Unless the parties agree to confer such power on the tribunal, the tribunal has no power to order consolidation of proceedings or concurrent hearings.

36   Legal or other representation

Unless otherwise agreed by the parties, a party to arbitral proceedings may be represented in the proceedings by a lawyer or other person chosen by him.

37 Power to appoint experts, legal advisers or assessors

(1) Unless otherwise agreed by the parties –

    (a) the tribunal may –

        (i) appoint experts or legal advisers to report to it and the parties, or

        (ii) appoint assessors to assist it on technical matters,

        and may allow any such expert, legal adviser or assessor to attend the proceedings; and

    (b) the parties shall be given a reasonable opportunity to comment on any information, opinion or advice offered by any such person.

(2) The fees and expenses of an expert, legal adviser or assessor appointed by the tribunal for which the arbitrators are liable are expenses of the arbitrators for the purposes of this Part.

38 General powers exercisable by the tribunal

(1) The parties are free to agree on the powers exercisable by the arbitral tribunal for the purposes of and in relation to the proceedings.

(2) Unless otherwise agreed by the parties the tribunal has the following powers.

(3) The tribunal may order a claimant to provide security for the costs of the arbitration.

This power shall not be exercised on the ground that the claimant is –

    (a) an individual ordinarily resident outside the United Kingdom, or

    (b) a corporation or association incorporated or formed under the law of a country outside the United Kingdom, or whose central management and control is exercised outside the United Kingdom.

(4) The tribunal may give directions in relation to any property which is the subject of the proceedings or as to which any question arises in the proceedings, and which is owned by or is in the possession of a party to the proceedings –

    (a) for the inspection, photographing, preservation, custody or detention of the property by the tribunal, an expert or a party, or

    (b) ordering that samples be taken from, or any observation be made of or experiment conducted upon, the property.

(5) The tribunal may direct that a party or witness shall be examined on oath or affirmation, and may for that purpose administer any necessary oath or take any necessary affirmation.

(6) The tribunal may give directions to a party for the preservation for the purposes of the proceedings of any evidence in his custody or control.

39 Power to make provisional awards

(1) The parties are free to agree that the tribunal shall have power to order on a provisional basis any relief which it would have power to grant in a final award.

(2) This includes, for instance, making –

    (a) a provisional order for the payment of money or the disposition of property as between the parties, or

    (b) an order to make an interim payment on account of the costs of the arbitration.

(3) Any such order shall be subject to the tribunal's final adjudication; and the tribunal's final award, on the merits or as to costs, shall take account of any such order.

(4) Unless the parties agree to confer such power on the tribunal, the tribunal has no such power.

This does not affect its powers under section 47 (awards on different issues, &c).

40   General duty of parties

(1)   The parties shall do all things necessary for the proper and expeditious conduct of the arbitral proceedings.

(2)   This includes –

(a)   complying without delay with any determination of the tribunal as to procedural or evidential matters, or with any order or directions of the tribunal, and

(b)   where appropriate, taking without delay any necessary steps to obtain a decision of the court on a preliminary question of jurisdiction or law (see sections 32 and 45).

41   Powers of tribunal in case of party's default

(1)   The parties are free to agree on the powers of the tribunal in case of a party's failure to do something necessary for the proper and expeditious conduct of the arbitration.

(2)   Unless otherwise agreed by the parties, the following provisions apply.

(3)   If the tribunal is satisfied that there has been inordinate and inexcusable delay on the part of the claimant in pursuing his claim and that the delay –

(a)   gives rise, or is likely to give rise, to a substantial risk that it is not possible to have a fair resolution of the issues in that claim, or

(b)   has caused, or is likely to cause, serious prejudice to the respondent,

the tribunal may make an award dismissing the claim.

(4)   If without showing sufficient cause a party –

(a)   fails to attend or be represented at an oral hearing of which due notice was given, or

(b)   where matters are to be dealt with in writing, fails after due notice to submit written evidence or make written submissions,

the tribunal may continue the proceedings in the absence of that party or, as the case may be, without any written evidence or submissions on his behalf, and may make an award on the basis of the evidence before it.

(5)   If without showing sufficient cause a party fails to comply with any order or directions of the tribunal, the tribunal may make a peremptory order to the same effect, prescribing such time for compliance with it as the tribunal considers appropriate.

(6)   If a claimant fails to comply with a peremptory order of the tribunal to provide security for costs, the tribunal may make an award dismissing his claim.

(7)   If a party fails to comply with any other kind of peremptory order, then, without prejudice to section 42 (enforcement by court of tribunal's peremptory orders), the tribunal may do any of the following –

(a)   direct that the party in default shall not be entitled to rely upon any allegation or material which was the subject matter of the order;

(b)   draw such adverse inferences from the act of non-compliance as the circumstances justify;

(c)   proceed to an award on the basis of such materials as have been properly provided to it;

(d)   make such order as it thinks fit as to the payment of costs of the arbitration incurred in consequence of the non-compliance.

Powers of court in relation to arbitral proceedings

42   Enforcement of peremptory orders of tribunal

(1)   Unless otherwise agreed by the parties, the court may make an order requiring a party to comply with a peremptory order made by the tribunal.

(2)   An application for an order under this section may be made –

(a)   by the tribunal (upon notice to the parties),

(b)   by a party to the arbitral proceedings with the permission of the tribunal (and upon notice to the other parties), or

(c)   where the parties have agreed that the powers of the court under this section shall be available.

(3)   The court shall not act unless it is satisfied that the applicant has exhausted any available arbitral process in respect of failure to comply with the tribunal's order.

(4)   No order shall be made under this section unless the court is satisfied that the person to whom the tribunal's order was directed has failed to comply with it within the time prescribed in the order or, if no time was prescribed, within a reasonable time.

(5)   The leave of the court is required for any appeal from a decision of the court under this section.

43   Securing the attendance of witnesses

(1)   A party to arbitral proceedings may use the same court procedures as are available in relation to legal proceedings to secure the attendance before the tribunal of a witness in order to give oral testimony or to produce documents or other material evidence.

(2)   This may only be done with the permission of the tribunal or the agreement of the other parties.

(3)   The court procedures may only be used if –

(a)   the witness is in the United Kingdom, and

(b)   the arbitral proceedings are being conducted in England and Wales or, as the case may be, Northern Ireland.

(4)   A person shall not be compelled by virtue of this section to produce any document or other material evidence which he could not be compelled to produce in legal proceedings.

44   Court powers exercisable in support of arbitral proceedings

(1)   Unless otherwise agreed by the parties, the court has for the purposes of and in relation to arbitral proceedings the same power of making orders about the matters listed below as it has for the purposes of and in relation to legal proceedings.

(2)   Those matters are –

(a)   the taking of the evidence of witnesses;

(b)   the preservation of evidence;

(c)   making orders relating to property which is the subject of the proceedings or as to which any question arises in the proceedings –

(i)   for the inspection, photographing, preservation, custody or detention of the property, or

(ii)   ordering that samples be taken from, or any observation be made of or experiment conducted upon, the property;

and for that purpose authorising any person to enter any premises in the possession or control of a party to the arbitration;

(d)   the sale of any goods the subject of the proceedings;

(e)   the granting of an interim injunction or the appointment of a receiver.

(3)   If the case is one of urgency, the court may, on the application of a party or proposed party to the arbitral proceedings, make such orders as it thinks necessary for the purpose of preserving evidence or assets.

(4)   If the case is not one of urgency, the court shall act only on the application of a party to the arbitral proceedings (upon notice to the other parties and to the tribunal) made with the permission of the tribunal or the agreement in writing of the other parties.

(5)   In any case the court shall act only if or to the extent that the arbitral tribunal, and any arbitral

or other institution or person vested by the parties with power in that regard, has no power or is unable for the time being to act effectively.

(6)   If the court so orders, an order made by it under this section shall cease to have effect in whole or in part on the order of the tribunal or of any such arbitral or other institution or person having power to act in relation to the subject-matter of the order.

(7)   The leave of the court is required for any appeal from a decision of the court under this section.

45   Determination of preliminary point of law

(1)   Unless otherwise agreed by the parties, the court may on the application of a party to arbitral proceedings (upon notice to the other parties) determine any question of law arising in the course of the proceedings which the court is satisfied substantially affects the rights of one or more of the parties.

An agreement to dispense with reasons for the tribunal's award shall be considered an agreement to exclude the court's jurisdiction under this section.

(2)   An application under this section shall not be considered unless –

(a)   it is made with the agreement of all the other parties to the proceedings, or
(b)   it is made with the permission of the tribunal and the court is satisfied –

(i)   that the determination of the question is likely to produce substantial savings in costs, and
(ii)   that the application was made without delay.

(3)   The application shall identify the question of law to be determined and, unless made with the agreement of all the other parties to the proceedings, shall state the grounds on which it is said that the question should be decided by the court.

(4)   Unless otherwise agreed by the parties, the arbitral tribunal may continue the arbitral proceedings and make an award while an application to the court under this section is pending.

(5)   Unless the court gives leave, no appeal lies from a decision of the court whether the conditions specified in subsection (2) are met.

(6)   The decision of the court on the question of law shall be treated as a judgment of the court for the purposes of an appeal.

But no appeal lies without the leave of the court which shall not be given unless the court considers that the question is one of general importance, or is one which for some other special reason should be considered by the Court of Appeal.

The award

46   Rules applicable to substance of dispute

(1)   The arbitral tribunal shall decide the dispute –

(a)   in accordance with the law chosen by the parties as applicable to the substance of the dispute, or
(b)   if the parties so agree, in accordance with such other considerations as are agreed by them or determined by the tribunal.

(2)   For this purpose the choice of the laws of a country shall be understood to refer to the substantive laws of that country and not its conflict of laws rules.

(3)   If or to the extent that there is no such choice or agreement, the tribunal shall apply the law determined by the conflict of laws rules which it considers applicable.

47   Awards on different issues, &c

(1)   Unless otherwise agreed by the parties, the tribunal may make more than one award at different times on different aspects of the matters to be determined.

(2)   The tribunal may, in particular, make an award relating –

(a)   to an issue affecting the whole claim, or
(b)   to a part only of the claims or cross-claims submitted to it for decision.

(3)   If the tribunal does so, it shall specify in its award the issue, or the claim or part of a claim, which is the subject matter of the award.

48   Remedies

(1)   The parties are free to agree on the powers exercisable by the arbitral tribunal as regards remedies.

(2)   Unless otherwise agreed by the parties, the tribunal has the following powers.

(3)   The tribunal may make a declaration as to any matter to be determined in the proceedings.

(4)   The tribunal may order the payment of a sum of money, in any currency.

(5)   The tribunal has the same powers as the court –

(a)   to order a party to do or refrain from doing anything;
(b)   to order specific performance of a contract (other than a contract relating to land);
(c)   to order the rectification, setting aside or cancellation of a deed or other document.

49   Interest

(1)   The parties are free to agree on the powers of the tribunal as regards the award of interest.

(2)   Unless otherwise agreed by the parties the following provisions apply.

(3)   The tribunal may award simple or compound interest from such dates, at such rates and with such rests as it considers meets the justice of the case –

(a)   on the whole or part of any amount awarded by the tribunal, in respect of any period up to the date of the award;
(b)   on the whole or part of any amount claimed in the arbitration and outstanding at the commencement of the arbitral proceedings but paid before the award was made, in respect of any period up to the date of payment.

(4)   The tribunal may award simple or compound interest from the date of the award (or any later date) until payment, at such rates and with such rests as it considers meets the justice of the case, on the outstanding amount of any award (including any award of interest under subsection (3) and any award as to costs).

(5)   References in this section to an amount awarded by the tribunal include an amount payable in consequence of a declaratory award by the tribunal.

(6)   The above provisions do not affect any other power of the tribunal to award interest.

50   Extension of time for making award

(1)   Where the time for making an award is limited by or in pursuance of the arbitration agreement, then, unless otherwise agreed by the parties, the court may in accordance with the following provisions by order extend that time.

(2)   An application for an order under this section may be made –

(a)   by the tribunal (upon notice to the parties), or
(b)   by any party to the proceedings (upon notice to the tribunal and the other parties),

but only after exhausting any available arbitral process for obtaining an extension of time.

(3)   The court shall only make an order if satisfied that a substantial injustice would otherwise be done.

(4)   The court may extend the time for such period and on such terms as it thinks fit, and may do so whether or not the time previously fixed (by or under the agreement or by a previous order) has expired.

(5)   The leave of the court is required for any appeal from a decision of the court under this section.

51   Settlement

(1)   If during arbitral proceedings the parties settle the dispute, the following provisions apply unless otherwise agreed by the parties.

(2)   The tribunal shall terminate the substantive proceedings and, if so requested by the parties and not objected to by the tribunal, shall record the settlement in the form of an agreed award.

(3)   An agreed award shall state that it is an award of the tribunal and shall have the same status and effect as any other award on the merits of the case.

(4)   The following provisions of this Part relating to awards (sections 52 to 58) apply to an agreed award.

(5)   Unless the parties have also settled the matter of the payment of the costs of the arbitration, the provisions of this Part relating to costs (sections 59 to 65) continue to apply.

52   Form of award

(1)   The parties are free to agree on the form of an award.

(2)   If or to the extent that there is no such agreement, the following provisions apply.

(3)   The award shall be in writing signed by all the arbitrators or all those assenting to the award.

(4)   The award shall contain the reasons for the award unless it is an agreed award or the parties have agreed to dispense with reasons.

(5)   The award shall state the seat of the arbitration and the date when the award is made.

53   Place where award treated as made

Unless otherwise agreed by the parties, where the seat of the arbitration is in England and Wales or Northern Ireland, any award in the proceedings shall be treated as made there, regardless of where it was signed, despatched or delivered to any of the parties.

54   Date of award

(1)   Unless otherwise agreed by the parties, the tribunal may decide what is to be taken to be the date on which the award was made.

(2)   In the absence of any such decision, the date of the award shall be taken to be the date on which it is signed by the arbitrator or, where more than one arbitrator signs the award, by the last of them.

55   Notification of award

(1)   The parties are free to agree on the requirements as to notification of the award to the parties.

(2)   If there is no such agreement, the award shall be notified to the parties by service on them of copies of the award, which shall be done without delay after the award is made.

(3)   Nothing in this section affects section 56 (power to withhold award in case of non-payment).

56 Power to withhold award in case of non-payment

(1) The tribunal may refuse to deliver an award to the parties except upon full payment of the fees and expenses of the arbitrators.

(2) If the tribunal refuses on that ground to deliver an award, a party to the arbitral proceedings may (upon notice to the other parties and the tribunal) apply to the court, which may order that –

(a) the tribunal shall deliver the award on the payment into court by the applicant of the fees and expenses demanded, or such lesser amount as the court may specify,

(b) the amount of the fees and expenses properly payable shall be determined by such means and upon such terms as the court may direct, and

(c) out of the money paid into court there shall be paid out such fees and expenses as may be found to be properly payable and the balance of the money (if any) shall be paid out to the applicant.

(3) For this purpose the amount of fees and expenses properly payable is the amount the applicant is liable to pay under section 28 or any agreement relating to the payment of the arbitrators.

(4) No application to the court may be made where there is any available arbitral process for appeal or review of the amount of the fees or expenses demanded.

(5) References in this section to arbitrators include an arbitrator who has ceased to act and an umpire who has not replaced the other arbitrators.

(6) The above provisions of this section also apply in relation to any arbitral or other institution or person vested by the parties with powers in relation to the delivery of the tribunal's award.

As they so apply, the references to the fees and expenses of the arbitrators shall be construed as including the fees and expenses of that institution or person.

(7) The leave of the court is required for any appeal from a decision of the court under this section.

(8) Nothing in this section shall be construed as excluding an application under section 28 where payment has been made to the arbitrators in order to obtain the award.

57 Correction of award or additional award

(1) The parties are free to agree on the powers of the tribunal to correct an award or make an additional award.

(2) If or to the extent there is no such agreement, the following provisions apply.

(3) The tribunal may on its own initiative or on the application of a party –

(a) correct an award so as to remove any clerical mistake or error arising from an accidental slip or omission or clarify or remove any ambiguity in the award, or

(b) make an additional award in respect of any claim (including a claim for interest or costs) which was presented to the tribunal but was not dealt with in the award.

These powers shall not be exercised without first affording the other parties a reasonable opportunity to make representations to the tribunal.

(4) Any application for the exercise of those powers must be made within 28 days of the date of the award or such longer period as the parties may agree.

(5) Any correction of an award shall be made within 28 days of the date the application was received by the tribunal or, where the correction is made by the tribunal on its own initiative, within 28 days of the date of the award or, in either case, such longer period as the parties may agree.

(6) Any additional award shall be made within 56 days of the date of the original award or such longer period as the parties may agree.

(7) Any correction of an award shall form part of the award.

58 Effect of award

(1) Unless otherwise agreed by the parties, an award made by the tribunal pursuant to an arbitration agreement is final and binding both on the parties and on any persons claiming through or under them.

(2) This does not affect the right of a person to challenge the award by any available arbitral process of appeal or review or in accordance with the provisions of this Part.

Costs of the arbitration

59 Costs of the arbitration

(1) References in this Part to the costs of the arbitration are to –

(a) the arbitrators' fees and expenses,
(b) the fees and expenses of any arbitral institution concerned, and
(c) the legal or other costs of the parties.

(2) Any such reference includes the costs of or incidental to any proceedings to determine the amount of the recoverable costs of the arbitration (see section 63).

60 Agreement to pay costs in any event

An agreement which has the effect that a party is to pay the whole or part of the costs of the arbitration in any event is only valid if made after the dispute in question has arisen.

61 Award of costs

(1) The tribunal may make an award allocating the costs of the arbitration as between the parties, subject to any agreement of the parties.

(2) Unless the parties otherwise agree, the tribunal shall award costs on the general principle that costs should follow the event except where it appears to the tribunal that in the circumstances this is not appropriate in relation to the whole or part of the costs.

62 Effect of agreement or award about costs

Unless the parties otherwise agree, any obligation under an agreement between them as to how the costs of the arbitration are to be borne, or under an award allocating the costs of the arbitration, extends only to such costs as are recoverable.

63 The recoverable costs of the arbitration

(1) The parties are free to agree what costs of the arbitration are recoverable.

(2) If or to the extent there is no such agreement, the following provisions apply.

(3) The tribunal may determine by award the recoverable costs of the arbitration on such basis as it thinks fit.

If it does so, it shall specify –

(a) the basis on which it has acted, and
(b) the items of recoverable costs and the amount referable to each.

(4) If the tribunal does not determine the recoverable costs of the arbitration, any party to the arbitral proceedings may apply to the court (upon notice to the other parties) which may –

(a) determine the recoverable costs of the arbitration on such basis as it thinks fit, or
(b) order that they shall be determined by such means and upon such terms as it may specify.

(5) Unless the tribunal or the court determines otherwise –

    (a) the recoverable costs of the arbitration shall be determined on the basis that there shall be allowed a reasonable amount in respect of all costs reasonably incurred, and

    (b) any doubt as to whether costs were reasonably incurred or were reasonable in amount shall be resolved in favour of the paying party.

(6) The above provisions have effect subject to section 64 (recoverable fees and expenses of arbitrators).

(7) Nothing in this section affects any right of the arbitrators, any expert, legal adviser or assessor appointed by the tribunal, or any arbitral institution, to payment of their fees and expenses.

64 Recoverable fees and expenses of arbitrators

(1) Unless otherwise agreed by the parties, the recoverable costs of the arbitration shall include in respect of the fees and expenses of the arbitrators only such reasonable fees and expenses as are appropriate in the circumstances.

(2) If there is any question as to what reasonable fees and expenses are appropriate in the circumstances, and the matter is not already before the court on an application under section 63(4), the court may on the application of any party (upon notice to the other parties) –

    (a) determine the matter, or

    (b) order that it be determined by such means and upon such terms as the court may specify.

(3) Subsection (1) has effect subject to any order of the court under section 24(4) or 25(3)(b) (order as to entitlement to fees or expenses in case of removal or resignation of arbitrator).

(4) Nothing in this section affects any right of the arbitrator to payment of his fees and expenses.

65 Power to limit recoverable costs

(1) Unless otherwise agreed by the parties, the tribunal may direct that the recoverable costs of the arbitration, or of any part of the arbitral proceedings, shall be limited to a specified amount.

(2) Any direction may be made or varied at any stage, but this must be done sufficiently in advance of the incurring of costs to which it relates, or the taking of any steps in the proceedings which may be affected by it, for the limit to be taken into account.

Powers of the court in relation to award

66 Enforcement of the award

(1) An award made by the tribunal pursuant to an arbitration agreement may, by leave of the court, be enforced in the same manner as a judgment or order of the court to the same effect.

(2) Where leave is so given, judgment may be entered in terms of the award.

(3) Leave to enforce an award shall not be given where, or to the extent that, the person against whom it is sought to be enforced shows that the tribunal lacked substantive jurisdiction to make the award.

The right to raise such an objection may have been lost (see section 73).

(4) Nothing in this section affects the recognition or enforcement of an award under any other enactment or rule of law, in particular under Part II of the Arbitration Act 1950 (enforcement of awards under Geneva Convention) or the provisions of Part III of this Act relating to the recognition and enforcement of awards under the New York Convention or by an action on the award.

67   Challenging the award: substantive jurisdiction

(1)   A party to arbitral proceedings may (upon notice to the other parties and to the tribunal) apply to the court –

    (a)   challenging any award of the arbitral tribunal as to its substantive jurisdiction; or
    (b)   for an order declaring an award made by the tribunal on the merits to be of no effect, in whole or in part, because the tribunal did not have substantive jurisdiction.

A party may lose the right to object (see section 73) and the right to apply is subject to the restrictions in section 70(2) and (3).

(2)   The arbitral tribunal may continue the arbitral proceedings and make a further award while an application to the court under this section is pending in relation to an award as to jurisdiction.

(3)   On an application under this section challenging an award of the arbitral tribunal as to its substantive jurisdiction, the court may by order –

    (a)   confirm the award,
    (b)   vary the award, or
    (c)   set aside the award in whole or in part.

(4)   The leave of the court is required for any appeal from a decision of the court under this section.

68   Challenging the award: serious irregularity

(1)   A party to arbitral proceedings may (upon notice to the other parties and to the tribunal) apply to the court challenging an award in the proceedings on the ground of serious irregularity affecting the tribunal, the proceedings or the award.

A party may lose the right to object (see section 73) and the right to apply is subject to the restrictions in section 70(2) and (3).

(2)   Serious irregularity means an irregularity of one or more of the following kinds which the court considers has caused or will cause substantial injustice to the applicant –

    (a)   failure by the tribunal to comply with section 33 (general duty of tribunal);
    (b)   the tribunal exceeding its powers (otherwise than by exceeding its substantive jurisdiction: see section 67);
    (c)   failure by the tribunal to conduct the proceedings in accordance with the procedure agreed by the parties;
    (d)   failure by the tribunal to deal with all the issues that were put to it;
    (e)   any arbitral or other institution or person vested by the parties with powers in relation to the proceedings or the award exceeding its powers;
    (f)   uncertainty or ambiguity as to the effect of the award;
    (g)   the award being obtained by fraud or the award or the way in which it was procured being contrary to public policy;
    (h)   failure to comply with the requirements as to the form of the award; or
    (i)   any irregularity in the conduct of the proceedings or in the award which is admitted by the tribunal or by any arbitral or other institution or person vested by the parties with powers in relation to the proceedings or the award.

(3)   If there is shown to be serious irregularity affecting the tribunal, the proceedings or the award, the court may –

    (a)   remit the award to the tribunal, in whole or in part, for reconsideration,
    (b)   set the award aside in whole or in part, or
    (c)   declare the award to be of no effect, in whole or in part.

The court shall not exercise its power to set aside or to declare an award to be of no effect, in whole or in part, unless it is satisfied that it would be inappropriate to remit the matters in question to the tribunal for reconsideration.

(4)   The leave of the court is required for any appeal from a decision of the court under this section.

69 Appeal on point of law

(1) Unless otherwise agreed by the parties, a party to arbitral proceedings may (upon notice to the other parties and to the tribunal) appeal to the court on a question of law arising out of an award made in the proceedings.

An agreement to dispense with reasons for the tribunal's award shall be considered an agreement to exclude the court's jurisdiction under this section.

(2) An appeal shall not be brought under this section except –

(a) with the agreement of all the other parties to the proceedings, or
(b) with the leave of the court.

The right to appeal is also subject to the restrictions in section 70(2) and (3).

(3) Leave to appeal shall be given only if the court is satisfied –

(a) that the determination of the question will substantially affect the rights of one or more of the parties,
(b) that the question is one which the tribunal was asked to determine,
(c) that, on the basis of the findings of fact in the award –

(i) the decision of the tribunal on the question is obviously wrong, or
(ii) the question is one of general public importance and the decision of the tribunal is at least open to serious doubt, and

(d) that, despite the agreement of the parties to resolve the matter by arbitration, it is just and proper in all the circumstances for the court to determine the question.

(4) An application for leave to appeal under this section shall identify the question of law to be determined and state the grounds on which it is alleged that leave to appeal should be granted.

(5) The court shall determine an application for leave to appeal under this section without a hearing unless it appears to the court that a hearing is required.

(6) The leave of the court is required for any appeal from a decision of the court under this section to grant or refuse leave to appeal.

(7) On an appeal under this section the court may by order –

(a) confirm the award,
(b) vary the award,
(c) remit the award to the tribunal, in whole or in part, for reconsideration in the light of the court's determination, or
(d) set aside the award in whole or in part.

The court shall not exercise its power to set aside an award, in whole or in part, unless it is satisfied that it would be inappropriate to remit the matters in question to the tribunal for reconsideration.

(8) The decision of the court on an appeal under this section shall be treated as a judgment of the court for the purposes of a further appeal.

But no such appeal lies without the leave of the court which shall not be given unless the court considers that the question is one of general importance or is one which for some other special reason should be considered by the Court of Appeal.

70 Challenge or appeal: supplementary provisions

(1) The following provisions apply to an application or appeal under section 67, 68 or 69.

(2) An application or appeal may not be brought if the applicant or appellant has not first exhausted –

(a) any available arbitral process of appeal or review, and
(b) any available recourse under section 57 (correction of award or additional award).

(3) Any application or appeal must be brought within 28 days of the date of the award or, if there

has been any arbitral process of appeal or review, of the date when the applicant or appellant was notified of the result of that process.

(4)   If on an application or appeal it appears to the court that the award –

    (a)   does not contain the tribunal's reasons, or
    (b)   does not set out the tribunal's reasons in sufficient detail to enable the court properly to consider the application or appeal,

the court may order the tribunal to state the reasons for its award in sufficient detail for that purpose.

(5)   Where the court makes an order under subsection (4), it may make such further order as it thinks fit with respect to any additional costs of the arbitration resulting from its order.

(6)   The court may order the applicant or appellant to provide security for the costs of the application or appeal, and may direct that the application or appeal be dismissed if the order is not complied with.

The power to order security for costs shall not be exercised on the ground that the applicant or appellant is –

    (a)   an individual ordinarily resident outside the United Kingdom, or
    (b)   a corporation or association incorporated or formed under the law of a country outside the United Kingdom, or whose central management and control is exercised outside the United Kingdom.

(7)   The court may order that any money payable under the award shall be brought into court or otherwise secured pending the determination of the application or appeal, and may direct that the application or appeal be dismissed if the order is not complied with.

(8)   The court may grant leave to appeal subject to conditions to the same or similar effect as an order under subsection (6) or (7).

This does not affect the general discretion of the court to grant leave subject to conditions.

71   Challenge or appeal: effect of order of court

(1)   The following provisions have effect where the court makes an order under section 67, 68 or 69 with respect to an award.

(2)   Where the award is varied, the variation has effect as part of the tribunal's award.

(3)   Where the award is remitted to the tribunal, in whole or in part, for reconsideration, the tribunal shall make a fresh award in respect of the matters remitted within three months of the date of the order for remission or such longer or shorter period as the court may direct.

(4)   Where the award is set aside or declared to be of no effect, in whole or in part, the court may also order that any provision that an award is a condition precedent to the bringing of legal proceedings in respect of a matter to which the arbitration agreement applies, is of no effect as regards the subject matter of the award or, as the case may be, the relevant part of the award.

Miscellaneous

72   Saving for rights of person who takes no part in proceedings

(1)   A person alleged to be a party to arbitral proceedings but who takes no part in the proceedings may question –

    (a)   whether there is a valid arbitration agreement,
    (b)   whether the tribunal is properly constituted, or
    (c)   what matters have been submitted to arbitration in accordance with the arbitration agreement,

by proceedings in the court for a declaration or injunction or other appropriate relief.

(2)   He also has the same right as a party to the arbitral proceedings to challenge an award –

(a) by an application under section 67 on the ground of lack of substantive jurisdiction in relation to him, or

(b) by an application under section 68 on the ground of serious irregularity (within the meaning of that section) affecting him;

and section 70(2) (duty to exhaust arbitral procedures) does not apply in his case.

73 Loss of right to object

(1) If a party to arbitral proceedings takes part, or continues to take part, in the proceedings without making, either forthwith or within such time as is allowed by the arbitration agreement or the tribunal or by any provision of this Part, any objection –

(a) that the tribunal lacks substantive jurisdiction,
(b) that the proceedings have been improperly conducted,
(c) that there has been a failure to comply with the arbitration agreement or with any provision of this Part, or
(d) that there has been any other irregularity affecting the tribunal or the proceedings,

he may not raise that objection later, before the tribunal or the court, unless he shows that, at the time he took part or continued to take part in the proceedings, he did not know and could not with reasonable diligence have discovered the grounds for the objection.

(2) Where the arbitral tribunal rules that it has substantive jurisdiction and a party to arbitral proceedings who could have questioned that ruling –

(a) by any available arbitral process of appeal or review, or
(b) by challenging the award,

does not do so, or does not do so within the time allowed by the arbitration agreement or any provision of this Part, he may not object later to the tribunal's substantive jurisdiction on any ground which was the subject of that ruling.

74 Immunity of arbitral institutions, &c

(1) An arbitral or other institution or person designated or requested by the parties to appoint or nominate an arbitrator is not liable for anything done or omitted in the discharge or purported discharge of that function unless the act or omission is shown to have been in bad faith.

(2) An arbitral or other institution or person by whom an arbitrator is appointed or nominated is not liable, by reason of having appointed or nominated him, for anything done or omitted by the arbitrator (or his employees or agents) in the discharge or purported discharge of his functions as arbitrator.

(3) The above provisions apply to an employee or agent of an arbitral or other institution or person as they apply to the institution or person himself.

75 Charge to secure payment of solicitors' costs

The powers of the court to make declarations and orders under section 73 of the Solicitors Act 1974 or Article 71H of the Solicitors (Northern Ireland) Order 1976 (power to charge property recovered in the proceedings with the payment of solicitors' costs) may be exercised in relation to arbitral proceedings as if those proceedings were proceedings in the court.

Supplementary

76 Service of notices, &c

(1) The parties are free to agree on the manner of service of any notice or other document required or authorised to be given or served in pursuance of the arbitration agreement or for the purposes of the arbitral proceedings.

(2) If or to the extent that there is no such agreement the following provisions apply.

(3)   A notice or other document may be served on a person by any effective means.

(4)   If a notice or other document is addressed, pre-paid and delivered by post –

(a)   to the addressee's last known principal residence or, if he is or has been carrying on a trade, profession or business, his last known principal business address, or

(b)   where the addressee is a body corporate, to the body's registered or principal office,

it shall be treated as effectively served.

(5)   This section does not apply to the service of documents for the purposes of legal proceedings, for which provision is made by rules of court.

(6)   References in this Part to a notice or other document include any form of communication in writing and references to giving or serving a notice or other document shall be construed accordingly.

77   Powers of court in relation to service of documents

(1)   This section applies where service of a document on a person in the manner agreed by the parties, or in accordance with provisions of section 76 having effect in default of agreement, is not reasonably practicable.

(2)   Unless otherwise agreed by the parties, the court may make such order as it thinks fit –

(a)   for service in such manner as the court may direct, or

(b)   dispensing with service of the document.

(3)   Any party to the arbitration agreement may apply for an order, but only after exhausting any available arbitral process for resolving the matter.

(4)   The leave of the court is required for any appeal from a decision of the court under this section.

78   Reckoning periods of time

(1)   The parties are free to agree on the method of reckoning periods of time for the purposes of any provision agreed by them or any provision of this Part having effect in default of such agreement.

(2)   If or to the extent there is no such agreement, periods of time shall be reckoned in accordance with the following provisions.

(3)   Where the act is required to be done within a specified period after or from a specified date, the period begins immediately after that date.

(4)   Where the act is required to be done a specified number of clear days after a specified date, at least that number of days must intervene between the day on which the act is done and that date.

(5)   Where the period is a period of seven days or less which would include a Saturday, Sunday or a public holiday in the place where anything which has to be done within the period falls to be done, that day shall be excluded.

In relation to England and Wales or Northern Ireland, a 'public holiday' means Christmas Day, Good Friday or a day which under the Banking and Financial Dealings Act 1971 is a bank holiday.

79   Power of court to extend time limits relating to arbitral proceedings

(1)   Unless the parties otherwise agree, the court may by order extend any time limit agreed by them in relation to any matter relating to the arbitral proceedings or specified in any provision of this Part having effect in default of such agreement.

This section does not apply to a time limit to which section 12 applies (power of court to extend time for beginning arbitral proceedings, &c).

(2)   An application for an order may be made –

(a)   by any party to the arbitral proceedings (upon notice to the other parties and to the tribunal), or

(b)   by the arbitral tribunal (upon notice to the parties).

(3)   The court shall not exercise its power to extend a time limit unless it is satisfied –

(a)   that any available recourse to the tribunal, or to any arbitral or other institution or person vested by the parties with power in that regard, has first been exhausted, and

(b)   that a substantial injustice would otherwise be done.

(4)   The court's power under this section may be exercised whether or not the time has already expired.

(5)   An order under this section may be made on such terms as the court thinks fit.

(6)   The leave of the court is required for any appeal from a decision of the court under this section.

80   Notice and other requirements in connection with legal proceedings

(1)   References in this Part to an application, appeal or other step in relation to legal proceedings being taken 'upon notice' to the other parties to the arbitral proceedings, or to the tribunal, are to such notice of the originating process as is required by rules of court and do not impose any separate requirement.

(2)   Rules of court shall be made –

(a)   requiring such notice to be given as indicated by any provision of this Part, and

(b)   as to the manner, form and content of any such notice.

(3)   Subject to any provision made by rules of court, a requirement to give notice to the tribunal of legal proceedings shall be construed –

(a)   if there is more than one arbitrator, as a requirement to give notice to each of them; and

(b)   if the tribunal is not fully constituted, as a requirement to give notice to any arbitrator who has been appointed.

(4)   References in this Part to making an application or appeal to the court within a specified period are to the issue within that period of the appropriate originating process in accordance with rules of court.

(5)   Where any provision of this Part requires an application or appeal to be made to the court within a specified time, the rules of court relating to the reckoning of periods, the extending or abridging of periods, and the consequences of not taking a step within the period prescribed by the rules, apply in relation to that requirement.

(6)   Provision may be made by rules of court amending the provisions of this Part –

(a)   with respect to the time within which any application or appeal to the court must be made,

(b)   so as to keep any provision made by this Part in relation to arbitral proceedings in step with the corresponding provision of rules of court applying in relation to proceedings in the court, or

(c)   so as to keep any provision made by this Part in relation to legal proceedings in step with the corresponding provision of rules of court applying generally in relation to proceedings in the court.

(7)   Nothing in this section affects the generality of the power to make rules of court.

81   Saving for certain matters governed by common law

(1)   Nothing in this Part shall be construed as excluding the operation of any rule of law consistent with the provisions of this Part, in particular, any rule of law as to –

(a)   matters which are not capable of settlement by arbitration;

(b)   the effect of an oral arbitration agreement; or

(c)   the refusal of recognition or enforcement of an arbitral award on grounds of public policy.

(2)   Nothing in this Act shall be construed as reviving any jurisdiction of the court to set aside or remit an award on the ground of errors of fact or law on the face of the award.

82   Minor definitions

(1)   In this Part –

'arbitrator', unless the context otherwise requires, includes an umpire;

'available arbitral process', in relation to any matter, includes any process of appeal to or review by an arbitral or other institution or person vested by the parties with powers in relation to that matter;

'claimant', unless the context otherwise requires, includes a counterclaimant, and related expressions shall be construed accordingly;

'dispute' includes any difference;

'enactment' includes an enactment contained in Northern Ireland legislation;

'legal proceedings' means civil proceedings [in England and Wales in the High Court or the county court or in Northern Ireland] in the High Court or a county court;

'peremptory order' means an order made under section 41(5) or made in exercise of any corresponding power conferred by the parties;

'premises' includes land, buildings, moveable structures, vehicles, vessels, aircraft and hover-craft;

'question of law' means –

(a)   for a court in England and Wales, a question of the law of England and Wales, and

(b)   for a court in Northern Ireland, a question of the law of Northern Ireland;

'substantive jurisdiction', in relation to an arbitral tribunal, refers to the matters specified in section 30(1)(a) to (c), and references to the tribunal exceeding its substantive jurisdiction shall be construed accordingly.

(2)   References in this Part to a party to an arbitration agreement include any person claiming under or through a party to the agreement.

83   Index of defined expressions: Part I

In this Part the expressions listed below are defined or otherwise explained by the provisions indicated –

agreement, agree and agreed	section 5(1)
agreement in writing	section 5(2) to (5)
arbitration agreement	sections 6 and 5(1)
arbitrator	section 82(1)
available arbitral process	section 82(1)
claimant	section 82(1)
commencement (in relation to arbitral proceedings)	section 14
costs of the arbitration	section 59
the court	section 105
dispute	section 82(1)
enactment	section 82(1)
legal proceedings	section 82(1)
Limitation Acts	section 13(4)
notice (or other document)	section 76(6)
Party –	
– in relation to an arbitration agreement	section 82(2)
– where section 106(2) or (3) applies	section 106(4)
peremptory order	section 82(1) (and see section 41(5))
premises	section 82(1)
question of law	section 82(1)
recoverable costs	sections 63 and 64
seat of the arbitration	section 3

serve and service (of notice or other document)	section 76(6)
substantive jurisdiction (in relation to an arbitral tribunal)	section 82(1) (and see section 30(1)(a) to (c))
upon notice (to the parties or the tribunal)	section 80
written and in writing	section 5(6)

84 Transitional provisions

(1) The provisions of this Part do not apply to arbitral proceedings commenced before the date on which this Part comes into force.

(2) They apply to arbitral proceedings commenced on or after that date under an arbitration agreement whenever made.

(3) The above provisions have effect subject to any transitional provision made by an order under section 109(2) (power to include transitional provisions in commencement order).

SCHEDULE 1
Mandatory provisions of Part I

Section 4(1)

sections 9 to 11 (stay of legal proceedings);
section 12 (power of court to extend agreed time limits);
section 13 (application of Limitation Acts);
section 24 (power of court to remove arbitrator);
section 26(1) (effect of death of arbitrator);
section 28 (liability of parties for fees and expenses of arbitrators);
section 29 (immunity of arbitrator);
section 31 (objection to substantive jurisdiction of tribunal);
section 32 (determination of preliminary point of jurisdiction);
section 33 (general duty of tribunal);
section 37(2) (items to be treated as expenses of arbitrators);
section 40 (general duty of parties);
section 43 (securing the attendance of witnesses);
section 56 (power to withhold award in case of non-payment);
section 60 (effectiveness of agreement for payment of costs in any event);
section 66 (enforcement of award);
sections 67 and 68 (challenging the award: substantive jurisdiction and serious irregularity), and sections 70 and 71 (supplementary provisions; effect of order of court) so far as relating to those sections;
section 72 (saving for rights of person who takes no part in proceedings);
section 73 (loss of right to object);
section 74 (immunity of arbitral institutions, &c);
section 75 (charge to secure payment of solicitors' costs).

1.4

President's arbitration practice guidance (November 2015)[1]

ARBITRATION IN THE FAMILY COURT

Practice Guidance issued on 23 November 2015 by Sir James Munby, President of the Family Division

1. This Guidance concerns the interface between the Family Court and arbitrations conducted in accordance with the provisions of the Arbitration Act 1996 (AA96) where the parties to a post-relationship breakdown financial dispute have agreed to submit issues for decision by an arbitrator whose award is to be binding upon them.

2. It is a fundamental requirement of this Guidance that the arbitrator will decide the substance of the dispute only in accordance with the law of England and Wales. This Guidance does not apply to, or sanction, any arbitral process based on a different system of law nor, in particular, one where there is reason to believe that, whatever system of law is purportedly being applied, there may have been gender-based discrimination.

3. To avoid unnecessary complication this Guidance is directed towards what may well be the most common form of arbitration with which the Family Court will become concerned, where the issues between the parties involve relief or an award by way of one or more of the financial remedies listed in rule 2.3 of the Family Procedure Rules 2010 (FPR).

4. In order to be effective, elements of some arbitral awards (by comprehensive dismissal of claims to create a clean break, or so as to bind the provider to a pension split, for example) will require their terms to be reflected in a Family Court order. If enforcement of the award becomes necessary, doing so via Family Court processes will be available only if orders reflecting the award are obtained. (Paragraph 30 below describes an alternative route which may be available via section 66 of AA96 in the county court or in the Family Division of the High Court.)

5. But it should be borne in mind that not every award need be brought before the Family Court for a financial order to be made, and that it may be more appropriate for some to be brought (if necessary) before a court which does not exercise family jurisdiction. Thus, for instance, where an arbitrator has decided upon the title to or possession of property under the Married Women's Property Act 1882, or has determined the respective beneficial interests of the disputants in a property or fund, the parties may simply choose to operate in accordance with the award and thus have no need for a court order to reflect it. Or a Trustees of Land and Appointment of Trustees Act 1996 ('TOLATA') award might more appropriately be made the subject of an order in the County Court if it simply declares the interests of the parties and does not involve any financial remedy element. It should be noted, however, that (pending any

---

[1] Crown copyright material is reproduced here with the permission of the Controller of HMSO.

statutory changes to facilitate the Family Court hearing them) only the High Court and county court have jurisdiction to determine applications made under TOLATA or the Inheritance (Provision for Family and Dependants) Act 1975.

6.   Taking the most common example of an arbitration where the agreed issues are what periodical payments, lump sum and adjustment of property awards should be received by a claimant spouse, it is important first to establish whether or not financial remedy proceedings have already been instituted and a Form A issued.

A: Where there are subsisting proceedings seeking the same relief as is in issue in the arbitration

Stay of proceedings:

7.   The court should be invited to stay the financial remedy proceedings pending delivery of the award. The arbitration agreement (in the case of an IFLA Scheme arbitration, the Form ARB1) will in most instances only recently have been signed by both parties, and thus contested applications for a stay will likely be rare. CPR rule 62.3(2) provides that such an application 'must be made by application notice to the court dealing with those proceedings'.

8.   The Family Court has an obligation under FPR 3.3(1)(b) 'where the parties agree, to enable non-court dispute resolution to take place.' Section 9(4) of AA96 requires that the court 'shall grant a stay unless satisfied that the arbitration agreement is null and void, inoperative, or incapable of being performed' and makes it clear that a stay application should be made to the court where the subsisting proceedings are pending. By paragraph 6.2 of Form ARB1 the parties will have agreed that they 'will apply for or consent to a stay of any existing court proceedings, as necessary.'

9.   In such circumstances where the application to stay is by consent or unopposed it should be dealt with on paper and (absent any unusual circumstances indicating a need) without listing or hearing.

10. Parties seeking such a stay should (in person or through their solicitors, who need not for this purpose be on the court record in the financial remedy proceedings) lodge in the place where the proceedings have been commenced, and within those proceedings, clear evidence of their agreement (or lack of opposition) to the stay order, together with a copy of their signed arbitration agreement (such as the IFLA Form ARB1). One of the standard orders approved for use in conjunction with arbitrations provides for a stay, and a copy completed with the details of the case, and signed by both parties or their representatives to signify approval, should be lodged with the other documents. The file will then be placed before a judge for approval, or for queries to be raised and dealt with by correspondence, and/or (if necessary) a hearing listed. [. . .]

Applying for an order to reflect the award: by consent

11. The terms of the proposed consent order will be drafted to reflect the decisions and directions contained in the award. Insofar as financial remedy orders are involved, their form should follow the relevant paragraphs of the standard orders, which contain recitals apt for an arbitration award case. Together with a signed copy of the proposed order in the terms agreed, the parties, in order to take advantage of this accelerated procedure, should at the same time lodge their Forms A and D81, a copy of the arbitrator's award and (unless already on the court file) their Form ARB1. There is no reason in principle why unopposed applications for a consent order should not be dealt with on paper by a District Judge, although the court will always retain the ability to raise questions in correspondence or to call for a hearing.

12. Attention is drawn to my observations in *S v S (Financial Remedies: Arbitral Award)* [2014] EWHC 7 (Fam), [2014] 1 FLR 1257, about the attitude likely to be adopted by the court in

such cases: 'where the parties are putting the matter before the court by consent, ... it can only be in the rarest of cases that it will be appropriate for the judge to do other than approve the order.'

13. Draft orders submitted which invite the court to make orders it has no jurisdiction to make (or which are otherwise in unacceptable form) will, like any other defective consent order submitted, be returned for reconsideration. There is of course no objection to recitals which express the parties' agreement to provisions which fall outside the scope of the available statutory relief. Nor indeed is there anything to prevent parties agreeing to change the terms of an award if they are agreed upon a revised formulation. In that event, though, it would be sensible for the covering correspondence to make it clear which provisions of the award have been overtaken by what subsequent arrangement arrived at by the parties.

14. Parties anxious to preserve the privacy and to maintain the confidentiality of the award should lodge that document in a sealed envelope, clearly marked with the name and number of the case and the words 'Arbitration Award: Confidential'. The award will remain on the court file but should be placed in an envelope clearly marked as above, plus 'not to be opened without the permission of a judge of the Family Court.' The request for the award to be sealed once the order has been approved should be made prominently in the covering letter.

Applying for an order to reflect the award: opposed

15. The party seeking to have the award reflected in a court order will need to proceed adopting what at para.[25] of S v S was described as the 'notice to show cause' procedure. An alternative formulation of the arbitration recital for such a situation is contained in each standard order.

16. Similar documentation should be submitted with the application, except of course that the order proposed is likely to have been unilaterally drafted on behalf of the party seeking to obtain the order. An application of this sort will ordinarily be listed for a hearing before a judge of Circuit Judge or High Court Judge level.

17. Attention is drawn to my observations in S v S concerning the attitude likely to be adopted by the court in opposed cases:

> 'The court will no doubt adopt an appropriately robust approach, both to the procedure it adopts in dealing with such a challenge and to the test it applies in deciding the outcome. ... The parties will almost invariably forfeit the right to anything other than a most abbreviated hearing; only in highly exceptional circumstances is the court likely to permit anything more than a very abbreviated hearing.'

18. Applications for consent orders are specifically placed outside the scope of the MIAMs requirement by Practice Direction 3A, para.13(2). So, by virtue of the same provision, are proceedings 'for enforcement of any order made in proceedings for a financial remedy or of any agreement made in or in contemplation of proceedings for a financial remedy.' Parties who have agreed to arbitrate but have become engaged in any post-arbitral award dispute, as for instance a contested 'show cause' application, should not be required to deviate into a MIAM.

B: Arbitration claims

19. An 'arbitration claim' is a term of art, and its scope for the purposes of its application to arbitrations conducted under AA96 is defined by CPR rule 62.2(1) in these terms:

> [In relation to AA96] 'arbitration claim' means –
> (a) any application to the court under the 1996 Act;
> (b) a claim to determine –
> (i) whether there is a valid arbitration agreement;
> (ii) whether an arbitration tribunal is properly constituted; or what matters have been submitted to arbitration in accordance with an arbitration agreement;
> (c) a claim to declare that an award by an arbitral tribunal is not binding on a party; and
> (d) any other application affecting –
> (i) arbitration proceedings (whether started or not); or
> (ii) an arbitration agreement.

20. The court where 'arbitration claims' as so defined are to be commenced is governed by CPR PD62 para.2 and the High Court and County Courts (Allocation of Arbitration Proceedings) Order 1996 (S.I. 1996/3215) as amended (the 1996 Order), which do not currently cater for such claims to be launched in the Family Court. Pending changes made to CPR PD62 and/or the 1996 Order, an applicant for an 'arbitration claim' should issue the requisite Form (see below) in the Commercial Court and should at the time of issue seek transfer to the Family Division. Para.[6] of the 1996 Order does not as yet permit the transfer of any such application to the Family Court – the transfer must therefore be to the Family Division of the High Court.

21. The Form N8 initiating such a claim should be prominently marked 'Family business: direction sought for transfer to the Family Division of the High Court' and should detail (where there are subsisting Family Court proceedings, albeit stayed) the case title and number.

22. Attention is drawn to sections 42 (enforcement of peremptory orders of the arbitrator) and 43 (securing the attendance of witnesses) of AA96 which are the provisions in relation to which an 'arbitration claim' is most likely to be sought in the course of an ongoing post-separation financial arbitration. Attention is also drawn to the provisions of section 44 (court powers exercisable in support of arbitral proceedings). Standard orders have been issued to meet each of these contingencies [. . .].

23. As these are all within the CPR definition of 'arbitration claims,' pending changes to para.[2] of CPR PD62 such applications should (as described above) be issued in the Commercial Court and bear prominently upon them a request for speedy transfer to the Family Division (or, in the case of, for instance, a TOLATA claim which does not also invoke the family court jurisdiction, to the relevant county court).

24. In relation to applications under sections 42 and 43 the standard orders are self-explanatory. Such applications should be heard by a judge of High Court level.

C: Arbitrations conducted when there are no subsisting proceedings seeking relevant relief

Stay of proceedings:

25. An application to stay legal proceedings under section 9 of AA96 is in effect excluded from the definition of and procedural requirements for 'arbitration claims' by CPR rule 62.3(2), which provides that such an application 'must be made by application notice to the court dealing with those proceedings'.

26. In the case of an IFLA Scheme arbitration the parties will have agreed (by paragraph 6.2 of their Form ARB1) that they 'will not commence court proceedings ... in relation to the same subject matter'. If however such proceedings are thereafter initiated then it is open to either party to apply for a stay pursuant to section 9 of AA96 in the court where the proceedings have been commenced, and within those proceedings. If a stay remains opposed an early hearing will obviously be required to determine the application.

Applying for an order to reflect the award: by consent

27. The principles discussed in Part A apply, but if the relief awarded and sought to be reflected in an order includes one or more financial remedies only capable of being made on or after pronouncement of a decree, then it will be necessary for 'status proceedings' seeking divorce, judicial separation, nullity or (in the case of civil partners) dissolution to have been instituted, the relevant financial remedies applied for, and the stage in the proceedings reached when it will be appropriate for the court to make an order. In the case of divorce proceedings that would normally predicate a decree nisi having been pronounced, but see *JP v NP* [2014] EWHC 1101 (Fam), [2015] 1 FLR 659.

Applying for an order to reflect the award: opposed

28.   The section of Part A describing the 'show cause' procedure applies, and again it would be necessary to have the necessary status proceedings in being for financial remedy orders to be made.

29.   Where the aid of the Court is needed in support of a family financial arbitration in relation to which status proceedings have not yet been commenced, then the route suggested in paragraph 20 et seq. above must be followed, and transfer from the Commercial Court sought. It will however be necessary for the FPR Part 18 procedure to be adopted in order to bring the arbitration claim (for instance, under section 42 or section 43 of AA96) before the Family Division.

D: Enforcement

30.   Section 3 of CPR Part 62 (rules 62.17 and 62.18) make provision for the direct enforcement of awards. In some situations it may be possible to pray section 66 of AA96 in aid to enforce an award. Para.4 of the 1996 Order authorises the commencement in any county court of section 66 proceedings under which awards can, with the court's permission, be enforced in the same way as a judgment or order of the court to the same effect. This may prove effective in the case of a TOLATA award but is not appropriate in the case of a financial remedy award.

E: Challenging the Award under sections 67 to 71 of the Arbitration Act

31.   Some very specific bases for challenging arbitrations are contained in these sections of AA96. They are hedged about with preconditions and limitations, and the commercial experience in arbitration is that they are relatively rarely successful. In relation to an arbitration dealing with family financial issues, however, it would ordinarily be appropriate for a High Court Judge of the Family Division to hear them, and thus it is to be expected that applications commenced pursuant to these provisions will by the same route be transferred to that court.

F: Arbitration-specific standard court orders

32.   This suite now consists of three orders for use in conjunction with arbitrations. They are reproduced in their approved form within Annex A to this Guidance and comprise orders to:

   •   Stay pursuant to Arbitration Act 1996 section 9 and/or under the court's case management powers
   •   Enforce an arbitrator's peremptory order under section 42, Arbitration Act 1996
   •   Secure the attendance of witnesses under section 43, Arbitration Act 1996

33.   The forms of 'omnibus' orders already commonly in use for both Financial Remedy and Children Act Schedule 1 Final Orders each contain a recital to be completed where the order sought was to reflect an arbitral award. A slightly revised form for such recital is included in Annex B.

34.   Pending any new or revised Practice Direction to accompany Part 5, these formulations should be adopted for use, subject always to the proviso that their provisions may be varied by the court or a party if the variation is required by the circumstances of a particular case.

James Munby
President of the Family Division
23 November 2015

Appendix 2

Forms and precedents

Family Law Arbitration Financial Scheme: Form ARB1FS (2016 edition)[1]

Application for family arbitration

1. We, the parties to this application, whose details are set out below, apply to the Institute of Family Law Arbitrators Limited for the nomination and appointment of a sole arbitrator from the Family Arbitration Financial Panel ('the Financial Panel') to resolve the dispute referred to at paragraph 2 below by arbitration in accordance with the Arbitration Act 1996 ('the Act') and the Rules of the Family Law Arbitration Financial Scheme ('the Financial Scheme'):

Applicant's name	[*Name*]
Address	[*Address*]
Telephone	[*Tel*]
Mobile	[*Mobile*]
Email	[*Email*]
Fax	[*Fax*]
Represented by*	[*Name*]
Address	[*Address*]
Telephone	[*Tel*]
Mobile	[*Mobile*]
Email	[*Email*]
Fax	[*Fax*]

And:

Respondent's name	[*Name*]
Address	[*Address*]
Telephone	[*Tel*]
Mobile	[*Mobile*]
Email	[*Email*]
Fax	[*Fax*]

---

[1] © IFLA 2016. This form may be updated in future.

Represented by*	[Name]
Address	[Address]
Telephone	[Tel]
Mobile	[Mobile]
Email	[Email]
Fax	[Fax]

*Delete as applicable. Add, if necessary, the names of other parties on a separate sheet.

2.   **The dispute concerns the following issue(s):**

(Set these out on a separate sheet if preferred, but as concisely as possible.)

[*Issues*]

Please complete EITHER paragraph 3(a) OR 3(b) OR paragraph 4 below:

3(a)   **We wish to nominate the following member of the Financial Panel for appointment in this matter:**

(This paragraph applies if the parties agree that they would like the matter to be referred to a particular arbitrator and/or have approached a particular arbitrator directly. The appointment will initially be offered to the nominated arbitrator. If the appointment is not accepted by their first choice of arbitrator the parties may, if they agree, make a second or subsequent choice. Otherwise, it will be offered to another suitable member of the Financial Panel in accordance with paragraph 4 below.)

[*Nominate requested arbitrator*]

3(b)   **We wish the Institute of Family Law Arbitrators Limited to select one of the members of the Financial Panel from the agreed shortlist below for appointment in this matter:**

(This paragraph applies if the parties have agreed on a shortlist of arbitrators from the Panel any one of whom would be acceptable to them, and wishes IFLA to select one of the arbitrators on the shortlist without reference to any criteria. In this case, IFLA will offer the appointment to one of the shortlisted arbitrators chosen at random. If the appointment is not accepted by the first choice of arbitrator, IFLA will offer the appointment to a second or subsequent shortlisted arbitrator, similarly chosen at random. If none of the shortlisted arbitrators accepts the appointment, IFLA will inform the parties and invite them to submit further agreed names.)

[*Specify shortlisted arbitrators*]

4.   **We wish the Institute of Family Law Arbitrators Limited to nominate a member of the Financial Panel for appointment in this matter.**

(This paragraph applies if the parties have not identified a particular arbitrator to whom they wish the matter to be referred. Please set out below the nature of the dispute (insofar as it is not apparent from paragraph 2 above). Please also set out below any preferences as to the arbitrator's qualifications, areas of experience, expertise and/or any other attributes; or as to the geographical location of the arbitration; and any other relevant circumstances.)

[*Desired characteristics and considerations of IFLA-nominated arbitrator*]

5.   **If court proceedings are current, please identify the nature of the proceedings, in which court they are running and what stage they have reached.** (Please attach copies of any relevant documents and court orders.)

[*Court proceedings*]

6.   **We confirm the following:**

6.1   We have been advised about and understand the nature and implications of this agreement to arbitrate;

6.2 Once the arbitration has started, we will not commence court proceedings or continue existing court proceedings in relation to the same subject matter (and will apply for or consent to a stay of any existing court proceedings, as necessary), unless it is appropriate to make an application to the court arising out of or in connection with the arbitration, or some relief is required that would not be available in the arbitration;

6.3 We have read the current edition of the Rules of the Financial Scheme ('the Rules') and will abide by them. In particular, we understand our obligation to comply with the decisions, directions and orders of the arbitrator and, when required, to make full and complete disclosure relating to our financial circumstances;

6.4 We understand and agree that any award of the arbitrator appointed to determine this dispute will be final and binding on us, subject to the following:

    (a) any challenge to the award by any available arbitral process of appeal or review or in accordance with the provisions of Part 1 of the Act;

    (b) insofar as the subject matter of the award requires it to be embodied in a court order (see 6.5 below), any changes which the court making that order may require;

    (c) insofar as the award provides for continuing payments to be made by one party to another, or to a child or children, a subsequent award or court order reviewing and varying or revoking the provision for continuing payments, and which supersedes an existing award;

6.5 If and so far as the subject matter of the award makes it necessary, we will apply to an appropriate court for an order in the same or similar terms as the award or the relevant part of the award. (In this context, 'an appropriate court' means a court which has jurisdiction to make a substantive order in the same or similar terms as the award, whether on primary application or on transfer from another division of the court.) We understand that the court has a discretion as to whether, and in what terms, to make an order and we will take all reasonably necessary steps to see that such an order is made;

6.6 We understand and agree that although the Rules provide for each party, generally, to bear an equal share of the arbitrator's fees and expenses (see Art.14.4(a)), if any party fails to pay their share, then the arbitrator may initially require payment of the full amount from any other party, leaving it to them to recover from the defaulting party;

6.7 We agree to the arbitration of this dispute in accordance with the Financial Rules of the Scheme.

IMPORTANT

Parties should be aware that:

- by signing this form they are entering into a binding agreement to arbitrate (within the meaning of s.6 of the Arbitration Act 1996).
- after signing, neither party may avoid arbitration (unless they both agree to do so). Either party may rely on the arbitration agreement to seek a stay of court proceedings commenced by the other.
- arbitration is a process whose outcome is generally final. There are very limited bases for raising a challenge or appeal, and it is only in exceptional circumstances that a court will exercise its own discretion in substitution for the award.

Signed..
(Applicant *or* Applicant's legal representative, for and on behalf of Applicant)

Dated: [*date*]

Signed..
(Respondent *or* Respondent's legal representative, for and on behalf of Respondent)

Dated: [*date*]

Please send your completed form, preferably by email, to info@ifla.org.uk, or it can be sent by post to IFLA, PO Box 302, Orpington, Kent BR6 8QX.

Note that information provided on this form may be retained and reviewed by IFLA on a strictly confidential and anonymous basis, and used for the purposes of family arbitration training and/or research.

2.2

Family Law Arbitration Children Scheme: Form ARB1CS (2016 edition revised)[1]

Application for family arbitration

1.   We, the parties to this application, whose details are set out below, apply to the Institute of Family Law Arbitrators Limited for the nomination and appointment of a sole arbitrator from the IFLA Children Panel ('the Children Panel') to resolve the dispute referred to at paragraph 3 below by arbitration in accordance with the Arbitration Act 1996 ('the Act') and the Rules of the Family Law Arbitration Children Scheme ('the Children Scheme'). We confirm that all the persons who have parental responsibility for the child(ren) concerned are parties to this arbitration.

Applicant's name	[Name]
Address	[Address]
Telephone	[Tel]
Mobile	[Mobile]
Email	[Email]
Fax	[Fax]
Represented by*	[Name]
Address	[Address]
Telephone	[Tel]
Mobile	[Mobile]
Email	[Email]
Fax	[Fax]

And:

Respondent's name	[Name]
Address	[Address]
Telephone	[Tel]
Mobile	[Mobile]
Email	[Email]
Fax	[Fax]

---

[1]   © IFLA 2016. This form may be updated in future.

Represented by*	[Name]
Address	[Address]
Telephone	[Tel]
Mobile	[Mobile]
Email	[Email]
Fax	[Fax]

*Delete as applicable.

Add, if necessary, the names of other parties on a separate sheet.

2. **The child(ren) concerned is/are:**

    Please insert names and dates of birth and relationship of each child to the parties and whether (as regards each party) they have parental responsibility. Please also state the current location of each child.

    [*Children information*]

3. **The dispute concerns the following issue(s):**

    (Set these out on a separate sheet if preferred, but as concisely as possible.)

    [*Issues*]

Please complete EITHER paragraph 4(a) OR 4(b) OR paragraph 5 below:

4(a) **We wish to nominate the following member of the Children Panel for appointment in this matter:**

    (This paragraph applies if the parties agree that they would like the matter to be referred to a particular arbitrator and/or have approached a particular arbitrator directly. The appointment will be offered to the nominated arbitrator. If the appointment is not accepted by their first choice of arbitrator the parties may, if they agree, make a second or subsequent choice. Otherwise, it will be offered to another suitable member of the Children Panel in accordance with paragraph 5 below.)

    [*Nominate requested arbitrator*]

4(b) **We wish the Institute of Family Law Arbitrators Limited to select one of the members of the Children Panel from the agreed shortlist below for appointment in this matter:**

    (This paragraph applies if the parties have agreed on a shortlist of arbitrators from the Children Panel any one of whom would be acceptable to them, and wishes IFLA to select one of the arbitrators on the shortlist without reference to any criteria. In this case, IFLA will offer the appointment to one of the shortlisted arbitrators chosen at random. If the appointment is not accepted by the first choice of arbitrator, IFLA will offer the appointment to a second or subsequent shortlisted arbitrator, similarly chosen at random. If none of the shortlisted arbitrators accepts the appointment, IFLA will inform the parties and invite them to submit further agreed names.)

    [*Specify shortlisted arbitrators*]

5. **We wish the Institute of Family Law Arbitrators Limited to nominate a member of the Children Panel for appointment in this matter.**

    (This paragraph applies if the parties have not identified a particular arbitrator to whom they wish the matter to be referred. Please set out below the nature of the dispute (insofar as it is not apparent from paragraph 3 above). Please also set out below any preferences as to the arbitrator's qualifications, areas of experience, expertise and/or any other attributes; or as to the geographical location of the arbitration; and any other relevant circumstances.)

    [*Desired characteristics and considerations of IFLA-nominated arbitrator*]

6. **If any court proceedings are current in relation to the child(ren), or your marriage or**

relationship, please identify the nature of the proceedings, in which court they are taking place and what stage they have reached. (Please attach copies of any relevant documents and court orders.)

[*Court proceedings*]

7. Please read paragraphs 8.3(a)–(d) below and provide with this Form:

    - a Basic Disclosure from Disclosure Scotland in relation to each party;
    - a Safeguarding Questionnaire (as attached to this Form) completed and signed by each party, together with any relevant documentation;
    - any relevant letter or report prepared by CAFCASS or any local authority children's services department or similar agency in relation to the safeguarding or welfare of the child(ren) concerned (if there is one).

8. We confirm the following:

    8.1 We have been advised about and understand the nature and implications of this agreement to arbitrate;

    8.2 Once the arbitration has started, we will not commence court proceedings or continue existing court proceedings in relation to the same subject matter (and will apply for or consent to a stay of any existing court proceedings, as necessary), unless it is appropriate to make an application to the court arising out of or in connection with the arbitration, or some relief is required that would not be available in the arbitration;

    8.3 We have read the current edition of the Rules of the Children Scheme ('the Rules') and will abide by them. In particular, we understand our obligations:

        (a) to provide accurate information regarding safeguarding in this Form and in the attached Safeguarding Questionnaire;

        (b) before the arbitration starts, to obtain a Basic Disclosure from Disclosure Scotland and promptly send it to the arbitrator and to every other party;

        (c) to send to the arbitrator and to every other party any relevant letter or report prepared by CAFCASS or any local authority children's services department or similar agency in relation to the welfare or safeguarding of the child(ren) concerned.

        (d) before the arbitration starts and at every stage of the process (as a continuing duty) to disclose fully and completely to the arbitrator and to every other party any fact, matter or document in our knowledge, possession or control which is or appears to be relevant to the physical or emotional safety of any party or to the safeguarding or welfare of any child the subject of the proceedings, or to a decision by the arbitrator whether to terminate the arbitration under Art.17.2.1. Such disclosure shall include (but not be limited to) any criminal conviction, caution or involvement (concerning any child) with children's services in respect of any party or any person with whom the child is likely to have contact;

        (e) at all stages of the process, to comply with the decisions, directions and orders of the arbitrator;

    8.4 We understand and agree that any determination of the arbitrator appointed to determine this dispute will be final and binding on us, subject to the following:

        (a) any challenge to the determination by any available arbitral process of appeal or review or in accordance with the provisions of Part 1 of the Act;

        (b) insofar as the subject matter of the determination requires it to be embodied in a court order (see 8.5 below), any changes which the court making that order may require;

        (c) any subsequent determination superseding the determination; or any changes to the determination or subsequent order superseding the determination which the Family Court considers ought to be made in the exercise of its statutory and/or inherent jurisdiction whether under the Children Act, 1989 or otherwise.

    8.5 If and so far as the subject matter of the determination makes it necessary, we will apply to an appropriate court for an order in the same or similar terms as the determination or the relevant part of the determination. (In this context, 'an appropriate court' means a court which has jurisdiction to make a substantive order in the same or similar terms as the determination.) We understand that the court has a discretion as to whether, and in what terms, to make an order and we will take all reasonably necessary steps to see that such an order is made;

8.6　We understand and agree that although the Rules provide for each party, generally, to bear an equal share of the arbitrator's fees and expenses (see Art.14.4(a)), if any party fails to pay their share, then the arbitrator may initially require payment of the full amount from any other party, leaving it to them to recover from the defaulting party;

8.7　We agree to the arbitration of this dispute in accordance with the Rules of the Children Scheme.

IMPORTANT

Parties should be aware that:

- By signing this form they are entering into a binding agreement to arbitrate (within the meaning of s.6 of the Arbitration Act 1996).
- After signing, neither party may avoid arbitration (unless they both agree to do so). Either party may rely on the arbitration agreement to seek a stay of court proceedings commenced by the other.
- Arbitration is a process whose outcome is generally final. There are very limited bases for raising a challenge or appeal, and it is only in exceptional circumstances that a court will exercise its own discretion in substitution for the determination.

Signed...
(Applicant *or* Applicant's legal representative, for and on behalf of Applicant)

Dated: [*date*]

Signed...
(Respondent *or* Respondent's legal representative, for and on behalf of Respondent)

Dated: [*date*]

Please send your completed form, preferably by email, to info@ifla.org.uk, or it can be sent by post to IFLA, PO Box 302, Orpington, Kent BR6 8QX.

Note that by submitting this Form, the parties consent to the processing by IFLA (and/or by Resolution, on IFLA's behalf) of the information and personal data provided in it and in associated documentation for the purposes of this Children Scheme arbitration. This includes retaining and storing the information and personal data for as long as is necessary in connection with this agreement. It may also be retained for research, training and statistical purposes in connection with family arbitration, but on the understanding that if so used, any information or details about individuals will have been removed so that they cannot be personally identified.

Family Law Arbitration Children Scheme – Form ARB1CS Safeguarding Questionnaire

Each party should complete and individually sign a copy of this Safeguarding Questionnaire. (Please make further copies as necessary.)

Name ....

Applicant/Respondent/Other Party ....

1.　Have there been any court proceedings in relation to the child(ren), or your marriage or relationship, other than as mentioned in paragraph 6 of Form ARB1CS?

Yes/No

(If 'Yes', please identify the nature of the proceedings, in which court they took place and the outcome. Please attach copies of any relevant documents and court orders.)

....

2.	Has a child protection plan been put in place by a local authority in relation to the child(ren), or have a local authority's children's services been involved in any way?

Yes/No, or not to my knowledge

((If 'Yes', please provide details and say whether the local authority's involvement is continuing.)

....

3.	Have you, or any person with whom the child(ren) is/are likely to have contact ever been convicted of an offence concerning a child, or ever been cautioned or investigated in that connection?

Yes/No

(If 'Yes', please provide full details.)

....

4.	Do you have any concerns that the child(ren) has/have experienced, or is/are at risk of experiencing, harm of any the following kinds from any person with whom the child(ren) is/are likely to have contact?

	• Any form of domestic violence	Yes/No
	• Child abduction	Yes/No
	• Child abuse	Yes/No
	• Drugs, alcohol or substance abuse	Yes/No
	• Other safety or welfare concerns	Yes/No

	(If 'Yes' to any of the above, please provide full details of your concerns.)

....

I confirm that the information I have provided in response to this Safeguarding Questionnaire is true and complete to the best of my knowledge and belief.

Signed ....

Dated ....

2.3

Draft letter by solicitor to client confirming confirmation of arbitration – Financial

Our ref:

Your ref:

Address

Date

Dear [*Name*]

Family Law Arbitration – Finance [or children]

I have pleasure to confirm the appointment of [Mr/Miss/Mrs/Ms] [*name*] as arbitrator.

I enclose [Mr/Miss/Mrs/Ms] [*name*]'s Terms of Engagement and draft ARB1FS [or draft ARB1CS].

I would appreciate if you could let me have your comments and telephone these offices to make an appointment to review.

Kind regards.

Yours sincerely

[*Name*], [Solicitor/Partner]
Family Law Arbitrator & Collaborative Lawyer

2.4

Draft letter by solicitor to client confirming confirmation of arbitration – Children

Our ref:
Your Ref:

Address

Date

Dear [Name]

Family Law Arbitration – Children

I thank you for confirming your agreement to pursuing the children dispute issues with [name] through the arbitration procedure.

I have spoken with your solicitors, [name of firm], and we have recommended [name] to be the nominated arbitrator OR will have the arbitrator nominated by one of the following options:

(a)   We each provide three nominations and if possible to agree one of those nominated.

(b)   To forward to the Institute of Family Law Arbitrators (IFLA) three nominations for them to nominate one of those three.

(c)   Request the IFLA to nominate.

When the arbitrator has been appointed they will provide their Terms of Engagement.

At this point all parties will need to decide whether they wish to undertake a pre-commitment meeting which will generally be free and will be an opportunity for the parties to get to know the arbitrator, agree procedure, review their Terms of Engagement and the Form ARB1CS.

By way of clarification, the ARB1CS is a document which constitutes a binding agreement between all parties. It sets out the issues in dispute. You need to be aware that by signing the Form ARB1CS you will be entering into a binding agreement to arbitrate and once signed neither you nor [name] may avoid arbitration. The arbitrator's award is final and binding and there are very limited bases for raising a challenge or appeal.

Alternatively, if you prefer and if everybody agrees, there is no need for a pre-commitment meeting. In that instance, you will both sign the arbitrator's Terms of Engagement and the ARB1CS and the arbitration will then commence by way of a preliminary meeting.

I appreciate that this letter contains a fair amount of detail and so I would be very happy to discuss the options set out above with you by phone.

In any event, I would also like to talk to you about the safeguarding requirements for children arbitration. Essentially, prior to the commencement of the arbitration, you will need to obtain a Basic Disclosure from Disclosure Scotland and send it to the arbitrator and [name]. I can talk you through how to deal with this and help you.

I look forward to hearing from you.

Kind regards.

Yours sincerely

[Name], [Solicitor/Partner]
Family Law Arbitrator & Collaborative Lawyer

2.5

Pre-commitment questionnaire – Financial[1]

Questionnaire for completion before appointment of the arbitrator is confirmed

1. This questionnaire is intended to provide the arbitrator with certain key information to enable him to determine whether to accept the appointment as arbitrator and the terms upon which the appointment is accepted (including any fixed or capped fees for any part of the arbitration).

2. It is most helpful if both parties incorporate their answers on a single version of this document. If possible, the party shown as applicant on Form ARB1 should complete the questionnaire and then email it to the respondent for completion and return to the arbitrator (copying it also to the applicant).

3. Lengthy or formal replies are not required.

4. You are not formally bound by the indications you give on this document. Once the arbitration has commenced each party will be able to make representations before any directions are given by the arbitrator.

Ref	Issue	Applicant's response	Respondent's response	Arbitrator's notes
1	Please confirm who represents you in the arbitration and that person's professional qualification and address. If you are unrepresented state 'acting in person'.			
2	If this questionnaire is completed by a representative, please confirm your authority to do so on behalf of the party.			
4	Please confirm that you understand paragraph 6.1 of Form ARB1 (that you have been fully advised about the process of arbitration and understand the consequences and binding nature of the agreement).			
5	Please confirm that you (and your representative) have read the current edition of the IFLA rules and that you agree to be bound by them.			
6	Please confirm that you understand that the arbitration must follow and apply the substantive law of England and Wales.			

---

[1] © FamilyArbitrator. This questionnaire is reproduced with the kind permission of the editors of FamilyArbitrator.com, Sir Peter Singer, Gavin Smith and Rhys Taylor.

Ref	Issue	Applicant's response	Respondent's response	Arbitrator's notes
7	Do you have a preferred venue for the arbitration hearing? If a venue has already been agreed please provide the address.			
8	Have any allegations of violence or significantly oppressive conduct been made by either party which may affect the suitability of the matter to be dealt with by arbitration? If so, please provide a brief summary of them.			
9	Meetings and hearings are ordinarily held with both parties together. Does this create any concerns for you?			
10	Do you have any special requirements and/or disability of which the arbitrator should be made aware?			
11	Please confirm as to preferred mode of communication between meetings (email 'to all' is the arbitrator's preference). Please include the email address you wish to use.			
12	Preferred mode of convening interim meetings: in person, by telephone (conference call), or Skype?			
13	Are you content that paragraph 2 of Form ARB1 clearly identifies the issue/s to be determined by this arbitration? If not, please append any alternative draft for discussion.			
14	Do the issues suggest that any other person, company or trust should be invited to join the arbitration?			
15	Please indicate whether you have agreed the terms and conditions of the appointment for the arbitrator. If not, please explain the points of disagreement.			
16	Save for the Form ARB1, have you agreed anything in writing which affects the procedure for the arbitration?			
17	Have you already exchanged financial disclosure/evidence?			
18	How long do you expect a first directions hearing with the arbitrator will take? Is it likely that directions will be agreed or dealt with without such a hearing?			
19	How long do you expect the final hearing is likely to take?			
20	Please indicate in general terms any areas of complexity, such as a foreign element, private company interests or trusts			

Ref	Issue	Applicant's response	Respondent's response	Arbitrator's notes
21	How many experts do you expect will be involved in the case? What are the disciplines of any expected experts? Is it anticipated that any expert will be required to give evidence?.			
22	Approximately how many pages do you expect will be required in the final hearing bundles for the arbitrator to read?			
23	If you have been or currently are engaged in legal proceedings concerning the same dispute, briefly state their nature, the stage reached, and the date of the next hearing if any has been fixed.			
24	Are there any other relevant features or factors which require the arbitration to be completed by a particular date.			
25	Any other procedural issues affecting the arbitration that you wish to raise?			
26	What is your estimated value of the assets concerned in the case (tick one)			
	Less than £500,000			
	£500,000 – £1,000,000			
	£1,000,000 – £5,000,000			
	£5,000,000 – £10,000,000			
	£10,000,000+			

Pre-commitment questionnaire – Children[1]

Questionnaire for completion before appointment of the children arbitrator is confirmed

1. This questionnaire is intended to provide the arbitrator with certain key information to enable him to determine whether to accept the appointment as arbitrator and the terms upon which the appointment is accepted (including any fixed or capped fees for any part of the arbitration).

2. It is most helpful if both parties incorporate their answers on a single version of this document. If possible, the party shown as applicant on Form ARB1CS should complete the questionnaire and then email it to the respondent for completion and return to the arbitrator (copying it also to the applicant).

3. Lengthy or formal replies are not required.

4. You are not formally bound by the indications you give on this document. Once the arbitration has commenced each party will be able to make representations before any directions are given by the arbitrator.

It is necessary for safeguarding to be fully considered before the arbitrator takes on a children arbitration so please ensure that you have read Article 17 of the Rules and considered completion of the Form ARB1CS paragraph 8 and completed the safeguarding questionnaire.

Ref	Issue	Applicant's response	Respondent's response	Arbitrator's notes
1	Please confirm who represents you in the arbitration and that person's professional qualification and address. If you are unrepresented state 'acting in person'.			
2	If this questionnaire is completed by a representative, please confirm your authority to do so on behalf of the party.			
3	Please confirm that you understand paragraph 8 of Form ARB1CS and that you have been fully advised about the process of arbitration and understand the consequences and binding nature of the agreement as well as the safeguarding procedure.			
4	Please confirm that you (and your representative) have read the current edition of the IFLA rules and that you agree to be bound by them.			

---

[1] © FamilyArbitrator. This questionnaire is reproduced with the kind permission of the editors of FamilyArbitrator.com, Sir Peter Singer, Gavin Smith and Rhys Taylor.

Ref	Issue	Applicant's response	Respondent's response	Arbitrator's notes
5	Please confirm that you understand that the arbitration must follow and apply the substantive law of England and Wales.			
6	Do you have a preferred venue for the arbitration hearing? If a venue has already been agreed please provide the address.			
7	Please read paragraph 8.3 of the Form ARB1CS and ensure that all of the safeguarding requirements have been complied with.			
8	Have any allegations of violence or significantly oppressive conduct been made by either party which may affect the suitability of the matter to be dealt with by arbitration? If so, please provide a brief summary of them.			
9	Meetings and hearings are ordinarily held with both parties together. Does this create any concerns for you?			
10	Do you have any special requirements and/or disability of which the arbitrator should be made aware?			
11	Please confirm as to preferred mode of communication between meetings (email 'to all' is the arbitrator's preference). Please include the email address you wish to use.			
12	Preferred mode of convening interim meetings: in person, by telephone (conference call), or Skype?			
13	Are you content that paragraph 3 of Form ARB1CS clearly identifies the issue/s to be determined by this arbitration? If not, please append any alternative draft for discussion.			
14	Do the issues suggest that any other person should be invited to join the arbitration?			
15	Please indicate whether you have agreed the terms and conditions of the appointment for the arbitrator. If not, please explain the points of disagreement.			
16	Save for the Form ARB1CS, have you agreed anything in writing which affects the procedure for the arbitration?			
17	How long do you expect the final hearing is likely to take?			
18	Please indicate in general terms any areas of complexity.			
19	How many experts do you expect will be involved in the case? In particular, please indicate whether you envisage an Independent Social Worker will be appointed.			

Ref	Issue	Applicant's response	Respondent's response	Arbitrator's notes
20	Approximately how many pages do you expect will be required in the final hearing bundles for the arbitrator to read?			
21	If you have been or currently are engaged in legal proceedings concerning the same dispute, briefly state their nature, the stage reached, and the date of the next hearing if any has been fixed.			
22	Are there any other relevant features or factors which require the arbitration to be completed by a particular date.			
23	Any other procedural issues affecting the arbitration that you wish to raise?			

Checklist of matters for discussion at an IFLA family arbitration first meeting/directions hearing[1]

1.   The arbitrator may use this checklist during the first meeting/directions appointment. It will assist him to focus on the key issues if each party is able to complete this checklist electronically prior to the meeting.

2.   The party shown as applicant on Form ARB1CS should complete the checklist first and then email it to the respondent for completion and return to the arbitrator (copying it also to the applicant).

3.   Lengthy responses are not required. Please note that at the outset of the arbitration some of these questions will not yet be capable of being answered. Please feel free to say so.

4.   You are not formally bound by the indications given in this document. The arbitrator will listen to the parties' representations and determine directions in due course.

5.   Both parties are encouraged to discuss this document with their legal advisers before it is completed and again once both parties have completed it.

It is necessary for safeguarding to be fully considered before the arbitrator takes on a children arbitration so please ensure that you have read Article 17 of the Rules and considered completion of the Form ARB1CS paragraph 8 and completed the safeguarding questionnaire.

Part I: Preliminary matters

Ref	Issue	Applicant's response	Respondent's response	Arbitrator's notes
1	Confirm that you have completed the pre-commitment questionnaire.			
2	Your preferred mode of address (Mr, Mrs, Miss, Ms, etc.) and how would you like to address the arbitrator? Formal or informal?			
3	Which party should be designated as the lead party in the arbitration?			

---

[1] © FamilyArbitrator. This checklist is reproduced with the kind permission of the editors of FamilyArbitrator.com, Sir Peter Singer, Gavin Smith and Rhys Taylor.

Part II: Procedural and interim matters

Ref	Issue	Applicant's position	Respondent's position	Arbitrator's notes
4	Save for the Form ARB1CS, have you agreed anything in writing which affects the procedure for the arbitration?			
5	Are there any particular points in the Rules which you wish to suggest might be amended or qualified for the purposes of this arbitration (save for Article 3)?			
6	Do the issues suggest that any other person should be invited to join the arbitration?			
7	Are you content with the costs rule at Article 14, or do you wish a different presumption to apply?			
8	What procedure should be adopted for the arbitration, i.e. Art.10 or Art.12 or some adaptation?			
9	Are there any preliminary issues or discrete findings of fact which would be more appropriately, conveniently or economically determined prior to a final hearing?			
10	Should there be an oral final (or interim) hearing or is this arbitration suitable for written submissions only?			
11	Any other points of concern or procedural/case management issues that need to be raised at first meeting?			

Part III: Evidence and experts

Ref	Issue	Applicant's position	Respondent's position	Arbitrator's notes
12	Are strict rules of evidence to be applied or a more flexible approach adopted?			
13	When and how (exchanged simultaneously or sequentially) should witness statements be supplied?			
14	Are expert witnesses to be appointed? In particular, do you envisage that an Independent Social Worker will be appointed?			
15	Is the arbitrator to receive evidence on oath? If yes, do you have a preference as to swearing (and upon what holy book) or affirming?			

Ref	Issue	Applicant's position	Respondent's position	Arbitrator's notes
16	How is evidence to be received? E.g. examination-in-chief limited to written statements only or are further questions to be permitted? Is there to be any time limit on cross-examination?			
17	May witnesses be in the hearing room when not giving evidence?			

Part IV: Contested interim and final hearings

Ref	Issue	Applicant's position	Respondent's position	Arbitrator's notes
18	Where do you wish any oral hearing to take place?			
19	Do you wish to undertake the costs of professional transcription of the final hearing, or any part of it?			
20	Please indicate your estimate of the length of hearing, to include final submissions (unless these are to be delivered in writing subsequently).			
21	How many witnesses do you wish to call? At this stage are you able to state what issue they go to? The parties will need to agree a witness template once this information has been provided.			
22	Need for skeleton arguments and/or written openings and/or chronologies and/or statement of issues? What do you suggest?			
23	Bundle format – PD27A?			
24	Do you wish to suggest draft directions? If so, these should be typed on a separate sheet and appended to this document.			
25	Do you wish expressly to exclude the right of appeal on a point of law (an option available under s.69(1) of the 1996 Act)?			
26	Do you wish to agree to dispense with reasons for the award? (Note that to do so is treated as an agreement to exclude the court's jurisdiction to appeal on a point of law: see s.69(1): it is strongly urged that the parties should require a reasoned award, so that any court will know the basis upon which the award has been reached.)			

Ref	Issue	Applicant's position	Respondent's position	Arbitrator's notes
27	Do you (upon payment of the balance then outstanding of the arbitrator's fees and any expenses jointly between the parties) wish to be provided with the award in draft so that you have an opportunity to suggest any factual corrections and any areas you maintain should have been covered in the reasons as then stated? [This provision does not afford the opportunity for further substantive argument upon points which have been determined.]			
28	Who has completed this document and on what date?			
29	If completed by a representative, please confirm your authority to do so on behalf of the party.			

2.8

Arbitrator's terms of engagement[1]

[Name of arbitrator] MCIArb

The terms and conditions upon which I accept appointment as a family arbitrator under the IFLA Family Arbitration Scheme are set out on the following pages.

Please note that before accepting the appointment I will normally require a meeting (which can be in person or via video-link or Skype) in which both you ('the parties') and your legal representatives participate, the purpose of which is to clarify and confirm the commitment involved in opting for arbitration and to explore the nature and scope of the issues.

This meeting is likely to last about one hour, is without commitment on any side, and is without charge on my part (save the reimbursement of any out-of-pocket expenses).

If at or after the conclusion of this pre-commitment meeting you wish to appoint me as arbitrator, you are requested to sign the Schedule where indicated on the final page of this document, and to sign (or re-sign) IFLA Form ARB1. The receipt by you of a copy of these terms counter-signed by me will constitute formal acceptance of the appointment for the purposes of rule 4.5 of the IFLA Rules (2015 4th edition), and the commencement of the arbitration.

Terms of appointment as a family arbitrator under the IFLA Scheme Rules

This document sets out the terms and conditions upon which I accept appointment as a family arbitrator under the IFLA Family Arbitration Scheme.

1. Appointment

I am and shall remain impartial and independent of the parties.

The parties confirm that they waive any possible objection to my appointment as arbitrator on the grounds of potential conflict of interest and/or lack of independence or impartiality in respect of matters known to me and/or disclosed to me by the parties at or before the date of my signature of these Terms of Appointment.

2. Immunity from suit etc.

In accordance with the mandatory provisions of section 29 of the Arbitration Act 1996 we agree that it is a term of this Appointment that:

- I am not liable for anything done or omitted in the discharge or purported discharge of my functions as an arbitrator unless the act or omission is shown to have been in bad faith;
- this immunity applies to any employee or agent of mine as well as to myself;

but that this immunity does not affect any liability which I may incur by reason of my resigning, as provided for by paragraph 14 below.

Save as provided by Statute and save as is set out herein, I shall not be made a party nor shall I be compelled by either party to become a witness in any judicial or other proceedings arising out of or relating in any manner to the arbitration the subject matter of these Terms of Appointment ('the arbitration').

In the event that any proceedings are brought by either of the parties against me or in the event that I am compelled to attend any proceedings as a witness, then I shall be entitled, without prejudice to any

---

[1] These model terms and conditions can be downloaded from **www.familyarbitrator.com**.

other rights I may have against that party whether under this agreement or otherwise in relation to the issue and pursuit of such proceedings or my requirement to attend any proceedings as a witness, to charge that party in accordance with my hourly and daily rates set out in these Terms of Appointment.

3.   Fees: generally

My fee rates are set out in the Schedule to these Terms of Appointment.

If you have any queries about my fees, please contact [me/my clerk/[*other*]].

4.   Value Added Tax

Where appropriate, Value Added Tax is added to all fees and disbursements at the rate prevailing when the work/disbursement is billed.

5.   Cancellation fees

When I am booked for a hearing and part or all of those days are vacated because of adjournment or settlement of the dispute the subject matter of the arbitration or because of a reduction in the number of days required for the hearing or because the hearing concludes within the time booked, then the following percentages of my aggregate fees (i.e. the number of days I have been booked multiplied by my daily rate) will be payable.

Where the booking is for up to 5 days and some or all of the days booked are vacated;

1.   on or after the first day booked – 100%

2.   within two weeks before the first day booked – 75%

3.   within four weeks before the first day booked – 50%

4.   within 6 weeks before the first day booked – 25%

5.   more than 6 weeks before the first date booked – 0%.

For details of the cancellation fees that apply to hearings listed for longer than five days please contact [me/ my clerk/[*other*]].

Cancellation fees are payable 10 days after the first of the cancelled days.

6.   Right to vary daily or hourly rates

To the extent that daily or hourly rates form the basis of the fee structure included in the Schedule, once agreed, then those rates will remain in force for work done prior to [*date*]. I reserve the right, on giving prior written notice to the parties, to vary the rates for work done after [*date*]. If I exercise this right, the varied rates will only apply to work done after the date notified for the variation.

7.   Disbursements

Disbursements are charged in addition to fees. Disbursements include such items as travel and accommodation charges, courier and (at the arbitrator's discretion) photocopying expenses and any communication expenses such as video-link or international phone charges.

Please note that the parties to the arbitration must by arrangement between themselves meet direct the costs of hiring premises for hearings, and of any transcription service they require. I will not incur any responsibility for such expenses.

Chargeable disbursements are payable on receipt of invoice.

It may be possible to hold a hearing at [my offices/my Chambers at [*location*]] depending on the nature of the dispute and the availability of the facilities but this can in no way be guaranteed.

8. Travelling time

[I reserve the right to charge for travelling time at the rate of £[*amount*] per hour if the parties require me to travel outside the area of Greater London for the purposes of this arbitration.] OR

[Unless the arbitration takes place within 3 miles of [*location*] I will be reimbursed in respect of all reasonable disbursements and charges incurred in connection with the arbitration including, but not limited to, travel expenses, business class air fares, first class rail fares, hotel accommodation, telephone, fax, couriers and copying.]

9. Joint and several liability for fees

Each of the parties to the arbitration is jointly and severally liable to me for the whole of my fees and disbursements in connection with this arbitration.

I shall be entitled, at any time, to direct the provision within a reasonable time of reasonable security for my fees and disbursements.

10. Billing and the time when fees are payable

Save as otherwise provided in the Schedule, I reserve the right to bill fees and disbursements from time to time during the course of the arbitration. Billings will be in arrears, but will not be more frequently than monthly.

Payment is to be made (i) as a pre-condition to delivery of the award; or (ii) within 10 days after notification that the award is ready for collection; or (iii) within 10 days after notice to the arbitrator that no award is required: whichever first occurs.

Save as otherwise provided herein and unless otherwise provided in the Schedule, payment is to be made within 28 days after billing.

11. Failure to comply with the payment provisions

Failure to pay billed fees in full by the date agreed gives rise to a right on my part to cease further work on the arbitration, or to decline to deliver the award as provided in rule 13.5 of the IFLA Rules. These rights are in addition to any other right that I may have under these terms, the terms of the IFLA Rules and/or the general law.

Interest will be charged on fees paid late at the rate of 8% per annum with quarterly rests.

12. Booking and diary arrangements

My arbitration practice is administered and my diary is managed by [[*name*]/the clerks at [*location*]], and I would invite you to contact them with all general and diary enquiries. [[*name*]/My [Senior] Clerk [*name*]] should be your requested point of contact in the first instance by telephone at [*telephone number*] or by email to [*email address*].

13. Resignation

I reserve the right, in my absolute discretion, to terminate the arbitration by resignation in writing at any point until two working days have elapsed after the first formal directions appointment held between myself and the parties. In the event that I exercise that right, what I determine as a fair proportion of my fixed fee shall be due in full up to the date of resignation, and upon such resignation I shall not be liable to the parties in any way.

In the event that I resign at any later stage, then in the absence of agreement between me and the parties as to my entitlement (if any) to fees or expenses and any liability incurred by me, my resignation and its consequences shall be governed by section 25(2) of the Arbitration Act 1996.

14. Conduct of the arbitration

During the course of the arbitration I agree to make myself available to assist the parties on reasonable notice and having regard to my other commitments.

Unless exceptional circumstances arise, I agree to make my award available to the parties promptly and in any event within 28 days of the conclusion of the hearing or the receipt of the parties' final submissions, whichever is the later.

15. Neutrality

I regard it as critically important that my neutrality is not put at risk or perceived by either party as being prejudiced. All communications between me or my clerks and the parties or their representatives **must** be transparent and **always** be copied to both parties.

16. Confidentiality

Arbitration proceedings are confidential. My [clerks/office colleagues and all staff] are used to dealing with cases confidentially, and moreover in such a way that if one or more [barrister members of these Chambers act or have acted for a party to an arbitration or proposed arbitration], then all effective steps are taken in the [Clerks Room] to preserve that confidentiality.

I will keep confidential all information provided to me in connection with the arbitration unless:

- I am required or permitted to disclose it by law (to include any duty I may owe under the Proceeds of Crime Act 2002), or by any other regulatory or fiscal authority or regime, in which case (and to the extent that I am permitted to do so) I will endeavour to give the parties as much advance notice as possible of any such required disclosure;
- I am authorised in writing by all parties to the arbitration to disclose it;
- the information is in or comes into the public domain without any breach of confidentiality on my behalf;
- any person (particularly a child) is at risk of significant harm, in which event I have a duty to contact the appropriate authorities;
- exceptionally, I disclose personal data in connection with the alleged or established commission of an unlawful act; or
- the parties or any or either of you makes a complaint about me to a regulatory authority concerning my conduct of the arbitration, in which event I may disclose relevant case papers to that authority.

I shall be permitted to make and retain copies of the arbitration papers and of any written material produced by the parties, subject to my duty of confidentiality.

I shall be entitled to, but not obliged, in circumstances in which I am issued with, or served with notice of, proceedings, brought by one of the parties in respect of the arbitration to give such disclosure to the Court about the course of the reference and about the evidence and submissions made therein, as I may consider reasonably necessary in order to enable me to deal properly with those proceedings.

17. Communication

The parties shall not engage in any oral or written communications with me without notice to the other party in connection with the subject matter of the arbitration save in respect of routine administrative matters where such communication should, at least in the first instance, normally be made with [my Clerk/[*name*]].

Written pleadings, submissions, written evidence and other formal documents which are the subject of any procedural Order shall normally be delivered to me by Document Exchange or first class post if sent within the United Kingdom or by courier if sent from outside the United Kingdom. Correspondence between the parties and me shall normally be by email.

The parties shall only send copies of correspondence between themselves to me if it pertains to a matter on which I am required to take some action or in order to make me aware of some relevant event. In the event correspondence is sent to me I am entitled to charge for the time I spend reading it and taking any necessary action (including informing the parties that I intend to take no action) at my normal hourly rate.

18.   Electronic communication

Unless otherwise directed by the parties, I may correspond by means of electronic mail, the parties agreeing hereby:

- to accept the risks of using electronic mail, including but not limited to the risks of viruses, interception and unauthorised access; and
- to use commercially reasonable procedures to maintain security of electronic mail; and
- to check for commonly known viruses in information sent and received electronically.

19.   Data protection

I am a data controller for the purposes of the Data Protection Act 1998 and am bound by that Act (amongst other considerations) to take appropriate technical and organisational measures against unauthorised processing of personal data and against accidental loss or destruction of, or damage to, personal data. I am entitled to process (which includes obtaining, consulting, holding, storing, using and disclosing) personal data of the parties to conduct the arbitration, to produce management data, to prevent crime, to comply with regulatory requirements, for research purposes ensuring at all times that personal identifying features of an arbitration are not disclosed, and as permitted or required by law. The parties each have a right of access and a right of correction in respect of their personal data which I hold about them, in accordance with data protection legislation.

20.   Intellectual property rights

All copyright and other intellectual property rights of whatever nature in or attaching to my awards and directions, including all documents, reports, or other materials ('work product') provided by me belong to me and remain mine. The parties and their representatives have the right and licence to use my work product for the particular arbitration and the particular purpose for which it is prepared. If the parties or their representatives wish to use copies of my work product for purposes other than those for which it is prepared, this will require my express written permission. My moral rights in respect of the work product are asserted.

21.   Waiver

Except where expressly stated, nothing done or not done by me or any party shall constitute a waiver of my or that party's rights under this Appointment.

22.   Severability

If any provision of this Appointment is found by a competent court or administrative body of competent jurisdiction to be invalid or unenforceable for any reason, such invalidity or unenforce-ability shall not affect the other provisions of this Appointment which will remain in full force and effect.

If any provision of this Appointment is found to be invalid or unenforceable but would be valid or enforceable if some part of the provision were deleted, the provision in question will apply with such deletions as may be necessary to make it valid and enforceable.

23.   Exclusion of rights of third parties

This Appointment governs my rights and obligations as arbitrator and those of the parties towards me and each other. It confers no benefit upon any third party. The ability of third parties to enforce any rights under the Contracts (Rights of Third Parties) Act 1999 is hereby excluded.

24.   Entire agreement

The provisions of this Appointment (other than this paragraph) may be varied if, but only if, expressly agreed by the parties and/or their representatives and by me in writing (including by exchange of emails).

Subject to the foregoing sub-paragraph this Appointment, incorporating these provisions, comprises the entire agreement between me and the parties to the exclusion of all other terms and conditions and prior or collateral agreements, negotiations, notices of intention and representations and the parties agree that they have not been induced to enter into the Appointment on the basis of any representation.

25.   Governing law, jurisdiction and dispute resolution

This Appointment and these provisions shall be governed by and construed in accordance with the law of England and Wales.

Unless you and I agree upon any alternative dispute resolution procedure, we agree to submit to the exclusive jurisdiction of the Courts of England and Wales in respect of any dispute which arises out of or under this Appointment.

I hope that the above is clear, but if you have any questions please contact me or [[*name*]/my Clerk] and we will endeavour to help.

[*Arbitrator's address and other contact details*]

The Schedule

These are [*name of arbitrator*]'s agreed fees for this arbitration:

Value Added Tax

Where appropriate, Value Added Tax is added to all fees and disbursements at the rate prevailing when the work/disbursement is billed.

1.   **Fees for hearing:**
   - £[*amount*] per normal sitting day (5 hours unless otherwise agreed)
   - Part-days charged at £[*amount*] per hour with a minimum of £[*amount*].

2.   **Additional hours engaged upon the arbitration:**

   E.g. for preparatory reading (including any time spent 'out of hours' during or between hearings); interlocutory hearings; inspections (if any); preparation of award:
   - £[*amount*] per hour [and incorporate reference to any upper time limits which may have been agreed].

   OR *here and below set out details of any fixed fee/brief and refresher/upper fee cap or other variant agreed.*

3.   Subject to the following provisions of this Schedule, a **fixed fee** of £[*amount*] and disbursements.
   - The fixed fee includes directions hearings, a final hearing and drafting the Award, provided that the final hearing does not exceed [one day/[*number*] days]. If the final hearing exceeds that duration a further fee of £[*amount*] per hour will be charged for each additional hour of hearing time.
   - It is agreed that if during the course of this arbitration one or more parties cease to be legally represented then, in recognition of the fact that significantly more time may necessarily be spent by me in bringing the arbitration to a conclusion I reserve the right in addition to this fixed fee to charge the unrepresented party or parties at the rate of up to £[*amount*] per hour for the additional time spent in and for the purposes of the arbitration which in my judgment is attributable to a party's lack of representation over the period in question.

- If settlement is agreed at any stage then the fixed fee remains due and payable and will include the delivery of a consent Award if the parties so request.

4. If the parties require me to travel for the purposes of this arbitration outside the area of Greater London then (in addition to disbursements) I reserve the right to charge for travelling time at the rate of £[*amount*] per hour.

If you wish to accept these terms, please sign and return one copy to me. Each party should retain a copy for reference.

We wish to appoint [*name of arbitrator*] as arbitrator on the terms and conditions set out in this document.

Signed by the parties:

....	....	....
Full name	Full name	Full name
Dated	Dated	Dated

Countersigned by [*name of arbitrator*]:

....

Dated

....

[*Arbitrator's address and other contact details*]

Final award checklist – Financial

Set out below are some suggested headings and a format for a Final Award in a Financial case. It is not necessary to follow this exact format but it would be helpful to make sure that all of the matters set out below have been considered somewhere in the Award.

General introduction

- Formalities
- Headings
- Reference to the Arbitration Act 1996
- Reference to the IFLA Scheme (Financial)
- Reference to parties' names
- Heading of the document in tramlines

General background

- Identifying
    - Parties/relationship
    - Dispute/issues – what is it that the parties are asking the arbitrator to decide?
    - Arbitration agreement – Form ARB1FS – when was it signed?
    - Appointment of arbitrator
    - Acceptance by arbitrator of appointment
    - Procedure adopted – oral hearings, telephone hearings, when and briefly what was decided
    - Place and date of hearing
    - Representation – Solicitors/Counsel
- Summary of the background in narrative form

General analysis

- Identifying common ground between the parties
- Identifying issues and points that will need to be decided by the arbitrator
- Evaluating the evidence/arguments – consideration of all that the arbitrator heard during the Final Hearing
- Knowledge of law and application – statutes/cases referred to and consideration by the arbitrator as to their relevance and arbitrator's view on the law. Remember to consider the Section 25 checklist if appropriate and any specific cases referred to in the arbitration.
- Conclusion on issues – what does the arbitrator think should happen bearing in mind all of the considerations above?

Award

- Heading/dated/signed
- Orders – financial
- Costs – will the normal rules of arbitration apply or will there be a change in relation to the costs position?
- Arbitrator's fees shared/reimbursement to one of the parties
- Schedule of Agreement (if any)

To consider

- In a financial case it is a good idea to include the asset schedule and the net effect schedule and to cross check that all of the assets listed in the asset schedule have been dealt with in the Award

Final determination checklist – Children

Set out below are some suggested headings and a format for a Final Determination in a Children case. It is not necessary to follow this exact format but it would be helpful to make sure that all of the matters set out below have been considered somewhere in the Determination.

General introduction

- Formalities
- Headings
- Reference to the Arbitration Act 1996
- Reference to the IFLA Scheme (Children)
- Reference to parties' names
- Heading of the document in tramlines

General background

- Identifying
  - Parties/relationship
  - Dispute/issues – what is it that the parties are asking the arbitrator to decide?
  - Arbitration agreement – Form ARB1CS – when was it signed?
  - Appointment of arbitrator
  - Acceptance by arbitrator of appointment
  - Procedure adopted – oral hearings, telephone hearings, when and briefly what was decided
  - Place and date of hearing
  - Representation – Solicitors/Counsel
- Summary of the background in narrative form

General analysis

- Identifying common ground between the parties
- Consider safeguarding issues
- Identifying issues and points that will need to be decided by the arbitrator
- Evaluating the evidence/arguments – consideration of all that the arbitrator heard during the Final Hearing to include expert evidence – independent social worker
- Knowledge of law and application – statutes/cases referred to and consideration by the arbitrator as to their relevance and arbitrator's view on the law. Remember to consider the welfare checklist and the no order principle
- Conclusion on issues – what does the arbitrator think should happen bearing in mind all of the considerations above?

Determination

- Heading/dated/signed
- Orders – children
- Costs – will the normal rules of arbitration apply or will there be a change in relation to the costs position?
- Arbitrator's fees shared/reimbursement to one of the parties
- Schedule of Agreement (if any)

2.11

Draft letter to HM Courts and Tribunals Service

[*Name of court*]

[*Date*]

Dear Sir

Re: Family Law Arbitration Award – [*name of case*]

We act on behalf of [*name*] the applicant in these proceedings and [*name of solicitor*] of [*address*] Solicitors on behalf of the respondent [*name*], and would ask you note this firm's interest.

We enclose:

1.   Form A.

2.   Form D81.

3.   Draft Minutes of Consent Order.

4.   Copy of respective clients' signed Form ARB1.

5.   Copy of [*name of arbitrator*]'s signed award.

6.   Copy of IFLA Scheme Rules.

7.   Court fee £[*amount*].

We respectfully refer the Honourable Court to Sir James Munby President of the Family Division's Judgment in *S v. S* [2014] EWHC 7 (Fam) at [23]:

> '... I can see no reason why the streamlined process applied by Coleridge J in *S v. P (Settlement by Collaborative Law Process)* [2008] 2 FLR 2040 in the context of a consent order which was the product of the collaborative law process should not be made similarly available in cases where the consent order is the product of an arbitral award under the IFLA Scheme or something similar. From now on, if they wish, parties should be able to avail themselves of that process whether the consent order is the product of the collaborative law process or an arbitral award under the IFLA Scheme or something similar.'

We invite the court, after considering the documentation, to take the view that the accelerated procedure should be adopted in this case.

The Draft Minutes of Consent Order reflect the terms of the award and in this regard we would very much request the court to grant the Consent Order.

We would appreciate hearing from the court in early course and if the court should require any further information please contact us.

Yours faithfully

2.12

Recitals for use where 'omnibus' orders to reflect an arbitral award are sought for either Financial Remedy or Children Act Schedule 1 Final Orders

For the Financial Remedy Final Order Omnibus:

...

Arbitration award recital

19.

(a)   The documents lodged in relation to this application include the parties' arbitration agreement (Form ARB1), their Form(s) D81, a copy of the arbitrator's award, and a draft of the order which the court is requested to make.

(b)   By their Form ARB1 the parties agreed to refer to arbitration the issues described in it which include some or all of the financial remedies for which applications are pending in this court. The issues were referred to [*name of arbitrator*] under the IFLA scheme, who made an arbitral award on [*date*].

(c)   **Either:**

[The parties have invited the court to make an order in agreed terms which reflects the arbitrator's award.]

or:

[There has been no agreement between the parties as to the form of an order to give effect to the arbitrator's award. The [applicant/respondent] has applied for the other party to show why an order should not be made in the terms of the draft proposed; and the court having considered the representations made by each party has directed that an order be made in the terms of this order.]

For the Children Act Schedule 1 Final Order Omnibus:

...

Arbitration award recital

18.

(a)   The documents lodged in relation to this application include the parties' arbitration agreement (Form ARB1), their Form(s) D81, a copy of the arbitrator's award, and a draft of the order which the court is requested to make.

(b)   By their Form ARB1 the parties agreed to refer to arbitration the issues described in it which encompass the application under Schedule 1 to the Children Act 1989 now pending in this court. The issues were referred to [*name of arbitrator*] under the IFLA scheme, who made an arbitral award on [*date*].

(c)   **Either:**

[The parties have invited the court to make an order in agreed terms which reflects the arbitrator's award.]

or:

[There has been no agreement between the parties as to the form of an order to give effect to the arbitrator's award. The [applicant/respondent] has applied for the other party to show why an order should not be made in the terms of the draft proposed; and the court having considered the representations made by each party has directed that an order be made in the terms of this order.]

2.13

Order to stay proceedings[1]

Stay pursuant to Arbitration Act 1996, s.9 and/or under the court's case management powers

No:

IN THE FAMILY COURT

Sitting at [*place*]

The Family Procedure Rules 2010 rules 3.2 and 3.3

The Marriage/Civil Partnership/Relationship/Family of [*XX*] and [*YY*]

After hearing [*name the advocate(s) who appeared*]

After consideration of the documents lodged by the parties

(In the case of an order made without notice) After reading the statements and hearing the witnesses specified in the recitals below

ORDER MADE BY [*NAME OF JUDGE*] ON [*DATE*] SITTING IN OPEN COURT/PRIVATE

The parties

1.   The applicant is [*XX*]

The respondent is [*YY*]

The second respondent is [*ZZ*]

Specify if any party acts by a litigation friend

[*Where undertakings have been given*]

Notice pursuant to PD 37A, para 2.1
You [XX], and you [YY], may be held to be in contempt of court and imprisoned or fined, or your assets may be seized, if you break the promises that you have given to the court.

Statement pursuant to PD 37A, para 2.2
I understand the undertaking that I have given and that if I break any of my promises to the court I may be sent to prison, or fined, or my assets may be seized, for contempt of court.
....
[XX]

I understand the undertaking that I have given and that if I break any of my promises to the court I may be sent to prison, or fined, or my assets may be seized, for contempt of court.
....
[YY]

Definitions

2.   IFLA is the Institute of Family Law Arbitrators.

3.   Form ARB1 is the arbitration agreement signed by the parties of which a copy has been lodged with the court.

---

[1] Crown copyright material is reproduced here with the permission of the Controller of HMSO.

4. The arbitration is an arbitration which is to be conducted in accordance with the rules of the IFLA arbitration scheme.

Recitals

5. *(In the case of an order made without notice)*

    (a) This order was made at a hearing without notice to the respondent. The reason why the order was made without notice to the respondent was [*set out*].

    (b) The Judge read the following affidavits/witness statements [*set out*] and heard oral testimony from [*name*].

6. *(In the case of an order made following the giving of short informal notice)*

    This order was made at a hearing without full notice having been given to the respondent. The reason why the order was made without full notice having been given to the respondent was [*set out*].

7. The applicant/respondent has applied to this court for financial remedies.

8. The court must by rules 3.2 and 3.3 of the Family Procedure Rules 2010 at every stage in proceedings consider whether alternative dispute resolution is appropriate and, if so, whether to adjourn those proceedings so to enable alternative dispute resolution to take place; and has power pursuant to its general powers of management under rule 4.1 to stay the whole or any part of proceedings either generally or until a specified date or event.

    …

Agreements

9. By their Form ARB1 the parties have agreed to refer to arbitration the issues described in it which include some or all of the financial remedies for which applications are pending in this court.

10. …

Undertakings to the court

11. …

12. …

IT IS ORDERED (BY CONSENT) THAT:

13. The pending application(s) for financial remedies is/are stayed pending receipt of the award in the arbitration (or until the parties may reach agreement in respect of the arbitration issues).

14. Upon receipt of the award (or upon reaching agreement) either party may in a form agreed with the other seek an order of this court to give effect to the award (or their agreement).

15. [*or if the parties cannot reach agreement upon the form of an order to give effect to the award*] Failing agreement between the parties as to the form of an order to give effect to the award either party may apply for the other to show why an order should not be made in the terms of the draft proposed.

16. Any application under either of the preceding 2 paragraphs shall be lodged together with a copy of the award, Form(s) D81 and with a draft of the order which the court is requested to make.

17. [*Provision for the costs of the stay application*]

Dated

2.14

Enforcement of an arbitrator's order[1]

Enforcement of an arbitrator's peremptory order under Arbitration Act 1996, s.42

No:

IN THE FAMILY COURT

Sitting at [*place*]

The Arbitration Act 1996 section 42
The Marriage/Civil Partnership/Relationship/Family of [*XX*] and [*YY*]

After hearing [*name the advocate(s) who appeared*]

After consideration of the documents lodged by the parties

(*In the case of an order made without notice*) After reading the statements and hearing the witnesses specified in the recitals below

ORDER MADE BY [*NAME OF JUDGE*] ON [*DATE*] SITTING IN OPEN COURT/PRIVATE

The parties

1.   The applicant is [*XX*]

       The respondent is [*YY*]

       The second respondent is [*ZZ*]

       Specify if any party acts by a litigation friend

[*Where undertakings have been given*]

Notice pursuant to PD 37A, para 2.1
You [*XX*], and you [*YY*], may be held to be in contempt of court and imprisoned or fined, or your assets may be seized, if you break the promises that you have given to the court.

Statement pursuant to PD 37A, para 2.2
I understand the undertaking that I have given and that if I break any of my promises to the court I may be sent to prison, or fined, or my assets may be seized, for contempt of court.
....
[*XX*]

I understand the undertaking that I have given and that if I break any of my promises to the court I may be sent to prison, or fined, or my assets may be seized, for contempt of court.
....
[*YY*]

Definitions

2.   IFLA is the Institute of Family Law Arbitrators.

3.   Form ARB1 is the arbitration agreement signed by the parties of which a copy has been lodged with the court.

---

[1]   Crown copyright material is reproduced here with the permission of the Controller of HMSO.

4. The arbitration is an arbitration which is to be conducted in accordance with the rules of the IFLA arbitration scheme.

5. The arbitrator is [*name*].

6. The arbitrator's order is a peremptory order made on [*date*] pursuant to section 41(5) of the Arbitration Act 1996 which required the respondent to comply with its terms [by [*date*]] *or* [without prescribing a date for compliance].

Recitals

7. *(In the case of an order made without notice)*

    (a) This order was made at a hearing without notice to the respondent. The reason why the order was made without notice to the respondent was [*set out*].

    (b) The Judge read the following affidavits/witness statements [*set out*] and heard oral testimony from [*name*].

8. *(In the case of an order made following the giving of short informal notice)*

    This order was made at a hearing without full notice having been given to the respondent. The reason why the order was made without full notice having been given to the respondent was [*set out*].

9. *(In the case of an application commenced elsewhere than in the Family Court)*

    This application was transferred to this court from the [*specify*] Division/Court by order of [*name of judge*] on [*date*].

10. The arbitration has commenced and is continuing.

11. The parties have by their Form ARB1 and their acceptance of the IFLA arbitration scheme rules agreed that the powers of the court under section 42 of the Arbitration Act 1996 (enforcement of peremptory orders of tribunal) are available, so that if one of them fails to comply with a peremptory order made by the arbitrator then another party may apply to the court for an order requiring compliance.

12. The arbitrator's order is (so far as relevant to this application) in the following terms:

    [*set out in the words of the arbitrator's order*]

13. This application is for an order under section 42 of the Arbitration Act 1996 for the enforcement of the arbitrator's order and is made:

    [by the applicant.] *(or)*

    [by the arbitrator, upon notice to the parties.]

14. This court is satisfied that:

    (a) the applicant has exhausted all available arbitral process in respect of the respondent's failure to comply with that/those provision(s) of the peremptory order; and

    (b) the respondent has failed to comply with that/those provision(s) of the peremptory order [within the time prescribed by the order] or [within a reasonable time, no time for compliance having been prescribed].

…

Agreements

15.

Undertakings to the court

16. …

IT IS ORDERED (BY CONSENT) THAT:

17.   The respondent shall comply with the peremptory order by no later than [*date*].

[*or*]

18.   [*Other orders*]

19.   [*If applied for*] Permission to appeal against this decision is [granted/refused].

20.   [*Provision for costs*]

Dated

2.15

Order securing the attendance of witnesses[1]

Order securing the attendance of witnesses under Arbitration Act 1996, s.43

No:

IN THE FAMILY COURT

Sitting at [*place*]

The Arbitration Act 1996, s.43
The Marriage/Civil Partnership/Relationship/Family of [XX] and [YY]

After hearing [*name the advocate(s) who appeared*]

After consideration of the documents lodged by the parties

(In the case of an order made without notice) After reading the statements and hearing the witnesses specified in the recitals below

ORDER MADE BY [*NAME OF JUDGE*] ON [*DATE*] SITTING IN OPEN COURT/PRIVATE

The parties

1.   The applicant is [XX]

      The respondent is [YY]

      The second respondent is [ZZ]

      Specify if any party acts by a litigation friend

[*Where undertakings have been given*]

Notice pursuant to PD 37A, para 2.1
You [XX], and you [YY], may be held to be in contempt of court and imprisoned or fined, or your assets may be seized, if you break the promises that you have given to the court.

Statement pursuant to PD 37A, para 2.2
I understand the undertaking that I have given and that if I break any of my promises to the court I may be sent to prison, or fined, or my assets may be seized, for contempt of court.
....
[XX]

I understand the undertaking that I have given and that if I break any of my promises to the court I may be sent to prison, or fined, or my assets may be seized, for contempt of court.
....
[YY]

Definitions

2.   IFLA is the Institute of Family Law Arbitrators.

3.   Form ARB1 is the arbitration agreement signed by the parties of which a copy has been lodged with the court.

---

[1]   Crown copyright material is reproduced here with the permission of the Controller of HMSO.

4. The arbitration is an arbitration which is to be conducted in accordance with the rules of the IFLA arbitration scheme.

5. The arbitrator is [*name*].

6. The witness[es] [is/are] [*name(s)*]

Recitals

7. *(In the case of an order made without notice)*

    (a) This order was made at a hearing without notice to the respondent. The reason why the order was made without notice to the respondent was [*set out*].
    (b) The Judge read the following affidavits/witness statements [*set out*] and heard oral testimony from [*name*].

8. *(In the case of an order made following the giving of short informal notice)*

    This order was made at a hearing without full notice having been given to the respondent. The reason why the order was made without full notice having been given to the respondent was [*set out*].

9. *(In the case of an application commenced elsewhere than in the Family Court)*

    This application was transferred to this court from the [*specify*] Division/Court by order of [*name of judge*] on [*date*].

10. The arbitration has commenced and is being conducted in England and Wales and the witness/witnesses are in the United Kingdom.

11. This application is for an order pursuant to section 43 of the Arbitration Act 1996 to secure the attendance before the arbitrator of the witness[es] in order:

    [to give oral testimony] *(and/or)*

    [to produce documents or other material evidence which the witness/witnesses can be compelled to produce in legal proceedings, namely [*specify*].]

12. This application is made:

    [by the applicant with the permission of the tribunal.] *(or)*

    [with the agreement of the other [party/parties] to the arbitration.]

Agreements

13. …

Undertakings to the court

14. …

IT IS ORDERED (BY CONSENT):

15. [*Insert the form of order or notice appropriate to secure the attendance of a witness in order to give oral testimony and/or to produce documents or other material evidence.*]

16. [*Other orders*]

17. [*Provision for costs*]

Dated

Appendix 3

Useful articles

3.1

Family Law Arbitration in Ontario, Canada (4 November 2016)[1]

1. Family law arbitration in Ontario was established by statute. Family law arbitrations are primarily governed by the Ontario Family Law Act, but where there are no specific family law provisions, the Ontario Arbitration Act, 1991 is the governing statute. In Ontario, as arbitration is statute based, there is a lack of flexibility which prevents development within its structure. However, family law arbitration does enjoy the benefit of judicial overview.

2. In Ontario there are three types of arbitrations used to resolve family law disputes. They are: arbitrations, mediation-arbitrations and secondary arbitrations.

3. The parties sign a mediation/arbitration agreement or an arbitration agreement. They can chose an arbitrator or the courts can appoint one.

4. Parties seeking to pursue their matters through arbitration are required to undertake independent legal advice before doing so. (See Arbitration Act, 1991, Ontario Regulation 134/07, s.2(1) and (3).) The Ontario requirements go further, in that if one or both parties do not receive independent legal advice before arbitration begins, the arbitration agreement may be set aside. (See Ontario Family Law Act, s.56(1), (4), (1.1).) Also, any award that arises from an arbitration conducted without both sides receiving independent legal advice is not enforceable by the court. (See Ontario Family Law Act, s.59.6 (1)(b).) The advising lawyer is required to complete a certificate of independent legal advice. (See Ontario Family Law Act, s.59.6(2).)

5. Prior to the commencement of mediation/arbitration or simply arbitration, the arbitrator must receive special training in arbitration and the parties must be screened for domestic violence and power imbalances. The mediator screens the parties in mediation/arbitration proceedings, whereas in an arbitration proceeding, screening may be performed by the arbitrator or a third party screener. The decision-maker, that is the mediator/arbitrator or the arbitrator, also certifies that the parties have been screened.

6. If the parties are engaged in mediation/arbitration, the mediation process must be exhausted before the parties proceed to arbitration.

7. The arbitrator's authority and powers stem from the arbitration agreement. His or her authority is limited to deciding only those questions that are set out in the arbitration agreement. The arbitrator is responsible for the conduct of the arbitration, in accordance with the arbitration agreement. If the agreement is silent on procedure, the arbitrator must determine the way in which evidence and arguments are presented.

8. The arbitration takes place with the parties and their lawyers in attendance.

    The arbitrator makes his or her award (decision), which must be in writing and, unless it is on consent, the award must state the reasons on which it is based. The arbitrator must keep a record of the arbitration. Each arbitration that has been conducted must be reported to the Ontario Attorney General.

9. An award binds the parties, unless it is set aside or varied under s.45 (appeals) or s.46 (setting aside awards) of the Ontario Arbitration Act, 1991.

10. Enforcement requirements of family arbitration awards are set out in s.59.6 of the Ontario Family Law Act.

11. At a later date, if a dispute arises, the parties may engage in a secondary arbitration. A

'secondary arbitration' arises when a separation agreement, a court order or an arbitration award provides for the arbitration of future possible disputes relating to the ongoing management or implementation of the agreement, order or award. (See Ontario Family Law Act, s.59.7(2).) The scope of a secondary arbitration can be narrow or broad, as determined by the parties.

12. It is not necessary for the parties to receive independent legal advice before participating in a secondary arbitration. (See Ontario Family Law Act, s.59.7(1)2.) Where the secondary arbitration arises from an arbitration award, this condition is waived, presumably, because the parties would have received legal advice before participating in the arbitration. Where the secondary arbitration arises from a separation agreement or court order, the requirement for independent legal advice is also waived. There is no requirement that the parties receive independent legal advice before executing the separation agreement or obtaining the court order, although it is considered highly advisable. Therefore it is possible that the parties entering a secondary arbitration have not had independent legal advice, where the secondary arbitration arises from a separation agreement or a court order, presumably a consent order.

13. All secondary arbitration agreements must now contain a declaration that the arbitrator has had the appropriate training and a certification that the parties have been screened for domestic violence or power imbalances and that the arbitrator has considered the results of the screening and will continue to do so throughout the arbitration.

3.2

ADR: wide focus and global view (Suzanne Kingston and Rachael Kelsey)[1]

Suzanne Kingston is a partner at Withers LLP and Rachael Kelsey is a director at Sheehan Kelsey Oswald, Edinburgh

Part one: wide focus

In the first of a two-part analysis, Suzanne Kingston and Rachael Kelsey take a comparative view of arbitration around the world

In September 2012 we spoke at the International Academy of Matrimonial Lawyers in Singapore about arbitration around the world. We are both arbitrators: Suzanne Kingston spearheaded the arbitration training in England and Wales and Rachael Kelsey was one of those instrumental in setting up the arbitration scheme in Scotland. This article deals specifically with the differences between England and Scotland in terms of the arbitration schemes and then extends to consider family arbitration worldwide. We then go on to discuss the applicability or otherwise of the New York Convention in terms of recognition and enforcement of arbitration in the family law context.

We appreciate that arbitration is no panacea. In both England and Wales and in Scotland it is a relatively new way of resolving disputes. It is an important and exciting new initiative. It could revolutionise the way we think about family law disputes, particularly bearing in mind the current pressure on court resources both in terms of time and funding. As with all things new, it may take some considerable time to be recognised. We believe there are a number of practical applications for arbitration, both within our domestic law and internationally, and we hope to expand on that during the course of this article so as to provide food for thought for solicitors who previously had not thought about referral to arbitration.

At the end of the day, however, we are acutely aware of the fact that there are different ways of dealing with disputes and so added to our armoury is what we hope to achieve by raising awareness of arbitration. Further, we wish to highlight at this point the work that Resolution has done in promoting all forms of dispute resolution. In particular we would urge practitioners to make use of the new publication 'Separating together – new advice guide' and the new-look options flyer entitled 'Divorce and Separation'. Both can be accessed online via the Resolution website (**www.resolution.org.uk**).

England and Scotland – so close yet so far!

Perhaps the most controversial difference between the two jurisdictions is the English court's ratification of an arbitral award under s.25 Matrimonial Causes Act 1973 (MCA 1973) on the basis that the court's jurisdiction cannot be ousted. The court has a duty to decide whether and how to exercise its powers. It is hoped that parties who enter into arbitration under the Institute of Family Law Arbitrators (IFLA) scheme with an accredited arbitrator and who have signed the form ARB1 will be bound by the arbitral award. The ARB1 specifically requires the parties to confirm that:

- they have been advised about and understand the agreement to arbitrate; and
- they have read the rules of the scheme and will abide by them – in particular, that they understand the obligation to comply with the decisions and orders of the arbitrator.

---

[1] This article appeared in two parts in *Family Law Journal*, December 2012/January 2013 and February 2013. Reproduced with the kind permission of Suzanne Kingston and Rachael Kelsey.

As well as the actual form that the parties sign, in England we take the view that we should be alive to the continuing shift in favour of individual and collective autonomy in arranging private family affairs as evidenced, for example in *Radmacher* v *Granatino* [2010]. This complements the approach taken in arbitration.

The Scottish system has no such constraints. The origins of the organisation set up in 2011 that now provides a family law arbitration scheme – Family Law Arbitration Group Scotland (FLAGS) – date back to 2004, when Rachael Kelsey and five others started to work on how to introduce a dispute resolution model for family cases that:

- provided a determination (unlike mediation, negotiation and collaborative family law models); and
- did away with many of the difficulties inherent in litigation: lack of control over the decision-maker, the vagaries of the court process, confidentiality issues, delay and expense.

The legal framework in Scotland, having more of a civil law than a common law feel, is well suited to the arbitration model, already allowing parties to oust the jurisdiction of the court and come to their own decision without any form of cross-check (this approach is, in fact, the norm in Scotland). This feeds into a potentially different approach in relation to the New York Convention. More on this later.

Another crucial difference is in relation to the scope of the potential arbitration. In England, the IFLA scheme deals only with financial and property issues to include:

- s.17 Married Women's Property Act 1882;
- Part 2 MCA 1973;
- Inheritance (Provision for Family and Dependants) Act 1979;
- s.12 Matrimonial and Family Proceedings Act 1984;
- Schedule 1 Children Act 1989;
- Trust of Land and Appointment of Trustees Act 1986; and
- Schedule 5 or Schedule 7 Part 1, paragraph 2 Civil Partnership Act 2004.

It is clear that a financial dispute between parents as to a child (to the extent that they could be dealt with by a court) is squarely within the scheme, but issues as to care and parenting are specifically excluded.

In Scotland, the arbitrator has the power to make such awards as the parties may agree, and therefore encompasses all issues as between the parties – whether relating to children or finances – with the exception of matters of status. As public law matters, these remain reserved to the state (courts). Unsurprisingly, in England and Wales, similarly, the status of the relationship cannot be determined by an arbitrator.

Insolvency, which will almost certainly involve a third party such as a trustee in bankruptcy, is not included in the IFLA scheme nor third-party involvement more generally, unless they are covered by the agreement to arbitrate. In Scotland, the FLAGS scheme allows such issues to be resolved through arbitration.

Finally, in England and Wales the arbitrator will not have the power to grant an interim injunction – the parties would be referred to the court for that purpose. This is not the case in Scotland. In Scotland not only can the arbitrator grant interim interdict (injunction), but they have a range of other remedies available to them, including the ability:

- to order the rectification of deeds;
- to require the parties to discharge statutory rights (for example succession or occupancy rights); and
- to make a transfer of property order.

There is provision within the FLAGS scheme to allow the arbitrator to obtain authority of the court to compel third parties (who are not parties to the arbitration) to attend as witnesses and/or produce information, just as would be the case in litigation.

The worldwide view

With help from our IAML colleagues in other jurisdictions, we have been able to prepare a comparative table setting out the answers to the following questions:

- What is the definition of arbitration?
- Do you have statutory provision for arbitration? If yes, please provide references.
- Is arbitration strictly legally binding in your jurisdiction?
- Does it cover all aspects of family law?
- Does the New York Convention apply in your jurisdiction?

Example sections of this table are set out [at the end of this section] covering Australia and Canada, with further international comparisons to follow in part two of this article.

When compiling the answers some interesting points became apparent:

- We need to be careful about definitions. When we first sent an email asking about arbitration, a number of respondents wrote about mediation. It is clear that in some jurisdictions there is an inter-changeability of definitions, even though it was acknowledged by the respondent that mediation was not an adjudication nor was it binding. The current table deals exclusively with arbitration, although we should state that there are a number of countries where there is a move towards mediation/arbitration – these are not dealt with in this article.
- Arbitration is a new concept and often misunderstood. In some jurisdictions, two lawyers responding to our questions set out contradictory answers. Most respondents were prepared to indicate that they knew little about the New York Convention and would be happy to receive more information about it. For this reason we have prepared a lengthy analysis for part two of this article.
- It is clear that, at the moment, only relatively few countries have arbitration as a form of dispute resolution in family matters. Even in countries where it has been available for some considerable time, e.g. Australia, it is little used. There seems to be a reluctance on the part of practitioners to embrace arbitration, and so we thought it would be helpful to set out some specific examples of where we believe that arbitration could be more widely used:

  - variation of maintenance applications where a flexible procedure could be used, especially in small cases where the parties could be assured of a speedy and economic resolution;
  - cases where there are discreet issues that, if resolved early, would free up settlement, which failing focus the dispute in hand and thereby restrict the scope of litigation – for example, the value of assets, or, in Scotland, the identity of the 'relevant date' (which is the lynchpin of financial provision);
  - big cases where the parties wish to select a decision-maker (or makers) with particular expertise and/or experience (under both schemes, for example, the tribunal could include, as well as the family law specialist arbitrator, arbitrators who are accountants or corporate specialists);
  - cases where the parties require confidentiality that could not be guaranteed within litigation; and
  - cases where the financial dispute resolution court hearing has failed but all of the paperwork is done and the parties want to deal with matters more quickly than waiting for trial.

Acknowledgements

We are of course extremely grateful to all of our IAML colleagues who have contributed to the international table on arbitration. Each of them is credited for their comments in the table.

Cases

Merrell v. *Merrell* (1987) 11 RFL (3d) 18 (BCSC)

Radmacher (formerly Granatino) v. *Granatino (pre-nuptial contract)* [2010] UKSC 42

Comparison of arbitration across international jurisdictions

Jurisdiction	Contributor	Matrimonial arbitration?	Governing legislation/ Code	Experience
Australia		Yes		
	Geoff Wilson of Hopgood Ganim	Yes	Family Law Act 1975 (as amended by the Family Law (Shared Parental Responsibility) Act 2006); Family Law Regulations 1984.	Australia has formal arbitration procedures, which for one reason or another, have been slow to be taken up. Traditionally family lawyers and clients in Australia have reluctantly embraced change to traditional forms of engagement. While mediation is now a popular form of dispute resolution it took many years to gain momentum. Arbitration, and now collaborative process, are languishing in the wake of mediation. There were some initial obstacles that kept litigants away (e.g. there were no rollover provisions for capital gains tax), but despite the fact that these have now been addressed (in 2006 the Tax Laws Amendment (2006 Measures No. 4) Act was passed) there is still a lack of engagement in the process.
	Michael Paul of PP Lawyers	Yes	Legislation in place.	Our system is enshrined in legislation and we all trained for it years ago, but no one uses it to my knowledge.
	See Ian Kennedy's chapter for Panel Discussion on 'Is mediation suitable in international cases?' http://www.iaml.org/cms_media/files/session_2.pdf	Yes	Mediation, arbitration and family dispute resolution in Australia are governed by the provisions of the Family Law Act 1975 (as amended) and associated statutory regulations and rules of court. ADR may be private, court-annexed or conducted through community-based non-profit organisations or government-funded family relationship centres.	
	Stuart Fowler of Family Court	Yes		Arbitration is available, but not commonly used in Australia for family law matters. The most common form of non-curial resolution short of negotiated settlement would be mediated or conciliated settlement. The conciliation model with positive input from a respected conciliator is perhaps perceived as the most successful. Presently the court is co-operating with the Law Society of New South Wales in a project which may lead to mandatory external mediation or conciliation prior to hearing. The courts are able to provide a limited service in this regard already but the resources are limited and alternatives are being sought. Initially the process will be limited to financial claims.

Jurisdiction	Contributor	Matrimonial arbitration?	Governing legislation/ Code	Experience
				There has been a traditional reticence about external mediation of children's matters although such mediation does occur within the court system using the mediators who form part of the court's complement of staff. Once again resources are a problem and some consideration is being given to using the proposed system for mediation in the simpler kinds of parenting issues, such as arrangements for handover when a child is spending time with a non-resident parent and perhaps also in cases where there is a dispute as to choice of school. It is probable that if the system is enlarged at all to cover parenting matters it will be done slowly and only after a trial has provided some comfort that the rights of children are reasonably protected.
	Stephen O'Ryan	Yes	The relevant statutory provisions relating to arbitration are found in Division 4 of Part II of the Family Law Act 1976 (Cth) and Division 4 of Part IIIB and Part 5 of the Family Law Regulations	The following is a useful summary of the relevant provisions of the Family Law Act and the Family Law Regulations prepared by Mr Rick Jones, a very experienced Australian family law practitioner: 'The amendments came into operation in December 2000. The regulations came into effect on 1 March 2001 thereby creating private arbitration as an option to resolve matrimonial, property and financial disputes. The regulations are clear in their intent, although there are some inconsistencies which will presumably need amendment as arbitration unfolds and with the passage of time. The Australian scheme has the following features: (a) There can be no arbitration unless the parties consent; (b) A court can suggest that arbitration is appropriate, but cannot order the parties to arbitrate; (c) The parties can only arbitrate under the Family Law Act on disputes between them about property and/or spousal maintenance; (d) Disputes about child support or child residence (custody) or contact (access) predictably cannot be arbitrated at all;

Jurisdiction	Contributor	Matrimonial arbitration?	Governing legislation/ Code	Experience
				(e) Presumably, some disputants will choose to arbitrate on one aspect of a conflict (e.g. valuation of a business) and then use the decision of the arbitrator as the basis for settling by negotiation all other elements of the property dispute such as percentage, timing of distribution and apportionment of debts etc. Alternatively of course, they can use the arbitration process to settle the whole of their property and financial matters in dispute; (f) Disputes over property with third parties (e.g. creditors or relatives claiming a share of the matrimonial property) cannot be arbitrated under the Family Law Act. This is because: (i) the arbitrator has no procedural power to join third parties; and (ii) the arbitrator has limited substantive power under the Family Law Act to make orders which affect the property rights of third parties. (g) disputes over the property rights of a third party can be arbitrated if the third party consents, enters into a written Arbitration Agreement and that "third party" part of the order is registered under a state Commercial Arbitration Act; (h) Only certain arbitrators can arbitrate and register his/her award under the Family Law Act. Who is eligible to be a family arbitrator? Regulation 67B sets out the prescribed requirements for an arbitrator: • A legal practitioner who is either accredited as a family law specialist or has practised as a legal practitioner for at least five years with at least 25% of work done in that time in relation to family law. • Has completed specialist arbitration training conducted by a tertiary institution or professional association of arbitrators. • Is included in a Law Council of Australia list of practitioners approved by the Council. The parties to the dispute must pay the costs of the arbitration directly to the arbitrator (not into court). The arbitrator must give pre-arbitration written information about fees.

Jurisdiction	Contributor	Matrimonial arbitration?	Governing legislation/ Code	Experience
				Once the arbitral award is registered in the family court, it has the same effect as an order of the family court. (This is subject to a provision, which currently allows 28 days to object after an award has been served.)
				An arbitrator can refer a question of law arising from the arbitration to the family court or to the Federal Magistrates Court and await the court's decision.
				How final is an arbitration award? On the fact of the legislation, it is very final. The Family Law Act however, provides that the award of an arbitrator can be:
				(a) reviewed on a question of "law" by a single judge of the family court or the Federal Magistrates Court;
				(b) varied by a judge of the family court or the Federal Magistrates Court, where:
				(i) the award or agreement was obtained by fraud; or
				(ii) the award or agreement is void, voidable or unenforceable; or
				(iii) in circumstances that have arisen since the award or agreement was made it is impracticable for some or all of it to be carried out; or
				(iv) the arbitration was affected by bias, or there was a lack of procedural fairness in the way in which the arbitration process, as agreed between the parties and the arbitrator, was conducted.
				The primary advantage of arbitration is the opportunity for a dispute to be heard much sooner than if it went to court and the parties can choose their decision-maker and make their own rules for their hearing.'
				My experience, and the outcome of inquiries of others, is that arbitration is not used by family law practitioners in Australia and there is no, or no credible explanation for why this is so. My observation is that it would be a very appropriate way to resolve many financial disputes, particularly financial proceedings pending in the Federal Magistrates Court of Australia.

Jurisdiction	Contributor	Matrimonial arbitration?	Governing legislation/ Code	Experience
Canada		Yes		
British Columbia	Lorne Wolfson of Torkin Manes LLP	Yes	British Columbia has legislation pending that will expressly provide for family law arbitration. I expect that their statute will be similar to Ontario's. Currently in British Columbia, s.2(2) of the Commercial Arbitration Act (which provides a provision of an arbitration agreement that removes the jurisdiction of a court under the Divorce Act (Canada) or the Family Relations Act has no effect) has been read by some lawyers as excluding family law arbitration. Despite *obiter dicta* in the 1987 case of *Merrell* v. *Merrell* that s.2 of the Commercial Arbitration Act 'preserves the jurisdiction of the court' in family law cases, subsequent courts have applied the Act in family law matters.	

Jurisdiction	Contributor	Matrimonial arbitration?	Governing legislation/ Code	Experience
Ontario	Lorne Wolfson of Torkin Manes LLP	Yes	Each province and territory has its own arbitration statute. These statutes establish the rules for creating enforceable arbitration agreements, provide for the appointment and removal of arbitrators and the procedure for arbitration, and define the role of the courts. With a few exceptions, most of these statutes are very similar. Only three statutes (Quebec, Ontario, and British Columbia) contain specific references to family law: the Quebec Civil Code specifically prohibits the use of arbitration in family law matters. In 2006, significant amendments were made to the Ontario Arbitration Act which incorporated special rules and procedures for use in family law cases. These amendments, although specifically designed to prevent the use of religious tribunals in family law cases and to protect the rights of vulnerable parties, have weakened the enforceability of arbitral awards and generated many procedural uncertainties. In Ontario, the law to be applied in family law arbitration is the law of Ontario or another Canadian jurisdiction. In Alberta, British Columbia, Manitoba, Saskatchewan, and New Brunswick, the parties are free to select the applicable substantive law. The other statutes are silent on this point.	

Jurisdiction	Contributor	Matrimonial arbitration?	Governing legislation/ Code	Experience
			In the Northwest Territories and Nunavut, the commissioner may make rules of practice and procedure. In all of the other jurisdictions, the arbitrator may determine the procedure in arbitration unless the arbitration agreement provides otherwise. All of the statutes either expressly permit the admission of hearsay evidence in arbitration or are silent on the point. Similarly, all of the statutes either permit the arbitrator to conduct a mediation with the consent of the parties or are silent on the point. Only Ontario, Manitoba, New Brunswick and Saskatchewan provide for minimum appeal rights (appeal on a question of law, with leave) that cannot be waived. All of the statutes give the court the power to set aside an award based on the grounds of procedural unfairness or lack of jurisdiction.	

Jurisdiction	Contributor	Matrimonial arbitration?	Governing legislation/ Code	Experience
Ontario	Stephen Grant of Grant & Sadvari	Yes	No national statute or regulation but ADR proceedings in Ontario are covered by the provincial Arbitration Act. No specific statute or legislation dealing with mediation. Mediation is a consensual process and is not mandatory (in Ontario at least) under the Family Law Rules. The ADR Institute of Canada has become important for training and certification of mediators/arbitrators and has promulgated the National Mediation Rules & Code of Conduct for Mediators. We also have special provisions in the Family Law Statute Amendment Act that covers family arbitrations specifically.	Panel Discussion on 'Is mediation suitable in international cases?': http://www.iaml.org/cms_media/files/session_2.pdf Includes information on: Hong Kong by Robin Egerton Canada by Stephen Grant South Africa by Jacqueline Julyan Australia by Ian Kennedy

Part two: global view

In the conclusion to a two-part analysis, Suzanne Kingston and Rachael Kelsey examine the New York Convention and international arbitration

In part one we examined the differences between arbitration in England and Scotland before extending the comparisons to family arbitration worldwide. In this concluding part we will discuss the applicability, or otherwise, of the New York Convention as to the recognition and enforcement of arbitration and set out the remainder of the comparative table for the jurisdictions of England and Wales, France, Germany, Ireland, Scotland, Switzerland and various US states.

The New York Convention

The Convention on the Recognition and Enforcement of Foreign Arbitral Awards of 1958 (330 UNTS 3) is arguably the key document in international arbitration. It came out of the United Nations Conference on International Commercial Arbitration and is more commonly known as 'the New York Convention'. To our knowledge, the New York Convention has not been used in relation to the recognition and enforcement of any family law arbitral awards to date. Use of the New York Convention in relation to arbitral awards made in family law cases has significant scope and may be of great benefit, albeit it is recognised that this may be in relatively few cases. In particular, it may have application where there is agreement between the parties as to the most appropriate course to be followed but where practical difficulties are encountered, or envisaged, with the authorities or other third parties in other states in relation to recognition of court orders. For example, if the parties wish to close a bank account in Thailand and encounter difficulties doing so of consent as they are non-nationals, it is submitted that recognition and enforcement of a very simple arbitral award – arising from a very restricted remit to arbitrate, where the parties seek an agreed determination – would be significantly easier using the Convention than trying to enforce a, say, Scottish court order.

The 146 states that are parties to the Convention, have undertaken to recognise and enforce arbitral awards made in states other than their own. This has significant implications, particularly for those of us who now find our practices routinely involving multi-jurisdictional work. There are opportunities here for clients and agents who want a more 'commercial' way to deal with family disputes.

The Convention provides a simple, quick and straightforward mechanism to have recognition given to, and enforcement taken in respect of, arbitral awards – in contrast, for example, to the many complexities that arise ordinarily in relation to the recognition and enforcement of non-domestic court orders. Even where there has been inter-state cooperation to try to find a uniform recognition and enforcement regime between EU member states there remains significant complexity, i.e. the EU maintenance regulation.

Operation

Essentially, the Convention requires member states to incorporate into their domestic legislation provision that ensures that the non-domestic arbitral award is:

- given the recognition that a court order would have; and
- can be enforced as would a domestic court order.

So, for example, a solicitor in Edinburgh, dealing with a (properly issued) arbitral award issued by a tribunal in Benin, Africa, can take steps to enforce the award 'as if it were an extract registered decree bearing a warrant for execution granted by the court' (s.19(2) Arbitration (Scotland) Act 2010). Contrast this situation with being asked to advise on the recognition and enforcement of a court order from Benin where there is no reciprocal recognition and enforcement of court orders treaty in place with the UK.

Of course, there are complexities: there is the scope for contracting states to make the 'reciprocity reservation' (Article 1(3) of the Convention), which limits recognition and enforcement to awards made in other contracting member states (although as there are so many contracting states this is not a significant limiting factor); and there is also scope for states to make the 'commercial reservation' (Article 1(3) of the Convention), which restricts recognition and enforcement to awards made only in the context of

> … legal relationships, whether contractual or not, which are considered as commercial under the national law of the State [in which recognition/enforcement is sought].

The commercial reservation is obviously more significant in the context of family law arbitration, as, presumably, in some states arbitral awards made in the context of the dissolution of a relationship, even if having 'commercial' consequences, would not benefit from the fast track recognition and enforcement mechanisms provided by the Convention.

There are more things to be considered if recognition and enforcement under the Convention was envisaged, including a need to ensure that the potential enforcing state was not going to refuse to recognise any award under the (limited) grounds that exist in the Convention (Article 5(2)) – if the potential enforcing state did not recognise arbitration as a method capable of settling the dispute between the parties or if the potential enforcing state regarded recognition and enforcement as being contrary to public policy.

Opportunities (and challenges) arise from arbitration as a dispute resolution model in family cases. These are early days and, as with anything new, first reactions have been predictable: curiosity, excitement, fear, rejection and *ennui*. It is not suggested that family arbitration will replace negotiation, litigation, mediation or collaborative family law. It does, though, enhance the menu of options we can offer clients and offers a radically better dispute resolution model in the right cases. We are seeing the first cases coming through and we say the future's bright!

Cases

Campbell v *Campbell* [2010] WL 391841

IAML arbitration

Country	Contributor	Matrimonial arbitration?	Governing legislation/code	Experience
England & Wales	Sir Peter Singer	Yes	Part I of the Arbitration Act 1996 contains an entire code. Family law is neither included expressly nor whether by implication or expressly excluded from the range of disputes to the governance of which the Act may apply. Some aspects of family law, e.g. the status of marriage and the residence and contact to children are thought to be non arbitrable, i.e. simply not suitable for arbitration because of their nature.	Currently the only Scheme Rules for arbitrations under the Arbitration Act 1996 in the family sphere are those elaborated and operated by IFLA (the Institute of Family Law Arbitrators) in conjunction with and under the aegis of the Chartered Institute of Arbitrators, of which all arbitrators accredited under the IFLA scheme are members. In Articles 2 and 3 of the Rules (2012) the permissible ambit of arbitrations under the Scheme are established. Issues relating to children (other than financial issues) and status are excluded, and the scheme is directed against a broad range of financial disputes, both under the Matrimonial Causes Act 1973 (upon divorce or the now rare judicial separation) and other statutes bearing on financial issues.
France	Veronique Chauveau of CBBC Avocats	No	None	'We do not have arbitration in family law in France.'
Germany	Werner of Kanzlei Pollzien & Martens	Yes for finances	Legislation includes: Süeddeutsche Familienschiedsgericht (www.familienschiedsgericht.de/)	'German law allows arbitration in family law for division of property law and alimony and support. arbitration as overseen by the Süeddeutsche Familienschiedsgericht (the South German Family Court of Arbitration) is managed by three retired judges. There have been and are attempts in various other venues within Germany to establish arbitral tribunals for family law with varying degrees of success.' (German law allows arbitration in family law for division of property law and alimony and support. I have not done it as of now but my colleague I Schlaich used the Süeddeutsche Familienschiedsgericht several times and she was happy.

Country	Contributor	Matrimonial arbitration?	Governing legislation/code	Experience
				Three excellent retired judges are in charge of it. There is another link (www.schiedsgericht-fam.de/ index.php?rub=cooperation) for arbitration but I have no experience with them and there are only a few publications about them.)
Ireland	Jennifer O'Brien	Arbitration is not generally used in the context of family law matters.	Ireland's Arbitration Act 2010 (SI 1/2010) came into operation on 8 June 2010 repealing all previous arbitration legislation in Ireland including the Arbitration Act 1954 (SI 26/1954), Arbitration Act 1980 (SI 7/1980) and Arbitration (International Commercial) Act 1998 (SI 14/ 1998). The 2010 Act applies to all arbitrations held in Ireland after the date of entering into force, both international and domestic. The main purpose of the 2010 Act is to bring Irish law into line with international best practice by adopting the UNCITRAL Model Law and applying it to all arbitrations which take place in Ireland.	Arbitration is not generally used in the context of family law matters.
Scotland	Rachael Kelsey; Scott F Cochrane of Brodies LLP	Yes	Arbitration (Scotland) Act 2010; Schedule 1 – mandatory and default rules; and FLAGS Arbitration Rules 2011 (FLAGS is Family Law Arbitration Group Scotland).	
Switzerland	Rolf P Steinegger of Steinegger Rechtsanwaelt	Yes	Part 3 of the Swiss Civil Procedure Code; Swiss Federal Law on Private International Law – Chapter 12.	Arbitration is a formalised proceeding before a non-governmental arbitral tribunal where the judges are appointed by the parties. The award has the effect of a legally-binding and enforceable judicial decision. In general, aspects of family law (i.e. marriage, paternity, divorce, separation, etc.) cannot be settled by arbitration. Only exceptions are financial claims such as matrimonial property and maintenance claims. However, in this field for the arbitrators' award to be enforceable, a mandatory approval by a governmental judge is necessary.
US				
California	Thomas Wolfrum of Wolfrum Law	Yes		Family law arbitration in the State of California is rare because Californian arbitration law makes it all but impossible to appeal from even a biased arbitration award.

Country	Contributor	Matrimonial arbitration?	Governing legislation/code	Experience
				There are two exceptions to this. First, arbitration of attorney fees, especially in family law is common, because when there are disputes that concern less than £1,500, arbitration is the only effective resolution process. Fee disputes less than that amount are assigned to a single arbitrator, whereas if the amount is greater there is a trio of arbitrators on the panel. Arbitration over fees greater than £1,500 is also common because arbitration is considered effective. The second exception is mediation/arbitration. Parties mediate and, if there is no resolution, the mediator becomes an arbitrator who then has discretion whether to use what was said in mediation (confidential under Californian law) in the arbitration. This can save the matter going to trial if the mediation fails, however, it is not often used. On the other hand, mediation (facilitative, evaluative, therapeutic) is common in Californian family law cases.

Country	Contributor	Matrimonial arbitration?	Governing legislation/code	Experience
Connecticut	Arthur Balbirer	Yes except children		Child support and parenting issues may not be arbitrated in Connecticut but arbitration is available for all other matrimonial matters. Despite being highly efficient, however, it is rarely employed in practice.
Kentucky	Bonnie Brown of BMB Family Law	No	Kentucky is anomalous and never had a separate family law statute or settled tradition. Arbitration is now illegal for family law. Statutory regime contained in KRS 417.045 et seq.	The Court of Appeals ruled in *Campbell* v. *Campbell* [2010] that arbitration in family law cases was illegal. The issues were strictly financial, with no child-related matters. The Kentucky Supreme Court (Kentucky's highest court) was prepared to review the decision so as to address the issue one way or the other. However, the estate for the wife who was appealing decided not to proceed and requested the case be dismissed before it could be heard. As a result, the Kentucky Supreme Court depublished the Court of Appeal's Opinion, so the case was prevented from becoming law, but the court was unable to affirmatively review and clarify the legality of arbitrating family cases. With the issue remaining in limbo, most family law attorneys consider it too dangerous to arbitrate.
Maryland	Stephen Moss of Delaney McKinney	Yes	Federal Arbitration Act. Uniform Arbitration Act in effect in Maryland. Revised Uniform Arbitration Act of the District of Columbia.	A number of arbitrators have been trained and certified by the American Academy of Matrimonial Lawyers. Arbitration is less prevalent in the Washington Metropolitan area than one might think because of the situs of the Federal government and the American Arbitration Association. For family law cases, the AAA is not frequently used because their fees are primarily based upon the amount in controversy. Members of the academy have often discussed using other fellows to arbitrate important family law cases but this has not occurred with any frequency. Cost may be one factor; however, more importantly, one can never be assured of the predisposition of the fellows on particular issues and furthermore the basis for challenging an arbitration award is extremely limited, even if the result is contrary to the law. This can be seen from the Uniform Arbitration Act in effect in Maryland and the Revised Uniform Arbitration Act of the District of Columbia.

Country	Contributor	Matrimonial arbitration?	Governing legislation/code	Experience
Minnesota	Nancy Zalusky Berg of Walling Berg & Debele	Yes	This link is to the enacting statute: www.revisor.mn.gov/statutes/?id=484.76 www.revisor.leg.state.mn.us/statutes/?id=572&view=chapterstatutes/?id=572&view=chapter	I believe every state in the US is different with regard to the use of arbitration in family court proceedings. My comments are specific to Minnesota, where we do not typically use arbitration in family court proceedings. If we want to avoid using a judge to decide a matter we typically use a consensual special magistrate as defined in our r.114 [. . .]. I believe we do favour arbitration because the application of law is not required in making the determination. A judge cannot overturn a binding arbitration decision because the arbitrator failed to follow the law. A consensual special magistrate, often called a private judge, still must apply the law. Their decisions are approved by the judge assigned to the case and can be appealed from that judge's approval. Generally we use the variety of processes available through our r.114 for alternative dispute resolution (ADR).
Nevada	Robert Cerceo of The Abrams Law Firm LLC	Yes	A uniform Arbitration Act has been adopted – though not specific to family law.	Nevada has a family division in two counties (Clark/Las Vegas and Washoe/Reno). The other counties have general jurisdiction courts, which handle all manner of cases. The two family divisions have mandatory mediation for child custody matters (no financial issues) with a rarely used 'opt out' provision (only for the most contested cases where it is obvious mediation will not work). The target is for a full or partial parenting agreement to cover legal custody (decision making) and physical custody (primary or jointly shared custody, holiday division, all aspects of coordinating parenting). A binding arbitrator can be appointed for high conflict cases for all aspects of divorce. In those instances, the court has developed a stipulation between the parties to essentially delegate the judicial role to one arbitrator to hear the case and to render a final order, which is appealable under only very narrow circumstances.

Country	Contributor	Matrimonial arbitration?	Governing legislation/code	Experience
				A uniform arbitration act has been adopted; however, it is not specific to family law. Arbitration remains the least used option in the State of Nevada.
New York	Initially: Sylvia Goldschmidt of Goldschmidt & Genovese LLP Later contribution from: Matthew Feigin, Peter Bronstein, Pamela Sloan, Alton Abramovicz, Harold Meyerson, John Teitler, Nicholas Loventhal, Nancy Murphy, Kenneth David Burrows, John A Pappalado, Howard Roy	Yes	No specific matrimonial arbitration legislation. Agreements to arbitrate generally are governed by Article 75 Civil Practice Law and Rules. Pre- and post-nuptial agreements are enforceable under Domestic Relations Law Section 236 Part B subdivision 3.	NY State allows for voluntary binding arbitration. It is not a frequently utilised mechanism in matrimonial matters; however, in addition to attorneys many retired judges have become involved and offer services as arbitrators on a private (unrelated to the court system) basis.
North Carolina			North Carolina Family Law Arbitration Act (www.law.justia.com/codes/north-carolina/2005/chapter_50/article_3.html). According to this article: www.aaml.org/sites/default/files/AAML%20HOT%20TIPS.pdf	www.aaml.org/sites/default/files/AAML%20HOT%20TIPS.pdf 'The North Carolina Family Law Arbitration Act (enacted in 1999 and revised in 2005) permits all issues incident to a marriage or breakup of a marriage, except for the absolute divorce itself, to be submitted to binding arbitration, if a husband and wife agree to it.' 'On October 1, 1999, North Carolina joined at least nine other states with specific legislation authorising arbitration of matrimonial cases and became the first state to adopt an arbitration statute specifically designed for such cases.'

Country	Contributor	Matrimonial arbitration?	Governing legislation/code	Experience
				'The North Carolina statute is unique among the nine states because it provides comprehensive authority and guidance to the parties by statute embodied within the matrimonial law chapters and by model forms and rules archived with the North Carolina Bar Association. While the project was technically conducted under the auspices of the North Carolina Bar Association for political reasons, all of the non-academic committee members were AAML fellows.'

3.3

Family arbitration (Sir Hugh Bennett)[1]

Lecture to the Worshipful Company of Arbitrators

1. You may feel that the title that I have chosen for my talk this evening, 'Family Law Arbitration: A better way to Justice?' is perhaps rather prosaic. But it is a question that practitioners in family law are going to have to ask themselves more and more, for the reasons that will appear from my talk. The title, of course, begs the question 'better than what other ways'? Mediation? Collaborative law? Litigation?

2. I shall concentrate on comparing family financial arbitration with litigation about family financial disputes. I shall exclude from my talk mediation and collaborative law for 2 reasons. (1) I know very little about either mechanisms, but (2) I know enough to say that although both may well have an important part to play in any particular case, mediation and collaborative law have one significant weakness – neither guarantee that the dispute will end – it all depends upon the parties reaching an agreement. If they do not, much time and money may have been wasted. By contrast, both arbitration and litigation do guarantee that the disputes will be resolved; in an arbitration by the award, in litigation by a judgment.

3. For centuries family law was the preserve of the legislature, the church and finally the secular courts. Divorce was the preserve of the wealthy either by a private Act of Parliament, or by decree of the church authorities. In later times, Parliament empowered the secular courts to pronounce decrees of divorce and ancillary orders. Because marriage was viewed as one of the bedrocks of society, the courts jealously guarded their jurisdiction. In the latter half of the 20th century things began to change. Divorce became much easier to obtain with the passing of the Divorce Reform Act, 1969. Gradually the courts ceased to focus on the grounds of divorce – cruelty, desertion, adultery, etc. – and began to focus much more on the consequences of divorce, namely disputes about the children, money and property of the parties. But here, too, the only avenue open to a divorcing couple to obtain a binding resolution of their disputes was the court, i.e. a judgment of a judge. Arbitration, known to the commercial world since the Middle Ages and the subject of several Acts of Parliament in the last 100 years or so culminating in the Arbitration Act, 1996, was a species of resolution completely and utterly foreign and unknown to the world of family law, its practitioners and judges. I speak here of the secular world, not of those religions who have their own internal dispute resolution mechanisms.

4. What has changed? The old paternalistic grip of the family courts has been very considerably loosened. It is now recognised by the courts of England and Wales, led by the Supreme Court in its seminal decision in *Radmacher* v *Granantino* in 2010 that the paternalistic approach of the courts – best summed up by the phrase 'we know best' – is dying if not dead, at least in family disputes about money and property. At the heart of *Radmacher* v *Granantino* was the standing in English law of a pre-nuptial agreement, that is to say an agreement entered into by a couple intending to marry which would regulate the disposition of their assets if they divorced. The Supreme Court emphatically endorsed both pre-nuptial and post-nuptial agreements. Para.78 of the judgment of 7 of the 9 Justices is headed 'autonomy' and reads as follows: 'The reason why the court should give weight to a nuptial agreement is that there should be respect for individual autonomy. The court should accord respect to the decision of a married couple as to the manner in which their financial affairs should be regulated. It would be paternalistic and patronising to override their agreement simply on the basis that the court

---

knows best. This is particularly true where the parties' agreement addresses existing circumstances and not merely the contingencies of an uncertain future.'

5.   So, I suggest, that that steer of the Supreme Court must lead inexorably to this proposition – if nuptial agreements between couples who thereby agree the disposition of their assets upon divorce are now a judicially recognised mechanism of matrimonial financial disengagement, the parties should be free to agree the forum in which they would like their disputes to be decided. And now they can, thanks to the scheme propounded by the Institute of Family Law Arbitrators, which has been emphatically endorsed by Sir James Munby, the President of the Family Division of the High Court in a case *S v S* in 2014 together with the Practice Guidance issued by the President last November.

6.   Before I attempt to compare the merits or otherwise of litigation against arbitration, let me first tell you, as briefly as I can, about the IFLA scheme of arbitration.

7.   The scheme is designed to resolve by arbitration disputes which are financial and/or involve property, for example financial and property remedies under the Matrimonial Causes Act 1973 as amended, the equivalent provisions in the Civil Partnership Act 2004 and Schedule 1 of the Children Act 1989. It does not cover the granting of a divorce or matters to do with status, and, as yet, does not cover disputes involving the upbringing of children, although this development is almost up and running.

8.   Next, the scheme specifically incorporates the relevant provisions of the Arbitration Act, 1996. In the form ARB1, which is the agreement to arbitrate, the parties specifically agree that their arbitration will be conducted in accordance with the 1996 Act.

9.   The Rules of the scheme, to which the parties bind themselves under ARB1, make it mandatory for the law of England and Wales to be applied. The parties cannot contract out of that provision. There is no room for the parties to agree that the arbitrator will apply the laws of their choice, whether secular or religious. That is because it is essential that the law applied by the arbitrator is to be English law which in turn will be applied by the family courts of England and Wales when converting the award into orders of the court.

10.   The final overarching ingredient of the scheme is that the parties agree in ARB1 that they will apply to the family court to convert the award into court orders where it is necessary to do so, and furthermore, they acknowledge in ARB1 that the court has a discretion as to whether, and in what terms, it will make orders arising out of the award. Why is this? First, all the Acts of Parliament, which give the court power to make financial and property provision orders, specifically give to the court a discretion whether to make such orders and in what terms. Second, in many cases a court order will be necessary to convert the award into orders which can be enforced. Let me give you just 3 examples. (1) The applicant gains an award of £X by way of a lump sum against the respondent, (2) the respondent in turn gains an award that the lump sum of £X is to be on the basis of a 'clean break', i.e. the lump sum when paid satisfies the applicant's claim for not only capital but also income provision so that the applicant's claim to continuing periodical payments is extinguished, and (3) the applicant also gains an award that the respondent's pension should be shared, i.e. there should be a pension sharing order. In each of these examples, unless the court makes the appropriate orders, there is no means of the rights gained by the parties under the award being enshrined in law and thus enforced.

11.   I am now going to turn my spotlight on litigation, i.e. the court process in family financial and property disputes. I want to make it absolutely clear that I have the greatest admiration for all the talented and dedicated judges, courtroom staff and backroom staff in the family justice system. All that they do is to be applauded. But the system is under colossal strain. Its weakness is that it is funded by the state, which in reality means the government of the day, and like many other parts of the body politic is being starved of resources. For instance, there are simply not enough judges to carry the load. This leads to a major deficiency. Cases fixed months ahead of the final hearing are at risk of being cancelled at the last moment due to there being no judge available. This can lead to unjustifiable delay and greater expense and dissatisfaction on the part of the parties.

12.   In litigation the parties have little or no autonomy as to the procedure to be adopted or as to what issues they want decided. In essence the case is judge led. Judges are now, and are encouraged to be, interventionist, overriding if necessary the parties' agreed course of action. Despite the innovation of Mr Justice Coleridge, as he then was, in *OS v DS*, discrete issues are

not often isolated for decision. The pattern of the court going through the whole gamut of the case persists. Although the court is likely to adopt a course of action, for instance limiting discovery of documents, agreed between the parties, the concept of 'party autonomy' is unknown in litigation.

13.   The latest guidance issued on 1 February 2016 entitled 'Efficient Conduct of Financial Hearings in the High Court . . .' basically limits the type of money case to be heard by a High Court Judge to cases where the overall net assets exceed £15m and/or the overall net earned income exceeds £1m. There are, it is true, exceptions for cases exceeding £7.5m of net annual assets if certain stringent conditions are satisfied. But this must mean that the vast majority of financial provision cases are and will be heard by judges below High Court level, most probably by District Judges who are the very level of judges most under the cosh of overwork. To add to this is the abolition of public funding for financial provision cases which has led to a very large rise in litigants in person.

Thus, if the hapless litigant cannot afford legal representation, he or she must represent him or herself, with all the disadvantages, both for the litigant and judge, we know so well. Cases are and will take longer because the judge must act not only as adjudicator but also a sort of shepherd to the litigant in person. Delay can then result in hearing other cases.

14.   In family cases before a court accredited members of the media can now be admitted into court to report the proceedings in the interests, it is said, of transparency. In my personal opinion, this is an unwelcome development. It cannot be a pleasant experience for any litigant, whether known locally, nationally or internationally, to have to run the gauntlet of having their privacy and intimate family affairs spread over the media, whether national or local. I do not believe that this development has done anything for transparency in family money cases. I suspect that if and when an analysis is carried out, it will be found that the only cases to have been reported in the media are the 'sensational' ones.

15.   There is, however, one area where the court process has no equivalent in arbitration. If a litigant has good grounds to apply for emergency relief, typically an injunction, without the knowledge of the respondent, he or she can literally turn up at the applications' court with the appropriate documentation and he will be heard. However, in arbitration, s.33 of the 1996 Act, as I understand it, precludes any such procedure since the arbitrator is under a duty to give to each party 'a reasonable opportunity of putting his case'. That, of course, would nullify the utility of applying for, say, a Mareva injunction, since the party to be injuncted could dispose of his assets before the grant of any injunction restraining him from so doing.

16.   Finally, there is the appeals' procedure. Permission to appeal from either the trial judge or from the Court of Appeal is necessary before an appeal can be launched. If permission to appeal is refused by the trial judge, which in a discretionary jurisdiction it is more often than not, application must be made to the Court of Appeal in writing, followed in the event of refusal by an oral hearing. If permission is granted then the oral appeal will follow. This elaborate procedure is both time consuming and therefore expensive. Typically a year or more can elapse between the judge's order and the decision of the Court of Appeal, leading to a very considerable increase in costs. And that may not be the end; an appeal to the Supreme Court may appear attractive to the losing litigant. Another year or more, with yet more expense, may then elapse.

17.   I am now going to look at what I believe to be the significant advantages of arbitration in family matters provided by the IFLA scheme over litigation, and then at what are perceived to be the disadvantages.

18.   I will take the advantages in no particular order. First, privacy and confidentiality. All the proceedings before the arbitrator are private and entirely confidential. The media and the public are not admitted. Rule 16 of the scheme makes it abundantly clear that the arbitration and its outcome are confidential. All documents, statements, information and other materials in the arbitration are confidential, as are all transcripts of evidence and/or submissions. I suggest that this is a real bonus for parties who do not relish their family disagreements, whether great or small, being bandied about in the national or local media. With the family courts now travelling at a gallop towards hearings being heard completely in open court, those couples caught up in a broken relationship who want their disputes adjudicated in private now have that option.

19. But what, you may say, happens when the award comes to the court for implementation? Will not the parties lose their privacy and confidentiality? Well, look at how the President dealt with the case of *S v S*. He simply said that he had read the necessary papers and approved the award and consequential orders. In para.22 of the judgment he said he did not propose to go into the details of the case as 'why, after all, in case like this should litigants who have chosen the private process of arbitration have their affairs exposed in a public judgment?' So, nobody was any the wiser as to the identity of the parties or the facts of the case. But that dicta was, of course, delivered in a case where both parties desired the award to be transformed into court orders. What, you may ask, is the court's likely attitude if one party challenges an award? Will the hearing be in open court with the media free to report what it likes, thus destroying the privacy and confidentiality the parties gained through the arbitral hearing? Does there have to be an unanonymised judgment? As to the hearing, I think the courts, following the President's lead, are going to have to be robust and respect the wishes of the parties, expressed in the arbitration agreement and the rules of IFLA, that they, by choosing arbitration as opposed to court based litigation, opted for privacy and confidentiality throughout. A situation cannot be allowed to develop whereby the dissatisfied party in challenging the award before the court thereby destroys the very privacy and confidentiality which he or she agreed to in the first place. As to the judgment, I see no difficulty in the judge so framing his judgment and anonymising it so that it does not identify the parties in any shape or form.

20. Flexibility as to procedure and as to issues to be arbitrated. Section 1(a) of the 1996 Act provides that one of the principles of the Act is that parties should be free to agree how their disputes are resolved. Section 34 of the Act provides that the tribunal shall decide all procedural and evidential matters 'subject to the right of the parties to agree any matter', and sub-section (2) sets out examples of those procedural and evidential matters. And we know that under s.68 an award can be challenged on the ground of 'serious irregularity' which includes under s.68(2)(c) 'failure by the tribunal to conduct the proceedings in accordance with the procedure agreed between the parties'.

21. The Rules of the scheme are faithful to the Act. Rule 9 provides that 'the parties are free to agree as to the form of procedure . . .' Rule 10 provides that the arbitrator will invite the parties to make submissions as to what are the issues and what procedure should be adopted.

22. As to flexibility of issues to be arbitrated, the parties can agree to define precisely what issues the arbitrator is to decide. Is he to decide the whole gamut of the case or is he to decide just those issues which the parties want him to decide? Let me give you an example. In an arbitration which I conducted the issue of control was involved of a private company in which the husband and wife each held 50% of the share capital. It was agreed that one of the parties would run the company. But they could not agree about the terms of the shareholder agreement to be executed by each of them. I was asked to, and did, determine that issue and that issue alone, all other issues (which had nothing to do with the company) being left to one side.

23. Thus the parties can submit to arbitration those issues which they see as the stumbling block to the resolution of their disputes, and done in a way which they desire, not in a way that a court may feel either that it has to impose on them or that it cannot permit.

24. Next, speed. The court system can be, for many family finance litigants, particularly those of modest means, impossibly slow. Of course, priority is rightly given to children cases, particularly those where a local authority takes proceedings in relation to a dysfunctional family or where one party is seeking the summary return of a child to a foreign jurisdiction pursuant to the Hague Convention. And, there is a limited pool of judges. Thus, what can happen is that finance cases may be adjourned almost at the last moment, because the courts are overworked, and in some courts adjourned not just once but more than once.

25. Compare that to what can happen under the IFLA scheme. I have done some research by asking Resolution, who collate the statistics, what is the longest and shortest arbitration, i.e. the period of time from the date of the appointment of the arbitrator to the date of the delivery of the award. The statistics are not complete because there are a number of uncompleted arbitrations. But I understand that the longest was one year and the shortest was 7 days. *S v S*, was completed from the date of the appointment of the arbitrator to the delivery of the award in 5 months.

The arbitration, in which I was the arbitrator to which I have referred, took no more than 4 weeks from start to finish. Five days after my appointment the oral hearing took place. There were further written submissions. Then no more than one month after my appointment the award, having been vetted by the lawyers for typos, etc., was delivered to the parties. I readily concede that the arbitration lasting 7 days concerned a very short point.

26. I venture to suggest that such speed, even if of 12 months and certainly if of 4 weeks (or 7 days) is quite unattainable in our court system.

27. Next, the arbitrator. Once the arbitrator is selected and accepts appointment, the arbitrator must see the arbitration through to its conclusion. There is no chopping or changing of the tribunal as can happen, sometimes all too often, in the court system. Although a judge may be allocated to a case at an early stage and conduct the interlocutory hearings, there is absolutely no guarantee that he will actually conduct the final hearing. He may be pulled out to conduct a more urgent case.

   Further, the parties to an arbitration select their arbitrator. They are given the opportunity, unavailable to them in the court system, of choosing the person to adjudicate their disputes in whom they and their advisers have confidence and consider the best person to be the arbitrator.

28. Let me now come to the perceived disadvantages, which I take again in no particular order of importance. First, an objection which I believe has now died away. It was said that the arbitrators under the scheme are unregulated, by which, I believe, it is meant that there is no recognised body to whom they are accountable. Let me lay this canard to rest, once and for all. What is IFLA? It is the Institute of Family Law Arbitrators which is a company limited by guarantee, with a board of directors chaired by Lord Falconer of Thoroton, a former Lord Chancellor. It is responsible for the implementation and administration of the family law finance arbitration scheme. The qualified arbitrators, now numbering over 200 with more to come, have all been trained in arbitral techniques and have a good working knowledge of the important and relevant parts of the Arbitration Act 1996. Each person so trained and wishing to practise as a family arbitrator must become a member of the Chartered Institute of Arbitrators and thus make him or herself subject to its disciplinary code. Solicitors, barristers, QCs, and retired judges, all of whom are, or were, full-time practising family lawyers, comprise the corps of arbitrators under the scheme. They are therefore real specialists in the field of family finance law.

29. Next, it is said 'the judge is free, the arbitrator must be paid'. The second part is true, the first part is only partially true. Litigants must pay court fees. But the better answer to the criticism of expense is that if parties engage in arbitration and get the hearing and the award through quickly, the saving in legal fees that would be otherwise expended whilst the case wends its way through the court system to a final hearing, will, I suggest, more than offset the cost of employing an arbitrator. If months, even years, of litigation can be avoided by choosing arbitration, the savings in legal costs will be huge and vastly outweigh the fees of the arbitrator and the cost of hiring a venue.

30. Next, it is said 'arbitration is only for the rich', by which I assume is meant that if only the rich can afford to pay an arbitrator, family arbitration can only be used by the rich. Not so. Among the qualified arbitrators are a large number who are prepared to, and have agreed to, take on arbitrations in cases of very modest means and tailor their fees accordingly, and indeed who are happy to agree a fixed fee. In any event, no doubt the choice of arbitrator will be influenced by the fees he proposes to charge and the parties can shop around.

31. I now come to 2 objections, which I have frequently heard, as to why some family practitioners advise their clients not to agree to arbitration. They are in a way linked. The first objection I have reduced to its bare essentials. It goes like this – 'If I advise my client to agree to arbitration with X as the arbitrator but then in his award he goes against my client I may get the blame. If, however, in litigation the judge (whom I cannot choose) decides the dispute contrary to my client's case, well, he gets the blame, not me'. The second objection is more nuanced! It is this – 'If the arbitrator decides the dispute contrary to my client's case there is no effective right of appeal'. Although the 1996 Act does stipulate grounds upon which an award can be challenged – see ss.67 to 70 inclusive – they are very circumscribed; see the judgment in the case of *DB* v *DLJ*, dated 24 February 2016, where Mostyn J described them as providing 'very limited rights of challenge'. Further, (the objection goes on) 'any challenge to the award

will face the hurdle that my client has agreed in the arbitration agreement that the award will be final and binding which can only encourage a family judge to enforce the award. By contrast, if my client has arguable grounds of appeal from an order of a judge, my client is likely to be given permission to appeal'.

32. I am going to take the 2nd objection first because it impacts on the first objection. It may be that it is easier to mount an appeal from a judgment than it is to mount a challenge to an arbitral award. But, if so, that is unsurprising. Arbitration is, after all, intended to be a one-stop shop. It is not there to provide a dry run for disaffected parties to rerun their cases before the courts, whether by way of appeal or rehearing or whatever. It is one of the attractions of arbitration that the 1996 Act gives very limited grounds of appeal or challenge, thereby cutting out much delay and expense. Surely, the party to an arbitration who is satisfied with the award should be pleased that the avenue to appeal under the 1996 Act is limited. It saves him or her from delay and further expense and discourages the unsuccessful party from challenging the award. Is not that an important factor for family practitioners to take into account when advising their clients? Nevertheless, in family law, the objection that there is no effective way of challenging an award outside the grounds in the 1996 Act, is, I believe, misplaced. If the unsuccessful party can persuade a court, which is asked by the successful party to convert the award into orders of the court, that the arbitrator has made an award which is wrong in principle or perverse (by which I mean that no reasonable tribunal, exercising its discretion and properly directing itself as to the law, could have come to the conclusion which it did), then no family court is going to convert the award into orders of the court. To do so would be an abdication of the court's exercise of discretion specifically placed upon it by Parliament.

33. In this respect I would like to comment briefly on parts of the judgment in *DB* v *DLJ* delivered by Mostyn J. The facts of the case are not important for the purpose of my talk. The wife sought to resist an application by the husband to turn the arbitrator's award into orders of the court on the grounds that the award was vitiated by a mistake or unforeseen event concerning the true value of a property in Portugal allocated to her. She failed.

34. This authority, like the President's decision in *S* v *S*, is very supportive of family law arbitration. I commend it to your attention. Much of the judgment I agree with. However, there are one or two passages in the judgment which appear to me to give an erroneous impression of the nature of a family arbitration agreement entered into by parties under ARB1. The judge first analyses the scope for challenging a commercial award under the 1996 Act. At para.6 he recites part of a paper given by Sir Bernard Eder in December 2014 to an International Arbitration Conference in Mauritius in which Sir Bernard said: '. . .the general approach of the Court is one which supports the arbitral process. By way of anecdote, it is perhaps interesting to recall what I was told many years ago by Michael Kerr, a former judge in the Court of Appeal and one of the leading figures in the recent development of the law of arbitration in England, when I was complaining about an arbitration that I had just lost and the difficulties in the way of challenging the award. I told him the award was wrong and unjust. He looked baffled and said: "Remember, when parties agree arbitration they buy the right to get the wrong answer". So, the mere fact that an award is "wrong" or even "unjust" does not, of itself, provide any basis for challenging the award or intervention by the Court. Any challenge or appeal must bring itself under one or more of the three heads which I have identified'.

35. In my personal opinion, as I shall demonstrate, I consider that the dicta of Michael Kerr leading to Sir Bernard's conclusion is not applicable to arbitral awards in family law.

36. Mostyn J then rightly states that the heads of challenge under the 1996 Act to an award are 'very circumscribed indeed' and illustrates that by reference to the grounds given in the Act.

37. In para.27 the judge rightly said that a family court, when exercising its discretion following an arbitral award, should adopt an approach of great stringency. The parties, having agreed to arbitrate, should understand that their dispute should end with the award. An arbitration is not a dry run prior to a court hearing.

38. However, in para.28 the judge went on ' . . .Outside the heads of correction, challenge or appeal within the 1996 Act these (I interpolate – the word "these" refers to a court refusing to implement an arbitral award on the grounds of mistake or supervening event) are, in my judgment, the only realistic available grounds of resistance to an incorporating order. An

assertion that the award was "wrong" or "unjust" will almost never get off the ground: in such a case the error must be so blatant and extreme that it leaps off the page'.

39.   If the judge there was saying or giving the impression that a party can never, or almost never, challenge an award on the ground that it is 'wrong' or 'unjust', then with the greatest of respect I disagree. It may be that the judge has misunderstood that part of Sir Bernard Eder's lecture to which I have referred. Sir Bernard was, as I understand it, referring to civil or commercial cases. I am led to believe by a retired commercial judge (now an arbitrator) that in such cases the arbitration clause in the contract may exclude any right of appeal to, or review by, a court of law. If so, then it may fairly be said that the parties in agreeing to arbitration have bought 'the right to get the wrong answer'. But, in sharp contrast to such arbitration clauses, in family law arbitrations under the IFLA scheme, the parties agree the very opposite. In ARB1, the arbitration agreement, the parties specifically agree and acknowledge the right of the family court to exercise its own discretion when invited by the parties, whether consensually or not, to convert the award into orders of the court. In family law, case after case from the House of Lords and Supreme Court downwards emphasises that it is the duty of the court to achieve a fair and just result. Under the Rules of the IFLA scheme the arbitrator is in precisely the same position. It is his duty to apply the law of England and Wales. If, therefore, Mostyn J was saying or implying that, notwithstanding that a court, asked to implement an award, is satisfied that the arbitrator's award may be wrong in principle or perverse so that the award can fairly be categorised as 'wrong' or 'unjust', cannot refuse to implement the award, then I profoundly disagree with him. For a court so to act would be an abdication of its duty. If he was saying, which in fact I believe he was when the whole of his judgment is considered, see in particular paras 17 to 22, that it will be a considerable uphill battle for a 'dissatisfied' party to an arbitral award to challenge it successfully before a family court, whether or not under the grounds in the 1996 Act, then I would have no quarrel with him.

40.   But it must follow that the parties in a family arbitration conducted under the IFLA scheme most emphatically do not buy into 'the right to get the wrong answer' from the arbitrator. Quite the reverse.

41.   I now return to the other objection, which is about the practitioner being blamed by his client for choosing the arbitrator in the event of an adverse award. It is, I believe, an irrational fear that will disappear in time as the culture of arbitration becomes embedded in family law. But in the meantime let me reassure the 'doubting Thomases'. First, challenges to an award are not limited to those under the 1996 Act, as I hope I have demonstrated. If a challenge to an award can be made good, even after applying what Mostyn J said was a stringent test, then why should the lawyer fear choosing the arbitrator? And conversely, the lawyer will have the comfort of knowing that if his client wins then the opposition faces an uphill battle in challenging the award.

42.   Second, I ask a rhetorical question of the fearful lawyer – is it not better for your client that he or she should have the opportunity to choose the arbitrator in whom he or she has confidence and who will see the case through to the end, rather than take a risk with a judge in whom he or she (or more likely, you) has little confidence or in whom they may have confidence but who is pulled from the case before the final hearing, sometimes at the 11th hour?

43.   Third, if all that I have said does not still anxieties, then the parties can submit to IFLA a shortlist of names and ask IFLA to nominate the arbitrator.

44.   Next, it may be said that 'if all arbitrations are confidential then no award in one can be cited in another, thus creating the risk of inconsistent awards being made'. I accept that an award in any particular arbitration cannot be cited in another, not at any rate without the express consent of both parties in the first arbitration. This is inherent in any system of arbitration where the principle of confidentiality prevails. So there is indeed the risk of inconsistency. But it is more apparent than real. In family finance cases, the inconsistency is likely to arise not by reason of the discretion given to tribunals under English law to determine the fair outcome, but by an arbitrator making a decision which is wholly outside the wide parameters of that discretion. That can be cured by the court. And just because two arbitrators may differ on roughly the same set of facts as to outcome does not under English family law mean that one is right and the other is wrong. It is only if one arbitrator makes an award which is indeed outside the wide ambit of the discretion given to the tribunal under English law, so that it can be said

that the award is wrong in principle or perverse, that the court is likely to uphold a challenge to it by the dissatisfied party. In that way the courts will be able to keep an eye on the arbitral process.

45. Finally, it is said 'the law cannot be developed in an arbitration'. That may be so. But the vast majority of family cases involve the application of existing principles to the facts of the particular case. For those very small number of cases where the law may need developing, then they can remain in the court system.

46. So, ladies and gentlemen, to my conclusions. We are fortunate in this country to have a good legal and judicial system. But it is under immense strain. Resources are constantly being cut or withdrawn. This leads to rigidity, delay, and expense and dissatisfaction. There is a lack of freedom in the court system for individuals to determine the procedure under which they themselves would like their differences to be adjudicated. Here for the first time is an arbitral scheme, applying English law, which empowers couples, suffering a terminal breakdown in their relationship, to opt to have their financial and property disputes adjudicated in the way that they consider suits them best. If the parties want privacy, arbitration will provide it. If they want speed, flexibility, and one 'adjudicator' (and a specialist at that) to take their case through from beginning to end, then arbitration provides all of that.

47. To return then to the title of my talk. Which is a better way to justice in family cases – litigation or arbitration? My question will, I suggest, only be answered definitively when arbitration gains the confidence of a significant body of family practitioners and their clients. My personal view is that arbitration under the IFLA scheme is the much more attractive path. The advantages of parties submitting their financial and property disputes to arbitration so outweigh what are said, very inaccurately, to be disadvantages, that I confidently predict that within the near future family finance arbitration will complement the court system just as private medicine complements the National Health Service.

Appendix 4

Case reports

4.1

S v. *S* [2014] EWHC 7 (Fam)

Neutral Citation: *S* v. *S* [2014] EWHC 7 (Fam)

Case No: GU12D00692

IN THE HIGH COURT OF JUSTICE

FAMILY DIVISION

Royal Courts of Justice

Strand, London, WC2A 2LL

Date: 14 January 2014

Before:

SIR JAMES MUNBY

President of the Family Division

Between:

S

Petitioner

and

S

Respondent

Hendersons for the Petitioner

Family Law in Partnership for the Respondent

No hearing: application dealt with on paper

Judgment

Sir James Munby, President of the Family Division:

1. I have before me an application, transferred to me from the Guildford County Court at my direction, for the approval of a consent order which has been lodged with the court following, and intended to give effect to, an arbitral award made by Mr Gavin Smith in an arbitration conducted under the IFLA (Institute of Family Law Arbitrators) Scheme.

2. There is no doubt that in this case the court should approve the consent order, as I do. But it seemed to me appropriate to give some guidance about the proper approach of the court to such applications.

The IFLA Scheme

3. The IFLA Scheme is described by Sir Peter Singer in '*Arbitration in Family Financial*

Proceedings: the IFLA Scheme: Part 1', [2012] Fam Law 1353, and '*Part 2*' [2012] Fam Law 1496. Up-to-date details about the Scheme and arbitrators accredited under it can be found on IFLA's website, **ifla.org.uk**.

4. For present purposes all I need say is that:

    (i)   IFLA is a not for profit organisation, created by the Chartered Institute of Arbitrators (CIArb), the Family Law Bar Association, and the family lawyers' group Resolution, in association with the Centre for Child and Family Law Reform;

    (ii)   IFLA arbitrations are conducted in accordance with the Arbitration Act 1996 and IFLA's Arbitration Rules (the Rules);

    (iii) IFLA arbitrators are all Members of the CIArb, that is, MCIArb;

    (iv) The IFLA Scheme covers financial and property disputes arising from relationship breakdown (Article 2 of the Rules);

    (v)   The Rules contain a mandatory requirement (Articles 1.3(c) and 3) that the arbitrator will decide the substance of the dispute only in accordance with the law of England and Wales.

This last point is significant.

The facts

5. I can take the relevant facts very briefly. The parties were married in 1986 and separated in 2012. Their only child is now 19. A decree nisi on the wife's petition was granted early in 2013. In June 2013 the parties signed IFLA's Form ARB1, agreeing to arbitration in accordance with the Rules by Mr Smith in relation to their claims for ancillary relief and thereby binding themselves to accept his award. The arbitrator's Final Award is dated 7 November 2013. On 9 December 2013 the parties applied to the Guildford County Court seeking approval of the consent order. In addition to the draft consent order they lodged the Form ARB1, the Final Award, a Joint Statement of Information in Form D81 and, marked for dismissal purposes only, their Forms A.

6. The facts relevant to the subject matter of the arbitration are set out, clearly and comprehensively, in the Final Award. They concern only the parties, so I say nothing more about them except to note that the Form D81 shows the matrimonial assets to be worth in excess of £1.5 but less than £2 million.

The legal context

7. The strong policy argument in favour of the court giving effect to an agreement that the parties have come to themselves for the resolution of their financial affairs following divorce has been recognised for a long time: see the discussion in *X* v. *X (Y and Z Intervening)* [2002] 1 FLR 508 of the line of authorities of which *Dean* v. *Dean* [1978] Fam 161, *Edgar* v. *Edgar* [1980] 1 WLR 1410, *Camm* v. *Camm* (1983) 4 FLR 577 and *Xydhias* v. *Xydhias* [1999] 1 FLR 683 were the most prominent.

8. Thus by the turn of the Millennium it was well established that the court would not lightly permit parties who had made an agreement between themselves to depart from it. Indeed, as a matter of general policy what the parties had themselves agreed would be upheld by the courts unless contrary to public policy or subject to some vitiating feature such as undue pressure or the exploitation of a dominant position to secure an unreasonable advantage.

9. In *X* v. *X*, para.103, I said that a formal agreement, properly and fairly arrived at with competent legal advice, should be upheld by the court unless there were 'good and substantial grounds' for concluding that an 'injustice' would be done by holding the parties to it. In propounding that formulation I adopted the language used by Ormrod LJ in *Edgar* v. *Edgar* in preference to that of Thorpe J in *Smith* v. *McInerney* [1994] 2 FLR 1077. I said that Thorpe J's references to 'the most exceptional circumstances' and 'overwhelmingly strong considerations' seemed to me, with respect, to put the matter perhaps a little too high. With the benefit of hindsight I was too questioning of what Thorpe J had said. Not for the first time he had seen, more clearly and presciently than others, the way in which the law was moving and, indeed, had to move.

10. There have of course been many significant developments in this area of the law since it was first set on its course by Ormrod LJ. Many have helpfully been identified by Baker J in *AI* v. *MT* [2013] EWHC 100 (Fam), paras.20-21, 30-31. For present purposes three developments demand particular notice.

11. First, there was the identification and subsequent elaboration by Thorpe LJ of the concept of the 'magnetic factor' – the feature(s) or factor(s) which in the particular case are of 'magnetic importance' in influencing or even determining the outcome: see, for example, *White* v. *White* [1999] Fam 304, 314 (affirmed, [2001] 1 AC 596) and *Crossley* v. *Crossley* [2007] EWCA Civ 1491, [2008] 1 FLR 1467, para.15. We see this approach, though not the label, carried forward in the fundamentally important statement of principle by the Supreme Court in *Radmacher (formerly Granatino)* v. *Granatino* [2010] UKSC 42, [2011] 1 AC 534, para.75:

> 'The court should give effect to a nuptial agreement that is freely entered into by each party with a full appreciation of its implications unless in the circumstances prevailing it would not be fair to hold the parties to their agreement.'

12. Secondly, mediation and subsequently other forms of alternative dispute resolution have become well established as a means of resolving financial disputes on divorce. As Thorpe LJ observed in *Al Khatib* v. *Masry* [2004] EWCA Civ 1353 [2005] 1 FLR 381, para.17, 'there is no case, however conflicted, which is not potentially open to successful mediation'. By 2008 use of the collaborative law approach was being encouraged by the court: see the observations of Coleridge J in *S* v. *P (Settlement by Collaborative Law Process)* [2008] 2 FLR 2040. The same year, writing extra-judicially in 'Statutory arbitration and ancillary relief', [2008] Fam Law 26, Thorpe LJ ventured the view that 'to extend the Arbitration Acts to reach all financial issues created by the breakdown of relationships is surely safe territory.' Indeed, there is nothing in the Arbitration Act 1996 which on the face of it would preclude arbitration as a permissible process for the resolution of disputes rooted in family life or relationship breakdown. The Family Procedure Rules 2010 now encourage resort to alternative dispute resolution procedures in this as in other areas of family law: see FPR rule 1.4(e) and FPR Part 3. It was against this background that the IFLA Scheme was introduced in February 2012.

13. Thirdly, the court has adapted and abbreviated its processes to facilitate the appropriately simple and speedy judicial approval of such agreements. Where the parties are agreed on the terms of the consent order the court has available to it the process adopted by the parties in the present case. But in the context of collaborative law, Coleridge J, with the support of Sir Mark Potter P, was willing to adopt an even more streamlined process in *S* v. *P (Settlement by Collaborative Law Process)* [2008] 2 FLR 2040.

14. Where, in contrast, one of the parties seeks to resile, the court has long sanctioned use of the abbreviated 'notice to show cause' procedure utilised in *Dean* v. *Dean* [1978] Fam 161, *Xydhias* v. *Xydhias* [1999] 1 FLR 683, *X* v. *X (Y and Z Intervening)* [2002] 1 FLR 508 and *S* v. *S (Ancillary Relief)* [2008] EWHC 2038 (Fam), [2009] 1 FLR 254. The approach here was well captured by Thorpe LJ in *Xydhias* v. *Xydhias* [1999] 1 FLR 683, 692:

> 'If there is a dispute as to whether the negotiations led to an accord that the process should be abbreviated, the court has a discretion in determining whether an accord was reached. In exercising that discretion the court should be astute to discern the antics of a litigant who, having consistently pressed for abbreviation, is seeking to resile and to justify his shift by reliance on some point of detail that was open for determination by the court at its abbreviated hearing.'

Moreover, in such a case the court, if need be of its own motion, can always, by the appropriately robust use of its case management powers, limit the ambit of the issues to be considered at the hearing; for example, as was done in both *Crossley* v. *Crossley* [2007] EWCA Civ 1491, [2008] 1 FLR 1467, and *S* v. *S (Ancillary Relief)* [2008] EWHC 2038 (Fam), [2009] 1 FLR 254, by focusing the hearing exclusively on those issues relevant to the magnetic factor(s).

15. Back of all this there is the increasing emphasis on autonomy exemplified by cases such as *MacLeod* v. *MacLeod* [2008] UKPC 64, [2010] 1 AC 298, and *Radmacher (formerly Granatino)* v. *Granatino* [2010] UKSC 42, [2011] 1 AC 534. As Lord Phillips PSC said in *Radmacher*, para.78:

> 'The reason why the court should give weight to a nuptial agreement is that there should be respect for individual autonomy. The court should accord respect to the decision of a married

couple as to the manner in which their financial affairs should be regulated. It would be paternalistic and patronising to override their agreement simply on the basis that the court knows best. This is particularly true where the parties' agreement addresses existing circumstances and not merely the contingencies of an uncertain future.'

I draw attention in the present context to the last sentence. I would accordingly respectfully endorse what was said by Charles J in *V* v. *V (Prenuptial Agreement)* [2011] EWHC 3230 (Fam), [2012] 1 FLR 1315, para.36:

> '[*Radmacher*] necessitates a significant change to the approach to be adopted, on a proper application of the discretion conferred by the MCA, to the impact of agreements between the parties in respect of their finances. At the heart of that significant change, is the need to recognise the weight that should now be given to autonomy, and thus to the choices made by the parties to a marriage ... The new respect to be given to individual autonomy means that the fact of an agreement can alter what is a fair result and so found a different award to the one that would otherwise have been made.'

The future

16. What, then, should be the approach in cases where there has been an arbitration award under the IFLA Scheme or something similar?

17. Two situations need to be considered: one where the parties come before the court seeking a consent order; the other where one or other party is seeking to resile from the arbitrator's award. In the present case I am, strictly speaking, concerned only with the first, but some provisional comments on the other may be helpful and not out of place.

18. The starting point in every case, as it seems to me, is that identified in characteristically arresting language by Sir Peter Singer in 'Arbitration in Family Financial Proceedings: the IFLA Scheme: Part 2' [2012] Fam Law 1496, 1503:

> 'I suggest that the "magnetic factor" perspective provides an appropriate analogy, and illuminates how applications (whether or not by consent) for orders to reflect an IFLA award should be viewed by the court: through the wrong end of a telescope rather than through a wide-angle lens. Such an approach respects the court's jurisdiction, but gives full force and effect to party autonomy by treating the parties' agreement to be bound by the award as the magnetic factor which should lead to a reflective order. Thus an arbitral award founded on the parties' clear agreement in their Form ARB1 to be bound by the award should be treated as a lodestone (more then than just a yardstick) pointing the path to court approval.'

19. While respectfully questioning whether it can ever be appropriate for a judge to look through the *wrong* end of a telescope, I agree with that approach. Where the parties have bound themselves, as by signing a Form ARB1, to accept an arbitral award of the kind provided for by the IFLA Scheme, this generates, as it seems to me, a single magnetic factor of determinative importance. As Sir Peter Singer said ([2012] Fam Law 1496, 1503):

> 'The autonomous decision of the parties to submit to arbitration should be seen as a "magnetic factor" akin to the pre-nuptial agreement in *Crossley* v. *Crossley*'.

I agree. This, after all, reflects the approach spelt out by the Supreme Court in *Radmacher* in the passages I have already quoted. In the absence of some very compelling countervailing factor(s), the arbitral award should be determinative of the order the court makes. Sir Peter had earlier suggested (1502) that:

> 'The scope for backsliding, resiling and indeed any space for repentance should ... be just as narrowly confined [as it was in *L* v. *L* [2006] EWHC 956 (Fam), [2008] 1 FLR 26] where what is in question is an attempt to wriggle out of the binding effect of an arbitral award.'

Again, I agree. There is no conceptual difference between the parties making an agreement and agreeing to give an arbitrator the power to make the decision for them. Indeed, an arbitral award is surely of its nature even stronger than a simple agreement between the parties.

20. It is worth remembering what the function of the judge is when invited to make a consent order in a financial remedy case. It is a topic I considered at some length in *L* v. *L* [2006] EWHC 956 (Fam), [2008] 1 FLR 26. I concluded (para.73) that:

> 'the judge is not a rubber stamp. He is entitled but is not obliged to play the detective. He is a watchdog, but he is not a bloodhound or a ferret.'

21. Where the consent order which the judge is being asked to approve is founded on an arbitral award under the IFLA Scheme or something similar (and the judge will, of course, need to check that the order does indeed give effect to the arbitral award and is workable) the judge's role will be simple. The judge will not need to play the detective unless something leaps off the page to indicate that something has gone so seriously wrong in the arbitral process as fundamentally to vitiate the arbitral award. Although recognising that the judge is not a rubber stamp, the combination of (a) the fact that the parties have agreed to be bound by the arbitral award, (b) the fact of the arbitral award (which the judge will of course be able to study) and (c) the fact that the parties are putting the matter before the court *by consent*, means that it can only be in the rarest of cases that it will be appropriate for the judge to do other than approve the order. With a process as sophisticated as that embodied in the IFLA Scheme it is difficult to contemplate such a case.

22. These are the principles that I have applied in the present case in deciding whether or not to approve the consent order. I do not propose to go into the details – why, after all, in a case like this should litigants who have chosen the private process of arbitration have their affairs exposed in a public judgment? Suffice it to say that I have no hesitation in approving the consent order in the form in which it has been put before me.

23. I should add that I can see no reason why the streamlined process applied by Coleridge J in *S v. P (Settlement by Collaborative Law Process)* [2008] 2 FLR 2040 in the context of a consent order which was the product of the collaborative law process should not be made similarly available in cases where the consent order is the product of an arbitral award under the IFLA Scheme or something similar. From now on, if they wish, parties should be able to avail themselves of that process[1] whether the consent order is the product of the collaborative law process or an arbitral award under the IFLA Scheme or something similar.

24. I add two points in relation to procedure. The first is that in every case the parties should, as they did here, lodge with the court both the agreed submission to arbitration (in the case of an arbitration in accordance with the IFLA Scheme, the completed Form ARB1) and the arbitrator's award. Second, the order should contain recitals to the following effect, suitably adapted to meet the circumstances:

> 'The documents lodged in relation to this application include the parties' arbitration agreement (Form ARB1), their Form(s) D81, a copy of the arbitrator's award, and a draft of the order which the court is requested to make.
>
> By their Form ARB1 the parties agreed to refer to arbitration the issues described in it which encompass some or all of the financial remedies for which applications are pending in this court; and the parties have invited the court to make an order in agreed terms which reflects the arbitrator's award.'

25. Where a party seeks to resile from the arbitral award, the other party's remedy is to apply to the court using the 'notice to show cause' procedure. The court will no doubt adopt an appropriately robust approach, both to the procedure it adopts in dealing with such a challenge and to the test it applies in deciding the outcome. In accordance with the reasoning in cases such as *Xydhias v. Xydhias*, the parties will almost invariably forfeit the right to anything other than a most abbreviated hearing; only in highly exceptional circumstances is the court likely to permit anything more than a very abbreviated hearing.

26. Where the attempt to resile is plainly lacking in merit the court may take the view that the appropriate remedy is to proceed without more ado summarily to make an order reflecting the award and, if needs be, providing for its enforcement. Even if there is a need for a somewhat more elaborate hearing, the court will be appropriately robust in defining the issues which are properly in dispute and confining the parties to a hearing which is short and focused. In most such cases the focus is likely to be on whether the party seeking to resile is able to make good

---

[1] The process is described in the headnote to the report as follows: 'This application for approval of draft consent orders could be dealt with [by a High Court judge] in the "urgent without notice" applications list, in order to shortcut the normal rather lengthier process of lodging consent orders ... and waiting for them to be approved and sent back ... The court would usually be prepared to entertain applications of this kind in the without notice applications list before the applications judge of the day on short notice. A full day's notice must be given to the clerk of the High Court judge in front of whom it was proposed to list the case; such notice could be given by telephone. The clerk of the rules should be informed that this was taking place. Use of the shortcut process was always subject to the consent of the urgent application judge. However, provided every aspect of documentation was agreed, the hearing was not expected to last more than 10 minutes, and the documentation was lodged with the judge the night before the hearing, this process had been approved by the President.'

one of the limited grounds of challenge or appeal permitted by the Arbitration Act 1996. *If* they can, then so be it. If on the other hand they can *not*, then it may well be that the court will again feel able to proceed without more ado to make an order reflecting the award and, if needs be, providing for its enforcement.

Concluding observations

27. I have already drawn attention to the fact that the IFLA Scheme requires the arbitrator to decide the dispute in accordance with the law of England and Wales. In this context it is important to remember the fundamental principles expounded by the House of Lords in *White* v. *White* [2001] 1 AC 596, 604–605, that in arriving at any financial order the objective must be to achieve a fair outcome and that, in seeking to achieve a fair outcome, there is no place for discrimination between husband and wife. My observations in this judgment are confined to an arbitral process such as we have in the IFLA Scheme. Different considerations may apply where an arbitral process is based on a different system of law or, in particular, where there is reason to believe that, whatever system of law is purportedly being applied, there may have been gender-based discrimination. The proper approach in that situation will have to be considered when such a case arises.

28. There is one final matter I must mention. New and emerging forms of alternative dispute resolution highlight the need for the court's processes to keep pace with the needs of litigants and their advisers, nowhere perhaps more so than where, as in this context, the mechanism for resolving a family financial dispute is arbitration conducted in accordance with the Arbitration Act 1996. For example, and no doubt there are other such matters, we need appropriate procedures to enable the Family Court, not the Commercial Court, to deal expeditiously (and if appropriate without the need for an oral hearing) with:

    (i)   applications for a stay of financial remedy proceedings pending the outcome of arbitration;
    (ii) applications seeking any relief or remedy under the Arbitration Act 1996, such as, for instance, under section 42 to enforce an arbitrator's peremptory order, or under section 43 to secure the attendance of witnesses.

29. Drafts of templates for such orders have been produced for consultation as part of the Family Orders Project being managed by Mostyn J. But alongside these innovations the need for procedural adaptation is becoming increasingly pressing. Whether such topics are most appropriately dealt with by rule changes (for example to the Family Procedure Rules 2010 and/or the Civil Procedure Rules 1998) or by the issue of Practice Directions or Practice Guidance is a matter for consideration. Initially, however, I would invite the Family Procedure Rules Committee to consider this as a matter of urgency.

4.2

DB v. *DLJ* [2016] EWHC 324 (Fam)[1]

Neutral Citation: [2016] EWHC 324 (Fam)

Case No: FD13D05331

IN THE HIGH COURT OF JUSTICE

FAMILY DIVISION

Royal Courts of Justice

Strand, London, WC2A 2LL

Date: 24 February 2016

Before:

MR JUSTICE MOSTYN

Between:

DB

Applicant

and

DLJ

Respondent

Martin Pointer QC and Jeni Kavanagh
(instructed by Kidd Rapinet LLP) for the applicant
Patrick Chamberlayne QC and Jacqueline Marks
(instructed by Blake Morgan LLP) for the respondent

Hearing date: 12 February 2016

Mr Justice Mostyn:

1. In this judgment I shall refer to the applicant as 'the husband' and to the respondent as 'the wife'.

2. This is my judgment on the husband's application dated 7 October 2015 that the wife do show cause why an arbitral award (as supplemented) made by Mr Gavin Smith dated 2 July 2015 should not be made an order of the court. The wife resists the application. She says that the award is vitiated by a mistake about the true value of the property in Portugal allocated to her. Alternatively, she says that events have occurred since the award which invalidate the finding made by the arbitrator as to the value of that property.

---

[1] This judgment was delivered in private. The judge has given leave for this version of the judgment to be published on condition that (irrespective of what is contained in the judgment) in any published version of the judgment the anonymity of the children and members of their family must be strictly preserved. All persons, including representatives of the media, must ensure that this condition is strictly complied with. Failure to do so will be a contempt of court.

Family arbitration

3. The arbitration procedure for family financial dispute resolution was launched by the Institute of Family Law Arbitrators in February 2012. A useful short guide (written by Gavin Smith and Sir Peter Singer) is to be found in Table 29 of At A Glance. It is described more fully by Sir Peter in 'Arbitration in Family Financial Proceedings: the IFLA Scheme' Part 1 [2012] Fam Law 1353 and Part 2 [2012] Fam Law 1496. A recent article explaining its undoubted merits and advantages written by Duncan Brooks appears in Resolution's 'The Review', Issue 180 at 32.

4. The scheme was intended to align the new family finance arbitration procedure as closely as possible with commercial arbitrations governed by the Arbitration Act 1996. Now divorcing couples were to be afforded the same advantages as had been made available to commercial people for over a century. Therefore, when parties agree to enter into arbitration they sign a document – ARB1 – which states that:

    'We, the parties to this application, whose details are set out below, apply to the Institute of Family Law Arbitrators Ltd for the nomination and appointment of a sole arbitrator from the Family Arbitration Panel to resolve the dispute referred to in paragraph 2 below by arbitration in accordance with the Arbitration Act 1996 ("the Act") and the rules of the Family Law Arbitration Scheme ("the scheme").'

5. Before I examine the differences, if any, that apply, or should apply, to a family arbitration I shall set out shortly the scope for challenging a commercial award governed exclusively by the 1996 Act.

6. In his excellent paper 'Challenges to Arbitral Awards at the Seat' given to the Mauritius International Arbitration Conference on 15 December 2014[2] Sir Bernard Eder explains at [6] that:

    '…the general approach of the Court is one which strongly supports the arbitral process. By way of anecdote, it is perhaps interesting to recall what I was once told many years ago by Michael Kerr, a former judge in the Court of Appeal and one of the leading figures in the recent development of the law of arbitration in England, when I was complaining about an arbitration that I had just lost and the difficulties in the way of challenging the award. I told him that the award was wrong and unjust. He looked baffled and said: "Remember, when parties agree arbitration they buy the right to get the wrong answer". So, the mere fact that an award is "wrong" or even "unjust" does not, of itself, provide any basis for challenging the award or intervention by the Court. Any challenge or appeal must bring itself under one or more of the three heads which I have identified.'

7. The grounds or heads of challenge are very circumscribed indeed. In addition to the three heads mentioned by Sir Bernard (to which I will turn below) there is the facility under section 57 to ask the arbitrator to correct his award. It is noteworthy that by virtue of section 57(1) the parties are free to agree on the powers of the tribunal to correct an award or make an additional award. As will be seen, in this case the parties agreed that certain matters could and should be corrected and clarified by the Tribunal. In the absence of agreement then by virtue of section 57(3) and (4) a party may apply to the arbitrator within 28 days of the award either (a) to correct an award so as to remove any clerical mistake or error arising from an accidental slip or omission or clarify or remove any ambiguity in the award; or (b) to make an additional award in respect of any claim (including a claim for interest or costs) which was presented to the tribunal but was not dealt with in the award.

8. This power is very limited. In *Ases Havacilik Servis Ve Destek Hizmetleri AS v Delkor UK Ltd* [2012] EWHC 3518 (Comm) Hamblen J (as he then was) stated at [21]:

    'Whilst the decision in *Craske v Norfolk CC* [1991] JPL 760 indicates that the power of the arbitrator under the slip rule contained in what is now s.57 of the 1996 Act (formerly s.17 of the Arbitration Act 1950) to correct errors in the award applies to errors which were attributable to the parties, as well as errors attributable to the tribunal, it also makes it clear that it does not extend to oversights or errors in production of evidence or argument before the arbitrator – see White Book 2012, Vol. 2, Note 2E-226 at page 648. S.57 does not apply to second thoughts, still less to second thoughts based on fresh evidence.'

9. An example of an arbitrator correcting an accidental slip or mistake is *Union Marine*

---

[2] www.judiciary.gov.uk/announcements/challenges-to-arbitral-awards-at-the-seat-december-2014

Classification Services LLC v *The Government of the Union of Comoros* [2015] EWHC 508 (Comm) where the arbitrator had, surprisingly, completely failed to deal with the Government of Comoros's counter-claim. The corrected award dealt with that and the challenge to such amended award was dismissed by Eder J. An application for leave to appeal against that decision was, I understand, recently dismissed by the Court of Appeal.

10. Aside from this limited corrective jurisdiction the only ways of contesting an award are by:

(i)   challenging an award of the arbitral tribunal as to its 'substantive jurisdiction' under s.67 of the 1996 Act; or

(ii) challenging an award on the ground of 'serious irregularity' under s.68 of the 1996 Act; or

(iii) an appeal to the Court on a 'question of law' arising out of an award made in the proceedings under s.69 of the 1996 Act.

By s.70, an applicant must first have exhausted all available arbitral processes of appeal and review. Further, any application or appeal must be brought within 28 days of the award.

11. There is a great deal of jurisprudence about these three heads and these are fully explained in Sir Bernard's paper. Challenges as to the tribunal's substantive jurisdiction go to the matters mentioned in section 30(1)(a)–(c) namely whether there is a valid arbitration agreement; or whether the tribunal is properly constituted; or what matters have been submitted to arbitration in accordance with the arbitration agreement. Serious irregularity is specified in nine sub-sections, viz:

(a) failure by the tribunal to comply with section 33 (general duty of tribunal to act fairly);

(b) the tribunal exceeding its powers (otherwise than by exceeding its substantive jurisdiction: see section 67);

(c) failure by the tribunal to conduct the proceedings in accordance with the procedure agreed by the parties;

(d) failure by the tribunal to deal with all the issues that were put to it;

(e) any arbitral or other institution or person vested by the parties with powers in relation to the proceedings or the award exceeding its powers;

(f) uncertainty or ambiguity as to the effect of the award;

(g) the award being obtained by fraud or the award or the way in which it was procured being contrary to public policy;

(h) failure to comply with the requirements as to the form of the award; or

(i) any irregularity in the conduct of the proceedings or in the award which is admitted by the tribunal or by any arbitral or other institution or person vested by the parties with powers in relation to the proceedings or the award.

I draw attention to (g) where, unsurprisingly, fraud is mentioned as a ground of serious irregularity entitling the court to set-aside an award.

12. An appeal on a question of law needs the leave of the court. Section 69(3) states that:

Leave to appeal shall be given only if the court is satisfied–

(a) that the determination of the question will substantially affect the rights of one or more of the parties,

(b) that the question is one which the tribunal was asked to determine,

(c) that, on the basis of the findings of fact in the award – (i) the decision of the tribunal on the question is obviously wrong, or (ii) the question is one of general public importance and the decision of the tribunal is at least open to serious doubt, and

(d) that, despite the agreement of the parties to resolve the matter by arbitration, it is just and proper in all the circumstances for the court to determine the question.

This is a stringent test indeed.

13. What amounts to 'a question of law' is, of course, capable of an expansive interpretation and might sweep up mixed questions of law and fact. However, in *Pioneer Shipping Ltd* v *BTP Tioxide Ltd (The Nema)* [1982] AC 724 leave to appeal was granted on the ground that an issue of frustration was a question of law. The decision of Goff J on the substantive appeal reversing the decision of the arbitrator that the charterparty in that case had been frustrated was set aside by the Court of Appeal, a decision upheld in the House of Lords, Lord Diplock proclaiming that leave to appeal ought never to have been granted and that the tide had turned in favour of finality as against 'meticulous legal accuracy'. Therefore, according to Sir Bernard

(at [40]) 'the result is that the Court will not generally give leave to appeal or substitute its own decision for that of the tribunal on points which might be said to involve a question of law (e.g., whether on the particular facts a party had wrongfully repudiated or renounced a contract) unless the Court decides that the arbitral tribunal had or might have misdirected itself in point of law'.

14. The traditional grounds for challenging a financial remedy award in family proceedings are mistake, fraud, non-disclosure and supervening event. Non-disclosure can be deliberate or innocent (see the recent decision of the Supreme Court in *Sharland* v *Sharland* [2015] UKSC 60, [2015] 3 WLR 1070 at [30]–[32]). Deliberate non-disclosure is a species of fraud. Innocent non-disclosure is a species of mistake (see below). Therefore, in essence, there are but three grounds of challenge in family proceedings, namely mistake, fraud and supervening event.

15. Fraud, of course, is a ground of challenge under section 68(2)(g), as has been seen. An alleged mistake can only be raised if it falls within section 57, and then will not extend to an error in production of evidence. The mistake alleged here would be impossible to raise in commercial arbitration proceedings. And a supervening event is completely impossible as a ground of challenge. In *The Nema* itself the arbitrator held that the award had been frustrated by the strike in Canada. He held that it would continue indefinitely. In fact it was settled a short time after the award but no-one suggested that that unexpected development could amount to a ground of appeal.

16. It can therefore be seen that when parties sign up to arbitration under the 1996 Act they 'buy' very limited rights of challenge. These rights do not extend to a challenge based on a mistake in the production of evidence or as a result of a supervening event. Mr Chamberlayne QC sought to argue that the wife could seek to argue a point of law under section 69, namely that the award had been frustrated by the later events, but this is impossible because (a) whether frustration has happened is in fact an un-appealable question of fact – see *The Nema*, and (b) the issue of law must relate to the facts as found by the tribunal – see section 69(3)(c).

17. However, I do not conclude that the door to relief is closed to the wife. This is because of certain important differences between the family and civil processes.

18. Following a civil arbitration the award is final and binding, unless the parties otherwise agree – see section 58(1) of the 1996 Act. It will amount to *res judicata* between the parties. One imagines that in the vast generality of cases no incorporating order will be sought from the court; rather, the parties will be content for their rights and obligations to speak from the award.

19. If a party does not comply with the award then it is open for the other party to apply under section 66 for enforcement by the court. Section 66(1) provides that 'an award made by the tribunal pursuant to an arbitration agreement may, by leave of the court, be enforced in the same manner as a judgment or order of the court to the same effect.' It might be thought that leave could be refused if the court thought that the award was wrong or unjust; but that would be a mistake. In *Middlemiss & Could* v *Hartlepool Corporation* [1972] 1 WLR 1643 Lord Denning MR stated at 1647:

> 'I would say that it is to be used in nearly all cases. Leave should be given to enforce the award as a judgment unless there is real ground for doubting the validity of the award.'

20. In contrast it is to be expected that in most family arbitration cases the parties will want an incorporating order. For example, the arbitrator may have awarded a clean break – that can only be achieved conclusively with a court order. The arbitrator may have awarded a pension share – again, that can only be achieved by a court order. It is trite law that where such an order is sought the court exercises an independent inquisitorial discretion. It is no rubber stamp: see *Jenkins* v *Livesey* [1985] AC 424.

21. In this case the terms of the form ARB1 signed by the parties stated:

> '5.4 We understand and agree that any award of the arbitrator appointed to determine this dispute will be final and binding on us, subject to the following:
> (a) any challenge to the award by any available arbitral process of appeal or review or in accordance with the provisions of Part 1 of the [1996] Act;

(b) insofar as the subject matter of the award requires it to be embodied in a court order (see 6.5 below (sic, recto 5.5)), any changes which the court making that order may require;

...

5.5 If and so far as the subject matter of the award makes it necessary, we will apply to an appropriate court for an order in the same or similar terms as the award all the relevant part of the award. ... We understand that the court has a discretion as to whether, and in what terms to make an order and we will take all reasonably necessary steps to see that such an order is made.'

22. It can therefore be seen that the parties have agreed in writing that challenges to an arbitral award would not be confined only to those available under the 1996 Act. In addition they specifically agreed that the court would retain an overriding discretion, and inferentially the parties agreed that they would each be enabled to argue that the court should not exercise its discretion to incorporate the award for reasons outwith those stated in the 1996 Act. In so doing they were agreeing, pursuant to section 58(1), an exception to the award being final and binding. In making such an agreement the parties were of course, doing no more than recognising what the general law already provided.

S v *S* and the Practice Guidance

23. I now need to refer to two important emanations from the President namely *S* v *S* *(Arbitral Award: Approval)* (Practice Note) [2014] 1 WLR 2299, and the Practice Guidance (Family Court: Interface with Arbitration) [2016] 1 WLR 59.

24. In *S* v *S* the President endorsed the 'notice to show cause' procedure, commonly used where a party is seeking to resile from an agreement, as the appropriate procedure where a party is seeking to resile from an arbitral award: see [25], and the Practice Guidance at [15].

25. The analogy with agreement cases was not merely procedural but was substantive. Thus he stated at [21]:

'Where the consent order which the judge is being asked to approve is founded on an arbitral award under the IFLA Scheme or something similar (and the judge will, of course, need to check that the order does indeed give effect to the arbitral award and is workable) the judge's role will be simple. The judge will not need to play the detective unless something leaps off the page to indicate that something has gone so seriously wrong in the arbitral process as fundamentally to vitiate the arbitral award. Although recognising that the judge is not a rubber stamp, the combination of (a) the fact that the parties have agreed to be bound by the arbitral award, (b) the fact of the arbitral award (which the judge will of course be able to study) and (c) the fact that the parties are putting the matter before the court by consent, means that it can only be in the rarest of cases that it will be appropriate for the judge to do other than approve the order. With a process as sophisticated as that embodied in the IFLA Scheme it is difficult to contemplate such a case.'

26. In fact his observations appear to suggest that it will be even more difficult for a party to resile from an arbitral award than from a negotiated agreement. At [26] he said:

'Where the attempt to resile is plainly lacking in merit the court may take the view that the appropriate remedy is to proceed without more ado summarily to make an order reflecting the award and, if needs be, providing for its enforcement. Even if there is a need for a somewhat more elaborate hearing, the court will be appropriately robust in defining the issues which are properly in dispute and confining the parties to a hearing which is short and focused. In most such cases the focus is likely to be on whether the party seeking to resile is able to make good one of the limited grounds of challenge or appeal permitted by the Arbitration Act 1996. If they can, then so be it. If on the other hand they cannot, then it may well be that the court will again feel able to proceed without more ado to make an order reflecting the award and, if needs be, providing for its enforcement.'

27. This would appear to suggest that the Family Court could only refuse to make the order if a challenge or appeal under the 1996 Act could be made out. I would not go that far, as this would appear to rule out a challenge on the ground of a vitiating mistake or a supervening event. If a challenge were to be made out on one or other such ground it would in my judgment be a plainly wrong exercise of discretion for the court to incorporate an award nonetheless. I agree with Mr Chamberlayne QC in this regard. However, I do agree with Mr Pointer QC that when exercising its discretion following an arbitral award the court should adopt an approach of great stringency, even more so than it would in an agreement case. In opting for arbitration the parties have agreed a specific form of alternative dispute resolution and it is important that

they understand that in the overwhelming majority of cases the dispute will end with the arbitral award. It would be the worst of all worlds if parties thought that the arbitral process was to be no more than a dry run and that a rehearing in court was readily available. Thus in the Practice Guidance at [12] the President stated:

> 'Attention is drawn to my observations in *S v S (Arbitral Award: Approval)* (Practice Note) [2014] 1 WLR 2299, para.21 about the attitude likely to be adopted by the court in such cases: "[where] the parties are putting the matter before the court by consent ... it can only be in the rarest of cases that it will be appropriate for the judge to do other than approve the order".'

In *Fage UK Ltd & Anor v Chobani UK Ltd & Anor* [2014] EWCA Civ 5, in the context of an appeal against a finding of fact, Lewison LJ stated at [114(ii)] 'the trial is not a dress rehearsal. It is the first and last night of the show.' Even more so, in my opinion, where the first instance decision is an arbitral award.

28. My conclusion is this. If following an arbitral award evidence emerges which would, if the award had been in an order of the court entitle the court to set aside its order on the grounds of mistake or supervening event, then the court is entitled to refuse to incorporate the arbitral award in its order and instead to make a different order reflecting the new evidence. Outside the heads of correction, challenge or appeal within the 1996 Act these are, in my judgment, the only realistically available grounds of resistance to an incorporating order. An assertion that the award was 'wrong' or 'unjust' will almost never get off the ground: in such a case the error must be so blatant and extreme that it leaps off the page.

29. In my opinion ARB1 should be modified to make this clear.

30. I now turn to consider the law relating to invalidating supervening events and mistake in financial remedy proceedings.

Barder: supervening events

31. In *Barder v Barder (Caluori intervening)* [1988] AC 20, the House of Lords stipulated the test that must be met before a set-aside could be granted. It has four conditions:

(i) New events have occurred since the making of the order invalidating the basis, or fundamental assumption, upon which the order was made.

(ii) The new events should have occurred within a relatively short time of the order having been made. It is extremely unlikely that could be as much as a year, and in most cases it will be no more than a few months.

(iii) The application to set aside should be made reasonably promptly in the circumstances of the case.

(iv) The application if granted should not prejudice third parties who have, in good faith and for valuable consideration, acquired interests in property which is the subject matter of the relevant order.

32. In *Cornick v Cornick* [1994] 2 FLR 530 at 537 Hale J explained that 'for the *Barder* principle to apply, it is a *sine qua non* that the event was unforeseen and unforeseeable.' Obviously, if the parties had actually foreseen a later event then it would not be unforeseeable. So, the question is usually confined to an analysis of (un)foreseeability. I agree with Hale J that the new or later event must have been unforeseeable. If relief were granted on the basis of the arrival of a foreseeable event then that would amount to exercising a disguised power of variation on proof of a mere change of circumstances, where Parliament has specifically declined to enact such a power.

33. In *Richardson v Richardson* [2011] EWCA 79, [2011] 2 FLR 244 Thorpe LJ emphasised that the jurisdiction is highly exceptional. At [86] he stated 'cases in which a *Barder* event ... can be successfully argued are extremely rare, should be regarded by the specialist profession as exceedingly rare, and should not be thought to be extendable by ingenuity or the lowering of the judicially created bar.' Earlier in *Walkden v Walkden* [2010] 1 FLR 174 Elias LJ had stated at [80]: 'given the importance attached to finality in settlements of this nature, the circumstances must be truly exceptional before a capital settlement can be re-opened.'

34. Even where the four conditions have been met it lies within the discretion of the court whether to grant the set-aside. A set-aside would be unlikely to be granted if alternative mainstream relief could be granted which broadly remedied the unfairness caused by the later event.

35.   The test for *Barder* relief, as propounded by the House of Lords, is a question of law. Whether it is satisfied is a question of fact. A finding that a later event was, or was not, foreseeable is an inference drawn from primary facts. Hitherto, every case where *Barder* relief has been granted is an appellate decision. Lord Brandon's speech is cast in the language and procedure of an appeal. So it is important to remember that every decision made by the Court of Appeal in the field since that seminal decision is a fact-finding decision. Certainly, the legal test has been explained in the appellate decisions, but none has sought to alter it. But occasionally the fact-finding exercise seems to have been driven more by considerations of the underlying merits than a faithful application of the question of law. The old cases of *Barber* v *Barber* [1993] 1 FLR 476 and *Heard* v *Heard* [1995] 1 FLR 970 and the recent case of *Critchell* v *Critchell* [2015] EWCA Civ 436 may be examples of this.

Unforeseeable

36.   I turn to the question of (un)foreseeability. Before I consider the *Barder* cases on this topic I allow myself a short excursion into this area as it arises in the civil sphere. Whether an event was reasonably foreseeable is a key question in deciding whether damages are recoverable in an action for negligence for breach of contract, negligence or nuisance, or whether they are too remote and therefore irrecoverable. The question is not whether a future event is literally incapable of being imagined. The capacity of homo sapiens to imagine fictive things is vast. The question is posed by the court standing retrospectively in the shoes of the actors and asking itself whether the then future, but by now past, event could reasonably have been predicted. The answer is generally given by linguistic tropes rather than by numeric assessments of future probability. The use of language rather than numbers led Lord Denning MR to say that he was swimming in a sea of semantics. In *Parsons (H) (Livestock) Ltd* v *Uttley Ingham & Co Ltd* [1978] QB 791 he stated at 801–802:

> 'Remoteness of damage is beyond doubt a question of law. In *C. Czarnikow Ltd.* v. *Koufos (The Heron II)* [1969] 1 AC 350 the House of Lords said that, in remoteness of damage, there is a difference between contract and tort. In the case of a breach of contract, the court has to consider whether the consequences were of such a kind that a reasonable man, at the time of making the contract, would contemplate them as being of a very substantial degree of probability. (In the House of Lords various expressions were used to describe this degree of probability, such as, not merely "on the cards" because that may be too low: but as being "not unlikely to occur" (see pp.383 and 388); or "likely to result or at least not unlikely to result" (see p.406); or "liable to result" (see p.410); or that there was a "real danger" or "serious possibility" of them occurring (see p.415).)
>   In the case of a tort, the court has to consider whether the consequences were of such a kind that a reasonable man, at the time of the tort committed, would foresee them as being of a much lower degree of probability. (In the House of Lords various expressions were used to describe this, such as, it is sufficient if the consequences are "liable to happen in the most unusual case" (see p.385); or in a "very improbable" case (see p.389); or that "they may happen as a result of the breach, however unlikely it may be, unless it can be brushed aside as far-fetched" (see p.422).)
>   I find it difficult to apply those principles universally to all cases of contract or to all cases of tort: and to draw a distinction between what a man "contemplates" and what he "foresees." I soon begin to get out of my depth. I cannot swim in this sea of semantic exercises – to say nothing of the different degrees of probability – especially when the cause of action can be laid either in contract or in tort. I am swept under by the conflicting currents. ...'

37.   I too found myself drowning when reading the old authorities. However, in *The Heron II* Lord Reid did set out what is to my mind a most helpful odds-based analysis. At 390 he stated:

> 'It has never been held to be sufficient in contract that the loss was foreseeable as "a serious possibility" or "a real danger" or as being "on the cards." It is on the cards that one can win £100,000 or more for a stake of a few pence – several people have done that. And anyone who backs a hundred to one chance regards a win as a serious possibility – many people have won on such a chance. And the *Wagon Mound (No. 2)* could not have been decided as it was unless the extremely unlikely fire should have been foreseen by the ship's officer as a real danger. It appears to me that in the ordinary use of language there is a wide gulf between saying that some event is not unlikely or quite likely to happen and saying merely that it is a serious possibility, a real danger, or on the cards. Suppose one takes a well-shuffled pack of cards, it is quite likely or not unlikely that the top card will prove to be a diamond: the odds are only 3 to 1 against. But most people would not say that it is quite likely to be the nine of diamonds for the odds are then

51 to 1 against. On the other hand I think that most people would say that there is a serious possibility or a real danger of its being turned up first and of course it is on the cards.'

38. Lord Reid is in effect saying here that in his opinion a probability of $P = 0.25$ would satisfy the test of reasonable foreseeability but a probability of $P = 0.02$ would not, although I acknowledge that he had earlier stated at 388 that 'it is hardly ever possible in this matter to assess probabilities with any degree of mathematical accuracy.' Thus, the test is now linguistically expressed as saying that a wrongdoer is responsible for damage which should have been foreseen by a reasonable person as being something of which there was a real risk, even though the risk would actually occur only in rare circumstances, unless the risk was so small that the reasonable person would feel justified in neglecting it or brushing it aside as far-fetched.

39. Although the numeric approach is generally eschewed one can confidently say that for damage to be held to be unforeseeable and therefore too remote the probability of it eventuating must be very low indeed (probably $P < 0.05$, I would guess). It is worth reflecting on the *Wagon Mound (No. 2)* [1967] 1 AC 617. The findings of Walsh J about the bunkering oil spilled from the *Wagon Mound* into Sydney harbour were:

'(1) Reasonable people in the position of the officers of the *Wagon Mound* would regard the furnace oil as very difficult to ignite upon water. (2) Their personal experience would probably have been that this had very rarely happened. (3) If they had given attention to the risk of fire from the spillage, they would have regarded it as a possibility, but one which could become an actuality only in very exceptional circumstances. (4) They would have considered the chances of the required exceptional circumstances happening whilst the oil remained spread on the harbour waters as being remote. (5) I find that the occurrence of damage to the plaintiff's property as a result of the spillage was not reasonably foreseeable by those for whose acts the defendant would be responsible.'

40. The Privy Council overturned finding No. 5. The risk may have been very small indeed but it was not such that a reasonable man would brush it aside as far-fetched. This points up just how unlikely a future event must be before it can be classed as 'unforeseeable'.

41. These civil cases are very important. In *Richardson v Richardson* at [53], Munby LJ stated that 'the Family Division is part of the High Court. It is not some legal Alsatia where the common law and equity do not apply.' Similarly, in *Prest v Petrodel Resources Ltd & Ors* [2013] UKSC 34, [2013] 2 AC 415 Lord Sumption at [37] said that 'Courts exercising family jurisdiction do not occupy a desert island in which general legal concepts are suspended or mean something different.' In my opinion 'unforeseeable' cannot mean one thing in the Queen's Bench Division and another in the Family Division.

42. And so I turn to some of the *Barder* cases and their treatment of the question of the (un)foreseeability of the later event. The first group of cases concern the death of an actor shortly after the order was made. *Barder* itself was just such a case. Shortly after the order the wife murdered the children and killed herself. Although the press reports a handful of such tragic cases each year the probability of such a thing happening must have been tiny. In terms of probability this was far more remote than drawing the nine of diamonds.

43. In *Barber v Barber* [1993] 1 FLR 476 the wife, aged 41, suffered from severe liver disease. The evidence was to the effect that there was a 'reasonable hope' that she would live for at least five years. In fact, she died within three months. The report of the judgment of Glidewell LJ does not show that he considered the question of the (un)foreseeability of a death of that ill woman within three months rather than five years. A similar criticism can be made of the factual findings in *Smith v Smith* [1991] 2 FLR 432 where the husband, aged 62, committed suicide shortly after the order. Nothing was said about the likelihood or otherwise of this later event, although inferentially the Court of Appeal appeared to accept that it came out of a clear blue sky. An even more surprising decision is *Critchell v Critchell* [2015] EWCA Civ 436 where the later event was the death of the husband's father shortly after the order and the consequential inheritance by the husband of a sum of money of around £100,000. The report does not state the age of the father, but the inference is that he was elderly. The finding of the circuit judge was that the death of the father was 'completely unforeseen'; that may have been so, but nothing was said about the requirement that it must have been unforeseeable. That crucial requirement is not mentioned in the judgment of Black LJ. It is very hard to see how this later event could have been found to be unforeseeable. Benjamin Franklin famously said that in this

world nothing can be said to be certain, except death and taxes. The death of an elderly man surely cannot be regarded as anything other than foreseeable and unremarkable.

44.   In contrast is the recent decision of Moor J in *WA* v *Executors of the Estate of HA & Ors* [2015] EWHC 2233 (Fam). There the husband committed suicide 22 days after the order which secured for him a substantial award. Moor J very carefully considered the available evidence concerning the husband's psychological condition but reached the clear conclusion that the death was not foreseeable. It is true that he did not have the civil authorities put before him, and one can speculate whether he may have reached a different decision had they been, but what cannot be disputed is that the court made a thorough examination, on the available evidence, of the central question of whether the death was foreseeable or not.

45.   In that case Moor J followed *Reid* v *Reid* [2004] 1 FLR 736 where the wife was aged 74 and had disclosed that she was registered blind, had high blood pressure, high cholesterol and was diabetic. She died two months after the date of the order. Wilson J found that her death was not foreseeable. At [20] he held that 'notwithstanding the possibility of death at any time, there was no material which should have placed the wife's death 2 months later into the minds of the parties as being a significant, i.e. more than a theoretical, possibility.' Again, I find myself in difficulty in squaring this decision with the civil authorities to which I have referred.

46.   In contrast are a number of cases where a death was not found to be a *Barder* event. I need only cite *Richardson* v *Richardson* where the wife, then aged 70, died 3 months after the order. Munby LJ held that this was not a *Barder* event as the death did not invalidate the order. The wife had earned her share; her award was not based on needs. Although Munby LJ referred to the death as being 'unexpected' he did not discuss whether it was technically 'unforeseeable'.

47.   The next group of cases concern those where at the time of the order a thing is known and assumed but in fact later eventuates to an extent that was not expected. These are the 'known unknown' cases, to use the celebrated language of Secretary Rumsfeld. Plainly it is very difficult to satisfy the test of unforeseeability in such a case.

48.   In *Walkden* v *Walkden* the wife sought to plead as a *Barder* event the fact that certain shares had subsequently been sold by the husband at a substantially higher value than, she said, had been anticipated. At [53] Thorpe LJ held that 'it could not possibly be said that the sale of the husband's shares was either unforeseen or unforeseeable'. At [89] Elias LJ held that 'it was plainly foreseeable that an asset of this nature might fluctuate dramatically.'

49.   The cases were all analysed in *Richardson* by Munby LJ. In that case there was a pending negligence action against the parties' partnership; the parties assumed that it was covered by insurance. It later transpired that the claim could be for £3m whereas cover was only for £2m. Moreover, the insurers had, after the order, avoided the policy. The former development was not a *Barder* event; neither was the latter, but it was a vitiating mistake. The avoidance of the policy was not foreseeable. The extent of the claim and the limit of the cover (before avoidance) was not even a later foreseeable event. It was a known unknown, and the husband with due diligence could have established the true facts. At [37] Munby LJ stated:

> 'The reality is that the husband, to adopt Sir Stephen Brown's words, knew "the essential facts" and by the exercise of due diligence could – would – have discovered the limit of the insurance cover. He has only himself to blame for the fact that he did not take these obvious steps. Faced with a known unknown he chose to proceed without further inquiry or investigation. He cannot now be heard to say that he was mistaken. There was no vitiating mistake he can rely upon. And just as in *Walkden* v *Walkden*, he cannot be heard to say that his discovery of the true position in relation to the limit of cover amounted to a new or *Barder* event. It quite plainly was not. In this case as in that the reasons which deny him relief under the one head serve equally to deny him relief under the other. But the reality is that this was simply not, and never could have been, a *Barder* event. The "problem" – the limit of the indemnity under the policy – had been there all along. Its belated discovery by the husband was not a new event; it reflected no more than his failure at the proper time to ask obvious questions about the existing state of affairs. In this case, as in both *Judge* v *Judge* and *Walkden* v *Walkden*, the husband either succeeds in mistake or not at all. For the reasons I have given he has no claim based on mistake; and that is the end of it.'

Mistake

50. The practice of framing what is in fact a case of mistake as a *Barder* event can be traced back to *Thompson* v *Thompson* [1991] 2 FLR 530. In *Cornick* v *Cornick* [1994] 2 FLR 530 Hale J, when setting out her famous categorisation at 535E, described the situation where:

> '(2) A wrong value was put upon that asset at the hearing, which had it been known about at the time would have led to a different order. Provided that it is not the fault of the person alleging the mistake, it is open to the court to give leave for the matter to be reopened. Although falling within the *Barder* principle it is more akin to the misrepresentation or non-disclosure cases than to *Barder* itself.'

51. In *Judge* v *Judge* [2008] EWCA Civ 1458, [2009] 1 FLR 1287 Wilson LJ at [3] explained that a case of a vitiating mistake (i.e. Hale J's category No. 2) does not fall within the *Barder* principles. In that case, five years after the order, the wife discovered that a tax debt which had been assumed in the proceedings to amount to about £14m had in fact eventuated at a mere £600,000. She sought to set the order aside on the ground of a vitiating mistake, alternatively on the ground of non-disclosure. Both grounds failed. As to mistake Wilson LJ at [43] stated:

> 'A judge's compilation of a balance sheet, usually necessary in order to enable him to address what is now the principle of equality, often requires him to confer a spurious specificity on the value of assets, or on the size of liabilities, in relation to which, on the evidence before him, he can reach no confident conclusion: his balance sheet demands figures so he inserts into it the figures which he considers to be the most probable or, more accurately, the least improbable. There is no evidence which enables us to override the judge's conclusion that he made no mistake in 2001 in that a liability of £600,000 fell within the spectrum of recognised outcomes. In his judgment in 2001 he expressly referred to the need to gaze into a crystal ball.'

52. In *Walkden* Elias LJ said this about the mistake ground at [83]:

> 'The second category of case arises where the settlement is reached on the basis of a false evaluation. That may be as a result of a mistake, or some misrepresentation or non-disclosure, innocent or fraudulent. The parties (and/or the judge) reaches a view on the value of the asset in the course of agreeing or fixing an appropriate settlement, or confirming a settlement, which would have been different had the full facts been known at the material time. In this category of case it is contended that the order reflecting the settlement should be set aside because it was not correct when made. The applicable legal principles are very different to those in the *Barder* case. For misrepresentation they are the principles enunciated by the House of Lords in *Jenkins* v *Livesey (Formerly Jenkins)* [1985] AC 424, [1985] 2 WLR 47, [1985] FLR 813. This second category involves no supervening event at all. The settlement is reopened because it was not sound when made; had the judge been in possession of the material facts he would have made an order for a different settlement. In *Cornick* Hale J placed mistake cases (but not misrepresentation or non-disclosure) into the first category. However, as Wilson LJ pointed out in *Judge* v *Judge* [2008] EWCA Civ 1458, [2009] 1 FLR 1287 para.[3], it does not properly fit into that category. That is because it does not rely upon new or supervening events at all.'

53. In *Richardson* the court classed the avoidance of the policy as a vitiating mistake. At the time that judgment was given in that case the insurers were considering whether to avoid the policy but had not reached a decision, let alone announced it. At [80]–[83] Rimer LJ stated:

> '80. Munby LJ explains, and I agree, why down to the delivery by His Honour Judge Raynor QC of his judgment on 25 September 2009 neither the husband nor the wife had actual or other relevant knowledge that there was a risk that the insurers might avoid the policy. That risk was, therefore, not something to which either could or should have disclosed to the court. What instead happened was that the trial proceeded down to judgment on the tacit assumption of both parties that the policy was an asset in the nature of an unflawed chose in action that would, if necessary, give the parties the benefit of an indemnity against any liability in the child's damages claim up to the limit of the cover.
>
> 81. In fact, the policy was not an unflawed chose in action, because at the time of the trial the insurers were already considering whether to avoid it. Had the parties known that, they would or should have disclosed it to the court and it is probable that His Honour Judge Raynor's order would have been adjusted (perhaps by the inclusion of some contingent provision) to cater for the risk that the policy would be successfully avoided.
>
> 82. In the event, and following His Honour Judge Raynor's order, the insurers have claimed to avoid the policy. That event has falsified the tacit assumption upon which the parties proceeded before His Honour Judge Raynor. In my view, it is analogous to the type of event that Hale J (as she then was) identified in *Cornick* v *Cornick* [1994] 2 FLR 530, at 536F, example (2), and

which, in *Judge* v *Judge* [2008] EWCA Civ 1458, [2009] 1 FLR 1287, at para.[3], Wilson LJ explained would nowadays be regarded not as a *Barder* event but as "vitiating mistake".'

54. As I see it, the crucial distinction between a mistake case and a true *Barder* case is that in the former the relevant facts will exist at the time of the order, but will be unknown; while in the latter, the relevant facts will arise after the order. One might think that in *Richardson* the relevant fact was the announcement on 18 December 2009, after the order, by the insurer that the policy would be avoided, so that the case was in true *Barder* territory. But, according to Rimer LJ (and somewhat to my surprise) the true relevant and unknown fact was that at the time of the judgment on 25 September 2009 the insurers were considering avoiding the policy even if they had not by then decided to do so, let alone announced a decision. That was an 'unknown unknown'.

55. Where a case of mistake, as opposed to supervening event, is being advanced the question of the ability of the claimant by exercising due diligence to have discovered the true facts is critically important. In this regard the burden will be on him to show that he could not have discovered the true state of affairs.

56. The recasting of Hale J's second category of case as a case of mistake rather than one falling within the *Barder* principles is relatively novel. I take it that the third and fourth *Barder* conditions will continue to apply. The first will not apply because there will not be any new event at all. The second is more problematic although I observe that in *Judge* no-one suggested that the five year passage of time of itself defeated the claim. Questions of foreseeability just do not arise.

57. Therefore I think that applicable principles in relation to the mistake ground can be formulated as follows:

    (i) The court may set aside an order on the ground that the true facts on which it based its disposition were not known by either the parties or the court at the time the order was made.

    (ii) The claimant must show that the true facts would have led the court to have made a materially different order from the one it in fact made.

    (iii) The absence of the true facts must not have been the fault of the claimant.

    (iv) The claimant must show, on the balance of probabilities, that he could not with due diligence have established the true facts at the time the order was made.

    (v) The application to set aside should be made reasonably promptly in the circumstances of the case.

    (vi) The claimant must show that he cannot obtain alternative mainstream relief which has the effect of broadly remedying the injustice caused by the absence of the true facts.

    (vii) The application if granted should not prejudice third parties who have, in good faith and for valuable consideration, acquired interests in property which is the subject matter of the relevant order.

This case

58. This was a second marriage for each of the parties. Both parties have children by their first marriages; they are now adult. The parties were married on 24 July 1999. They have a daughter who was born on 26 January 2005. They separated in November 2013. Both parties and their daughter are based in Portugal. The wife commenced divorce proceedings on 31 October 2013. Decree Nisi was pronounced on 16 April 2014; it has not yet been made absolute. (I am asked to grant the husband permission to make the decree absolute.) The wife commenced her claim for financial remedies on 10 January 2014. The parties signed ARB1 on 16 January 2015. The financial remedy proceedings were stayed to allow the arbitration to proceed.

59. Gavin Smith heard evidence on 27, 28 and 29 April 2015. Final submissions were made on 15 May 2015. Mr Smith circulated his award in draft on 2 June 2015. He invited submissions as to corrections and clarifications. These were duly supplied and on 2 July 2015 he promulgated his award and a supplemental award. I shall refer to the two awards collectively as 'the award'.

60. The award was a thorough, conscientious and clear piece of work. Its quality is a testament to

the merit of opting for arbitration. Mr Smith decided that the parties' property and cash should be shared equally. In order to achieve equality this required the husband to pay a lump sum of £158,142. This has been paid. Mr Smith decided that the pensions should be shared equally. This would require a court order. He decided that the husband's business (in which he was a 70% shareholder) should be shared 60:40 to reflect the fact that it was well established at the time that the parties commenced their relationship. The wife would receive her 40% share on the sale by the husband of his shareholding in the business. No end date was provided for that, so the wife might have to wait a long time before she received that further payment, and of course the actual amount could only be speculated about. Pending payment the wife was to receive periodical payments of £36,000 a year. Those would end when she received her payment from the business. The periodical payments were specifically made extendable, as the arbitrator could not foresee whether at the point of payment of her share of the business the wife could adjust without undue hardship to termination. Therefore, it was open to the wife to apply for an extension if she perceived that her payment from the business would not represent an adequate replacement for her loss of periodical payments. In fact, she has already applied for just such an extension.

61.   The effect of the arbitrator's award was as follows:

	Husband	Wife
Property and cash	409,866	409,866
Pensions	274,709	274,709
Business	741,420	494,280
	1,425,995	1,178,855
	55%	45%

The business valuation was, of course, the present value. The property and cash figures were after the payment of the lump sum. Within the wife's figure for property and cash was the value of her home in Portugal. The arbitrator referred to that property as QP, and I shall do likewise. The net figure for QP taken by the arbitrator was £375,797. The wife says that the correct figure at the time of the award was in fact £152,306, a fall of £223,491. Therefore there is a vitiating mistake. Alternatively, she says that by virtue of later events the value has fallen to £152,306, and this fall invalidates the basis of the award. Mr Chamberlayne QC says that the fall of £223,491 has 'devastated' and 'decimated' her financial position.

62.   If the wife's new figure for the value of QP is right, and if the award is not disturbed by me, then the effect is as follows:

	Husband	Wife
Property and cash	409,866	186,375
Pensions	274,709	274,709
Business	741,420	494,280
	1,425,995	955,364
	60%	40%

If the award is modified by me so that the new value of QP is used, but the arbitrator's technique otherwise maintained, then the figures become:

	Husband	Wife
Property and cash	298,121	298,121
Pensions	274,709	274,709
Business	741,420	494,280
	1,314,250	1,067,110
	55%	45%

Thus, based on her new figures, the wife seeks an additional lump sum award of £111,746 (£298,121–£186,375). It is worth reflecting, in the context of the overarching requirement of exceptionality, that the wife's ambition is to recover a further £111,746 out of a total pool of assets (on her new figures) of £2,381,360.

63.   I have seen a transcript of the wife's evidence to Mr Smith. Under cross-examination she stated she wished to keep QP and to will it to her children eventually. She stated:

> '…it belonged to me in my previous marriage and my first husband and the children have spent a great deal of time there. They are very attached to it, and it's my wish that they should inherit it. And it's also my first husband's wish. He agreed to the settlement, hoping that they would inherit it.'

Earlier she had stated:

> 'I don't know what my future plans are, other than to return to the UK for [our daughter's] education. In that case, if there was funds to put (sic) just a small property here so she could be educated in England, I may let it, to help maintain it but I can't do that until I have the legalisation, the habitation certificate, and a tourism licence is now required.'

64.   In his award Mr Smith made the following findings. At para.47(b) he dealt with its value as follows:

> 'For the purpose of these proceedings [QP] has an agreed value of €660,000. This value assumes that the house will have the benefit of a 'habitation licence' which the wife has been in course of applying for some years. It is her case that without it the property cannot be sold. Costs of sale are agreed at 5%. There is an issue as to the CGT, if any, which should be set against the net equity, and as to the building and other costs which the wife will or should reasonably incur in obtaining the habitation licence. I deal with these issues below. Ignoring CGT, there is a net equity of £445,000.'

Later in his award, and in the attached schedule of assets, Mr Smith dealt with the deductions and arrived at the net figure of £375,797.

65.   Mr Smith dealt with the wife's future housing needs as follows:

> '97. The wife's future is at present uncertain and it is thus difficult for her to quantify her housing need. She wishes to return to the UK with [the daughter] and to buy a home in Oxfordshire, and for [the daughter] to attend school there, probably at [school named]. That is a school which she and the husband had previously identified as one which [the daughter] might in the future attend. The wife has produced estate agents' details of 3 bedroomed houses costing in the bracket £500,000–£650,000. However, she is not in a position at the moment to relocate with [the daughter], as she requires either the permission of the husband, which is not currently forthcoming, or the permission of the Portuguese court. She has not yet issued her application and has been advised not to do so until next year. The husband's Portuguese lawyer has said that if an application were issued now it would not be heard until after June 2016.
> 98. I cannot predict or second-guess the order that may be made by the Portuguese court. I cannot assume that the wife will receive permission to relocate.
> 99. What is clear in my judgment is that her housing need are currently met at QP and would be if she remains in Portugal. If she is successful in obtaining leave to remove, she may well have to lower her sights in terms of accommodation in England and/or use some of the pension funds with which to rehouse herself.
> 100. She is very attached to QP and wishes to retain it if at all possible. However, it is not in my view realistic for the wife to envisage retaining QP while at the same time buying a property in England that would be suitable for her and [the daughter] if she obtained leave to remove, but that of course is a matter for her.'

66.   At para.132(h) Mr Smith determined that the wife should receive periodical payments of £36,000 annually, and he concluded that she could adjust without undue hardship to termination of those payments once she receives her interest in the business on final disposal. However, at para.132(f) he had held:

> 'On the sale of [the husband's] shares the wife should receive a lump sum equal to 40% of the proceeds after tax and the husband the balance and at that point there should be a clean break. I shall not order a s.28(1A) direction. This will be to provide a safety net in case the wife's share is substantially less than the current value would suggest and does not meet her needs.'

67.   It follows that the safety net is available if the wife's capital is not sufficient to meet all her needs, whether for housing or income, at the point of the sale of the business. If the value of one element of her estate has fallen, whether it be the value of QP or her share in the business, then the safety net is there to ensure that her needs in the long-term are met.

68.   In my judgment, the existence of the safety net inevitably leads me to refuse to interfere with the arbitrator's award, even if the threshold requirements for proof of mistake or supervening event are demonstrated. If the notional loss of £223,491 in the value of QP – which the wife is

presently not in fact intending to sell, and which she wishes to leave to her children – in fact eventuates in hard money terms then the court will have the facility to bring into operation the safety net both in relation to quantum and duration of periodical payments. I have mentioned that the wife has already applied for an extension of the term of periodical payments. The husband has applied, in effect, for a capitalisation of the periodical payments in that following receipt of the draft award he has tendered to her the sum of £494,280, which is the present value taken by the arbitrator of the wife's 40% share in the business. In his supplemental award Mr Smith rightly refused to deal with the husband's de facto capitalisation application. This would have to be heard as a fresh application either by means of arbitration or in court. At all events, there are now pending cross-applications for variation of the wife's award of periodical payments. In those proceedings the wife's assertions as to the fall in value of QP will fall to be adjudicated. If those assertions are found proved then I imagine that the arbitrator or court will wish to reconsider whether the periodical payments should terminate on receipt by the wife of her share of the business when it is sold.

69.   However, I will deal with the wife's primary case as it may be that others disagree with my view that the existence of the safety net inevitably means that the discretion to set aside the award should not be exercised.

70.   I take the facts largely from Mr Chamberlayne's skeleton argument. These are not seriously disputed.

71.   In 1992 the wife acquired QP, a Portuguese farmhouse sited on agricultural land. The original house was built prior to 1951 and does not require legalisation (planning consent). In the 1970s its previous owners constructed a separate annex (bedroom, kitchenette and swimming pool) and in the late 1980s they extended the main house. Planning consent was not granted for either additional construction. The total area of building construction is now 401.65 m².

72.   In 2007 the parties jointly engaged the services of an architect, Jaime Coutinho, to secure the necessary planning consent to legalise the property and to obtain a habitation licence. A habitation licence is required in order to be able to sell the property to a third party. A notary will not sign a deed of transfer of title without there being such a licence in existence.

73.   Two applications for planning have been submitted. The first application had been refused by the council on 4 October 2011 because 'the main building and pool were in conditions to be legalised but not the annex, for the main reason that [it] was located at a distance less than 5m from the boundary' and 'the annex is separated from the main building'.

74.   In 2012 or 2013 the parties acquired a strip of land from a neighbour to overcome the issue regarding the distance from the boundary. The second application for planning had been submitted by the architect on 27 November 2014 but had not been determined at the time of the arbitration. The wife had obtained quotations from two builders for the construction of a physical link – a 'pergola' – between the main building and the annex. The amounts involved were relatively small – £11,000.

75.   A SJE chartered surveyor, Ian Rostrum, was instructed to provide the market value of the property. He provided an initial valuation in his report dated 31 August 2014 and an updated valuation in a letter dated 2 April 2015 to take account of an increase in property prices. His evidence, which included his consideration about the issue of the likely legalisation of the property, was unchallenged.

76.   In summary Mr Rostrum's opinion was that once the property obtained a habitation licence it would be worth €660,000. Without the legalisation licence, but on the assumption that planning would be granted in due course, he valued the property at €630,000. The small difference in effect reflected the 'hassle factor' of having to obtain the licence, because, of course, the property could not be sold without it. He reports that based upon his discussion with the architect, all that was required by the council to grant a licence was a physical link between the main property and the annex. He stated:

> 'The local authority has so far raised two conditions that need to be addressed before they will consider approval. One was that the detached annex was within 5m of the original southern boundary and the other was that a physical connection by way of a pergola was needed between the detached annex and the main house. They are applying the conditions set out on the Plano Director Municipal (PDM), the master plan that deals with planning regulations.

A strip of land has already been purchased from the neighbouring property ensuring that the structure is five metres from the boundary and the construction of a pergola is simple and relatively inexpensive.

Arq. Jaime Coutinho has advised that he is convinced that when these two conditions have been met that no more conditions will be applied by the local authority. However, he has qualified this advice by adding that no one can be 100% sure that it will be approved. As a result two valuation figures have been provided for this property.'

77. The evidence, accepted by all, was that the habitation licence would in all likelihood be forthcoming, subject only to the construction of a structure deemed suitable by the council to connect the main house to the annex. The precise characteristics required by the council of the structure were all that was awaited according to emails from Mr Coutinho that formed part of the evidence at the hearing.

78. As stated above at [64] Mr Smith therefore attributed to the property the full value of €660,000 but deducted as a liability the building costs and fees that the wife would have to incur in obtaining the necessary planning consent. After deduction of other expenses this resulted in a net value to the wife of £375,797.

79. The award was promulgated on 2 July 2015. On 20 July 2015 the council determined the planning application by refusing it. The decision states that the permitted planning parameters for the built area are 300 m² and that the existing and proposed built area exceeds this limitation (401.65 m²).

80. On 17 August 2015 the architect Mr Coutinho sent an email to the wife clarifying the decision. He stated that the main house together with the extension was already bigger than the permitted area (324.20 m²), let alone the annex. Mr Coutinho stated 'this means that now even the main villa may not be totally approved due to excess of area'. On 16 October 2015 Marta Lopes from Mr Coutinho's office advised that 'the only way to continue the process to obtain a habitation licence is to reformulate the process and proceed with the demolition of the annex and the excess area of the villa to accommodate the PDM requirement.'

81. In the light of these developments the wife obtained new expert evidence from Peter Densham MRICS. She has adduced his evidence in these proceedings without having obtained the court's permission under FPR 25.4(2) although no strong objection was raised by Mr Pointer QC to my being referred to it. Obviously the status of the evidence is no more than indicative. It cannot be taken to be conclusive in circumstances where the rules have not been complied with. Further, if fresh valuation evidence was to have been relied on in any definitive way then it ought to have derived from a single joint expert: see PD25D para.2.1, which provides that 'wherever possible, expert evidence should be obtained from a single joint expert instructed by both or all the parties'.

82. In his letter dated 23 October 2015 Mr Densham has valued the property without planning consent at €225,000 but states that 'the probability of achieving a sale at all is doubtful'. The value of the property with a habitation licence with it reconstructed and with reduced size will be €400,000, in his opinion.

83. The cost of reducing the property in size, digging up the pool and making good the works is set out in a table in the statement of the wife's case. This calculates the current net residual value as £152,306.

84. It is not accepted by the husband that any of these gloomy predictions will come to pass. He asserts that this issue has been 'rumbling on' for nearly 10 years and that there is no firm or reliable evidence either way as to its eventual outcome.

85. I deal first with the contention that the decision of the council on 20 July 2015 was an unforeseeable later event which invalidated the decision of the arbitrator. I cannot agree that it was. The application was pending and although everyone was confident that it would be granted it must have been recognised that it might be refused. To my mind the decision, albeit unwelcome, was eminently foreseeable in the sense described by the House of Lords and the Privy Council in the cases to which I have referred. Even if the decision was unforeseeable I do not agree that it 'invalidated' the arbitrator's decision in circumstances where the scale of the loss, assuming that Mr Densham's evidence is correct, would reduce the wife's overall share of the capital from 45% to 40%. A 40% overall award was well within Mr Smith's discretion and to my mind invalidation is only demonstrated where it can be shown that the consequence

plainly falls outside the discretionary band. A claim for a further lump sum of £111,746 out of a total pool of assets of £2,381,359 does not come close to meeting the requirement of exceptionality.

86.   The wife's case on mistake is stronger and has similarities to the case of *Richardson*. It would certainly seem to be undeniable that on 2 July 2015 the council were considering refusing the application, just as in *Richardson* on 25 September 2009 the insurers were considering avoiding the policy. However, I am not satisfied on the evidence that the wife with due diligence could not have discovered that the council might well adopt a much harder line about unauthorised building developments. I have been given no evidence of any efforts made by her to find out what the council were actually contemplating. There seems to have just been a blithe assumption that all would be well. The possibility of rejection was specifically referred to by her architect and it is surprising in those circumstances that she was content to allow the arbitrator to proceed to judgment without nailing down the point one way or another.

87.   I therefore reject the wife's case on mistake.

88.   But either way, the wife's claim fails because there is available to her alternative mainstream relief which can broadly remedy any injustice caused to her by a fall in value in QP, if that actually eventuates.

89.   The husband's application is therefore granted and the order as drafted by Mr Smith will be made by me. I further allow the husband to make absolute the Decree Nisi so that the order can take immediate effect.

Two procedural points

90.   In this case the husband's notice to show cause was issued in the Central Family Court and came before Recorder Campbell on 27 October 2015. She transferred the matter to be heard by a High Court judge, but it has taken some time for this hearing to be listed. In the future any notice to show cause why an arbitration award should not be made an order of the court must, for London and the South Eastern Circuit, be issued in the Royal Courts of Justice and immediately placed before me for allocation to a High Court judge for speedy determination. If the application is issued outside London or the South Eastern Circuit then it must be immediately placed before the Family Division Liaison Judge who will arrange for it to be heard speedily by him or her or another High Court judge (including a section 9 judge). It is important for the promotion of the arbitration system that litigants should know that if a challenge to an arbitration award is raised that it will be heard by a High Court judge at the soonest opportunity.

91.   Finally, I wish to deal with a procedural point which is in fact not material to this case and therefore what I say is strictly speaking obiter. In *CS v ACS* [2015] EWHC 1005 (Fam) the President decided that an application to set aside an order on the basis of non-disclosure (or fraud or mistake) could, pursuant to FPR 4.1(6) and section 31F(6) Matrimonial and Family Proceedings Act 1984, be made to the original court and did not have to be made by way of appeal. He left open the question whether a *Barder* application could be made to the original court or whether it had to be by way of appeal. In my judgment, for the reasons set out in Financial Remedies Practice 2016 (Class Publishing) at paragraphs 4.12 to 4.20, a *Barder* application can be made to the original court.

Appendix 5

Further resources

5.1

Further resources

IFLA

Following the launch of the new children arbitration scheme, IFLA has produced revised editions of a number of its documents, which are downloadable from its website (**http://ifla.org.uk/resources-for-practitioners**).

Articles

'Arbitration in Family Financial Proceedings: the IFLA Scheme: Part 1', Sir Peter Singer [2012] Fam Law 1353
(**www.familyarbitrator.com/wp-content/uploads/FLJ_2012_11_Singer.pdf**)

'Arbitration in Family Financial Proceedings: the IFLA Scheme: Part 2' by Sir Peter Singer [2012] Fam Law 1496
(**www.familyarbitrator.com/wp-content/uploads/FLJ_2012_12_Singer.pdf**)

'*S* v. *S* Tales' by Sir Peter Singer, James Pirrie, Lynn Henderson and Gavin Smith
(**www.classlegal.com/news/12412_free_article_on_family_law_arbitration_after_s_v_s**)

Useful websites

Centre for Child and Family Law Reform
www.city.ac.uk/law/research/centre-on-child-and-family-law-reform

Chartered Institute of Arbitrators
www.ciarb.org

FamilyArbitrator
www.familyarbitrator.com

Family Law Bar Association
www.flba.co.uk

Institute of Family Arbitrators
http://ifla.org.uk

The Law Society
www.lawsociety.org.uk

Resolution
www.resolution.org.uk

Discussion groups

FamilyArbitrator group
www.linkedin.com/groups/FamilyArbitrator-4370850